Modern Hebrew Drama

MODERN HEBREW DRAMA

Glenda Abramson

Weidenfeld & Nicolson/London

First published in Great Britain by
Weidenfeld and Nicolson
91 Clapham High Street, London SW4

ISBN 0 297 77653 3

Designed by Sue Montalto Lee

Printed in Great Britain by Westerham Press Limited

My grateful thanks are due to the University of the Witwatersrand, Johannesburg, for Council's Faculty of Arts Research Grant which allowed me to proceed with research for this book. In addition I owe a debt of gratitude to the scholars, playwrights, directors and critics (not necessarily in that order) whose patience, advice and assistance were of inestimable value.

Title page quotations taken from an article by Eric Bentley entitled "What is Theatre?" from the book of the same name (Horizon Press, 1956).

To my mother and father

Contents

Introduction

The greatest problem concerning the evaluation of Hebrew drama in Israel today is its lack of a continuous past. After 1948 it emerged suddenly as an art form to be reckoned with but because of its youth it has no tradition from which to evolve certain necessary critical standards. Modern Israel has in effect been presented with an artistic baby of questionable parentage which demands attention and careful nurturing. Of all the Jewish arts only poetry and prose can claim a long and distinguished tradition while the drama may perhaps be regarded as their adopted child with its true ancestry in the Christian cultures of Eastern and Central Europe.

Although primitive ceremonies and rituals similar to those from which drama grew were practised in ancient Israel the rigid and traditional forms of emerging Judaism did not allow the dramas as such to take root. There were, in ancient times, Israelite ritualistic performances but liturgy was always more important than any abstract concept of art. In Israel and Judah the men who enthralled the masses were prophets, not poets or orators. The entire Jewish imagination was engaged in the overwhelming task of understanding the concept – and the desires and commands – of God. There was little left for creative art. The idea of a "Hebrew drama" was not formulated until the years immediately preceding the foundation of the State of Israel, nor were the periods of its creation seriously considered. It has since been customary for those studying the subject or writing about it to begin with the Bible and its apparent dramatic material and only then continue through the subsequent history of the Jews, for certain Biblical passages supply tantalising hints as to the existence of some form of ancient Hebrew drama.

The entire Old Testament is a continuing story of the development of a nation. It is, in a way, a chronicle of rebellion. The history of ancient Israel from the beginning to the end is motivated by defiance of God out of which the prophets were able to create their vision of a last judgement when human intransigence would come to an end. The story told by the Bible is a dramatic one, having Israel and God as the major protagonists; with the exception of the Wisdom Literature it can be regarded as one long drama with a single theme: how Israel acquired its land, lost it through its stubbornness and then reacquired it, with the two principal actors, God and Israel, having a covenant between them. However, the Bible as a whole shows little trace of conventional dramatic form despite its abundance of dramatic dialogue. There are indeed isolated dramas in the Biblical text such as the Book of Job, the Song of Solomon, the stories of Samson and Saul, the Book of Ecclesiastes, the Book of Jonah and some of the prophetic passages which utilise theatrical symbols and settings, for the methods of the major prophets were essentially histrionic.[1] The Song of Solomon is a romance with dramatically cohesive story and action. Dance and song are elements of drama and occur in the Bible a few times, for example Miriam led a dance in honour of the Lord and David danced with all his might before the Holy Ark.

[1] See for example Jeremiah Chapter 19.

Among all such examples the Books of Ecclesiastes and Job are the most interesting and the latter is certainly the most convincing in terms of dramatic form. Strictly speaking the Book of Job is not a drama but a dramatic situation, for it lacks visualised scenes and presents only voices. The world of Job is confined to a heap of ashes and there is no reference to time or place; in its stark setting it is reminiscent of the early works of Samuel Beckett for there is indeed something Absurd in Job's situation. He himself does not recount ideas, he is, rather, a dramatisation of suffering, yet his book achieves its purpose which is to question the nature of evil – and the evil of nature – just as some of the later Absurd "heroes" question the nature of life.

This book bears some analysis by the rules of dramatic form and it has long been the subject of intensive study from a dramatic standpoint. It may be part of a foreign drama, that is, its origin may not be Jewish at all, but, according to Horace Kallen,[2] it is more likely to be the work of a Hebrew poet aware of Euripides' tragic structure but departing from the Greek spiritual world while applying certain Euripidean principles in his own play. The form he gave to his tragedy would then have been transposed from the dramatic to the narrative when the Book of Job was added to the Canon, with other ideological changes rendering it suitable to the perspectives of the Judaism of its time.

[2] Horace M. Kallen. *The Book of Job as a Greek Tragedy*. Hill and Wang, N.Y., 1959.

The tragedy at the basis of "Job" is the fact of the protagonist's undeserved suffering which on the surface negates the comforters' doctrine of the law of just deserts.[3] Similar ideological conflicts are the source of all tragic situations: dogmatic public or social theory fails to account for the reality of the hero's situation, highlighted in the case of Job when he is seen against the comforters, or the Greek hero against the chorus, Lear against his court, modern man against society. The comforters, the chorus, the courtiers represent established dogma, the barrier between the hero and the truth he seeks. Job, in the early book, starts as a representative of virtue, as do

[3] תורת הגמול

Macbeth, Oedipus and so on. Then follows the gradual alienation of the hero from the group and he ends his days as an outcast. Job's direct challenge to God echoes all the tragic figures who cry out against their fate. As the hero's alienation increases he himself gains in stature for his real experience gives an answer or at least an argument to the group ideology and his response to suffering is ultimately heroic. These great heroes undergo a spiritual metamorphosis through their ordeals, leading to triumph which has the value of religious affirmation. Job and all the tragic heroes gained visionary knowledge, which has been called the "dark side" of knowledge, for suffering produces comprehension transcending ordinary knowledge: for example, physical blindness intensifies the vision of the soul.

"Job" seems to be the first consciously created non-Greek tragic hero, but nothing is known of his creator. His great spiritual tragedy has become a legacy of the Jews and their first major dramatic contribution to the world.

But for these isolated examples in the Old Testament, drama is one of the most forsaken sections of Israel's literature. Although more of it appeared in Italy in the sixteenth century it did not create a dramatic tradition nor begin a chain of dramatic works and authors. From the sixteenth century onwards many works were written in dramatic form without being dramas but merely monologues spoken between personified ideas, similar to the Book of Job in concept but not in brilliance or dramatic impact. There is not one viable theatrical drama among them.

Certain hypotheses have been offered to explain the lack of dramatic art in Israel's past. First of all the practice of theatrical performances was regarded by the religious leaders as being foreign to the traditional Jewish way of life; secondly, drama is a literary category which is especially linked to independent national and social conditions. Theatre has always been involved with the life of an independent nation. It requires long consolidation and development and moreover it requires for its perfection the consistent reciprocity between the artistic creator and his audience. Yet even in the period of its greatest security and consolidation the nation of Israel did not exhibit a special tendency to theatrical art. The third hypothesis relates to the nature of religious practice. In the pagan view the scene of the cosmic drama is the mythological with its clashing divine powers. In Israel, however, it is a moral drama, arising out of the tension between the will of the Almighty God and the will of man who is free to rebel and who does so. In respect of the early history of

Israel and the Jews the great dramatic story moved from the realm of myth to the realm of history: it began with the conflict between the will of God and man, the defiant pagan. And it ended with the Jews' realisation that for them there was no struggle, only absolute submission to the idea of God's absolute decree, their own place in His universal scheme of justice and obedience to all His laws. During this period the Greeks were creating drama and theatre out of man's struggle with the gods and fate, a theme that could not have been enacted by the Jews. Greek tragedy did not ever depend on absolute values – absolute good or evil; its hero could not embody either of these values exclusively. Judaism, with its emphasis on unquestionable good or unquestionable evil, was clearly unable to suit the spiritual conditions of tragedy. For example the story told in Genesis 22 of the binding of Isaac, although tragic in concept, does not conform to the idea of tragic drama. The possibility of choice is apparently given but from the start the reader knows the outcome in terms of the will of God, embodying the perfect value. There can be no drama when one of the protagonists is Almighty God. Buber says: "The nature of drama is fixed in the lack of justice which exists in every one of the characters functioning in the story, just as there exists an essential lack of justice in the very arbitrariness of fate . . ."[4]

[4]"On the Lack of Hebrew Drama" by Israel Eliraz. *Bamah* 48–49, Winter–Spring 1971.

Drama arose from the festivals celebrated by pre-Achaean cultures, always associated with some aspects of the life of the gods. The pagan festivals celebrated the life-processes of the deities to which were linked fertility of the soil and the tribe. Israel's rituals lacked the dramatic element of mythology because of the Jews' celebration of the sovereign God. Pagan ritual dramatised the recurring cycle of the life of the gods not merely as a memorial but as a magical rite. Its purpose was to affect the divine powers and to aid them, to work with them, so to speak. This kind of dramatic rite did not occur in Israelite religion. Only in the historical festivals do we find certain dramatic elements, those commemorating certain moments in the history of the nation when God manifested Himself, but these Biblical stories do not deal with the *life* of God as do those of the pagans, but with His relations to men. For example the ritual described in Exodus 12 for Passover contains a series of prescriptions for action, in other words, re-enactments of the events of the night of the Passover in Egypt. There is a certain dramatic element in the injunction to build booths (Succot) and live in them for seven days. Such dramatic elements are not found in the non-historicised or cosmic festivals (Sabbath, Yom Kippur) for dramatisation of a cosmic event could easily have become transformed into a representation of an event in the life of God, a motif that had no place in Israel. There was no danger in re-enacting what had happened to the *people*.

Dance, song, sacrifice, feasting and rejoicing are all present in Israelite festivals. There were always processions, singing, dancing, shouting, prostrating, but never any hint of drama. If there was a Dionysiac element in Israel's festivals – a legacy of Canaan, hinted at by many references to wine drinking and libation and, to an extent, the singing and dancing – the underlying idea is quite different from the pagan Dionysiac frenzy. In Israel God did not participate in and was not affected by the festival, the intoxications and the enthusiasm. He was not among the throng of His devotees and did not join their frenzy. The rejoicing was not with Him but *before* Him.

The ancient Jews appear to have known little themselves about the theatre or its implications in art and society and all that they did know seems to have been derived from the Greeks. Their records reveal no spontaneous and characteristic drama and no native stage. When the nation lost its independence in the first century of the common era any hope for a national theatre faded completely. The Jews then had to guard themselves against the influence of strange cultures, especially Hellenism, which was seen from the start as a threat to Judaism and its spiritual values. Everything relating to the Greeks was to be avoided, most of all the drama which had arisen from pagan revels, from idolatry which was the most formidable sin the Jews could commit.

Whereas Greek theatre had a firm share in the foundation of what we call Western culture, no dramatic or theatrical contribution was made relating to the Jewish religion. Later there were Jewish authors who wrote plays on Greek themes and in Greek form, but there was little indigenous Hebrew dramatic art. Reference is made to some kind of theatrical activity in the Jewish settlements on Greek territory, for example, Alexandria in the second century BC. Whatever Jewish drama there was in such areas of settlement was based on the material of the Old Testament recast in Euripidean tragic form. There was an Ezekiel, a "poet of Jewish tragedies" who composed a drama in Greek on the Exodus from the Old Testament account. It is only later, in the diaspora, that the stirring of interest in Jewish theatrical enterprise can be discerned; even this, however, was not to be the formation of a Jewish dramatic tradition.

For almost every reason given to explain the lack of Hebrew drama there is a valid counterargument, all hypotheses being supported by impressive authority. The conclusion on the simplest level is that for many reasons theatre was clearly alien to the spirit of the Jews, their religion, morality and cultural philosophy. Just as music and the visual arts were, for various reasons, not within their orbit, neither was the drama or theatre, until the foundation of Israel in 1948.

Part 1 The Development of the Drama

. . . we need a sense of where it all came from, this theatre of ours, and where it has been going . . .

1 Renaissance and Enlightenment

The Hebrew drama was always a faint echo of the dramatic activity taking place outside the ghetto walls. There had been nothing at all to parallel the monumental tragedy and comedy of the Attic, Hellenistic and Roman worlds and later, during the Middle Ages, Christian Europe brought down the curtain altogether, so that from AD 467 for almost a thousand years no theatre in the ordinary sense was to be seen. Roman theatrical traditions had been inherited in a small way by the mummers, jongleurs or minstrels who were ballad singers, acrobats, conjurers and musicians. At this time certain groups of Jewish jugglers, dancers and mimics joined together and began to entertain predominantly Jewish audiences despite the continuing strictures of the religious leaders. Jewish theatre might have begun to evolve very slowly from these troupes but it is more likely that its roots are to be found in the ancient ritualistic Purim celebrations which started approximately in the third century BC. Purim is a semi-religious holiday observed in early spring to celebrate the events recorded in the Scroll of Esther, one of the many books of the Bible possessing potentially dramatic elements. The Purim play – or Purimschpiel – was a dramatic version of the Book of Esther developed from a simple puppet show given in the courtyards of the synagogues. Later, during the Renaissance, actors took over, with improvisation, songs and masquerades in which they impersonated the characters of the Biblical story in one-act plays in verse and prose. Short comic interludes presented between performances were sometimes more popular even than the plays themselves. This shows clear influence of the Spanish *pasos* or *entremeses*, burlesques given between the acts of serious plays, which had been entertaining Spanish audiences from the time of Lope de Rueda until well into the seventeenth century. During similar sketches between performances of Purim plays actors were in their element clowning as comic rabbis, doctors, apothecaries, midwives and devils, at times severely criticising Jewish peculiarities but always ending with a final chorus foretelling Israel's salvation.

As time passed the subjects of the plays varied: whereas originally they had been confined to the ritual story of Esther, Persia's Jewish queen, now they told of the sale of Joseph by his brothers, Jacob's dream, the battle of David and Goliath and so on. Yet for all this the early Purim plays were themselves no more than dramatic dialogues, allegories on religious, ethical and mythical topics. In the ninth century a Purim play had been written down, arranged and edited according to the rules of drama but it could not then be performed, as women were not allowed to act on the stage, a prohibition not uncommon in theatrical history; in this case, however, it was more restrictive, for men were forbidden to replace them following an injunction in the Book of Deuteronomy that no man may wear women's clothing.[1]

[1] Deuteronomy 22, 5.

One reason for the lack of development of the Jewish drama was the continuing opposition of the communities' religious leaders to so pagan a manifestation. The Church was not any more enthusiastic about secular Christian playacting than were the rabbis about their own and it waged a constant war against the theatre because of its sources in polytheism and the accompanying indecency and licentiousness. However, this antipathy was resolved by the evolution of a liturgical drama to which Christian ritual was more suited than that of the Jews and this, moving towards the mystery, miracle and morality plays, left the Purimschpiel far behind. Nevertheless Purim plays occupy a place of distinction in Jewish theatrical history. They were being printed regularly in the seventeenth century, especially in Spanish and Italian and showed clear influence of the *commedia dell'arte*. In Frankfurt in the eighteenth century one of Beerman von Limburg's Purim plays – dealing with the story of David and Goliath – proved so popular that Christians were forbidden by their authorities to attend it.

In the sixteenth century there appeared signs of an embryonic theatre in the ghettos of Europe but this had a different purpose from that of the Christian societies of the time. In the ghettos all spiritual life was introverted; the community performed or viewed performances of Biblical tales on the festivals of the Jewish calendar, especially at Purim which later developed to become a carnival season. The spectators did not want to watch acted-out events of their everyday life for in these they merely saw the diaspora mirrored and it was depressing in the extreme. The only writing that could stir their enthusiasm was that of their past and of their longings for salvation, for the homecoming of the nation. "They . . . compensated for their alienation from pastoral surroundings by idealising nature's charms and allurements . . ."[2] by singing of beauty and freedom in the glory of God's fields and forests which few of them had ever seen. Their poetry and drama were not an abstract artistic concern but a means of education and propaganda, of expressing their yearning for release, and their hope. The playwrights or authors saw drama solely as literature and their emphasis was consequently on the literary and ideological rather than the dramatic-theatrical. Dramatic form was to

[2] Howard M. Sachar. *The Course of Jewish History*. Weidenfeld and Nicolson, 1958.

them merely a new literary way of expressing old ideas.

With the Renaissance in Europe all dramatists, like artists, poets, architects and sculptors, studied their ancient sources of inspiration, particularly the art and mythology of Greece and Rome. The Jews turned to their own classical sources, the Bible and later related writings but Jewish classicism could not fulfil the function that did Greek and Roman art and literature, for the Bible was regarded with too much awe to be used as a basis for any kind of subjective artistic interpretation and its holiness prevented writers from attempting to take the text as a source for anything other than direct religious exposition. Yet Hebrew drama had its formal, historical beginning during the European Renaissance with the first discoverable Jewish play, dating back to the sixteenth century and primarily performed on the festival of Purim. Its author was Jehuda Leone di Somi, a Jewish poet who was the playwright, choreographer and *maestro* at the Court of the Dukes of Gonzaga in Mantua. His real name and dates are not entirely certain; it is assumed from the extant evidence that he was born in 1529 and died in 1592. His play was in five acts in the style and using the conventions of popular Italian comedy and it was called *An Eloquent Marriage Farce*.

During the sixteenth century the court of Mantua achieved its greatest brilliance under the cultured patronage of the Dukes of Gonzaga. Palaces and villas were lavishly commissioned and a multitude of great writers and artists found employment and encouragement in them: Castiglione, Boiardo, Ariosto, Raphael, Leonardo, Titian, Monteverdi and the Jew, Leone di Somi. There were troupes of Jewish players in service at the Court, not always voluntarily, and di Somi had been taken in as their director. He was regarded as an important theatrical personality even at the time when the Jews, confined to ghettos, were allowed little part in the intellectual life of the country. He was producer, director, actor and playwright in Italian and an authority on the art of the theatre, having written a number of theoretical works on dramatic art, some of which were translated for the first time in the thirties of this century into Russian. They have subsequently been translated into English as well but only fragments have remained of the original writings for the rest were destroyed in a fire at the turn of this century. The most important text available to us is called *Conversations About Acting on the Stage* (circa 1565) and it takes the classical form of dialogue, in this case about theatrical design, performance and production. It is one of the few theoretical treatises on theatre and theatrical art since Aristotle.

Di Somi's Italian-Hebrew comedy was formally little different from other examples popular at that time but it nevertheless proves that he was in every way a man of the stage. It dates from approximately 1550 when Italian comedy was at the height of its development. It combined conventions of the *commedia erudita*, the *commedia dell'arte* and the morality plays. The "learned comedy" of the time had to observe strict formal conventions derived in the most part from Terence and Plautus, and di Somi had the added problem of suiting his own comedy to Jewish audiences, bearing in mind the severe restrictions placed by Jewish religious authorities on all aspects of the theatre. Di Somi was already unpopular in orthodox circles for having written a secular love poem to a woman but, determined to give the Jewish community a play, he wrote one in Hebrew, mingling in it Jewish and Italian elements. His language was unusually colloquial and, for a Hebrew writer, extraordinary in the sense that he suited the manner of speech to the personality of each character. He quoted from the Bible with new and sarcastic twists of meaning. C.N.Bialik, Israel's poet-laureate, who died in 1934, said that had he not known otherwise he would have been sure that di Somi's play was "modern" The play was revived in 1968 by the Haifa Municipal Theatre.

The central story of the play is based on a device fashionable in the sixteenth century – legend or folklore as a primary source. In this case the source was Jewish. The play conformed further to its Italian models in its use of the motifs of law and courts and justice which were also in vogue in the secular drama of the time and in this way di Somi achieved his desired link between Judaism and the current rage in the Italian theatre. The play combines four distinct plots, one of them the story of a young man, Shalom, whose father died while he – Shalom – was far away, and bequeathed all his possessions to his slave, Shuval. He left only one thing to Shalom but the boy was to choose this legacy himself from among his father's possessions. On the advice of Rabbi Ammitai the Wise, who understood the father's purpose, the young man chooses the slave and thus obtains him and his inheritance. Originally the Talmudists had turned the ancient legend into a moral maxim; di Somi made it into a witty play fulfilling every demand of Italian Renaissance comedy and of Jewish philosophical thinking. Or rather fulfilling almost every demand of Renaissance comedy, for di Somi's play, mindful of the Jewish audience, is devoid of licentiousness, *double entendres* and so-called bad language.

Mantua at the time of di Somi is considered to be the cradle of the *commedia dell'arte* in which, for example, the servants have exalted roles, as do the five slaves in di Somi's play; slaves had major roles in the learned comedy as well. The Rabbi is an innovation for no comparable character appeared in either form of Italian comedy, but Hamdan, the foil to the wise Rabbi Ammitai, is a synthesis between the pedant of the *commedia erudita* and the pompous, foolish Doctor of the *commedia dell'arte*. Other *commedia dell'arte* themes, for example those of thwarted love and intrigue, are present in di Somi's work which includes a multitude of characters, masques, a prologue, monologues, many exits and entrances and frequent changes of scene.

Di Somi was the first and last great Jewish playwright for many years. In the seventeenth century certain "foreign" influences penetrated into some Jewish communities and from then onwards there appears quite a large number of dramas written by Jews in various languages: Spanish, Italian, French and, later, Yiddish. Performances of burlesques and "modern" farces by Jewish authors had begun to attract general audiences in Spain and Italy. These plays and later variations of the Purimschpiel were certainly influenced by the Saturnalia and by the Fastnachtschpiele currently in vogue throughout Spain and Germany. However, the Jewish writers still suffered from the lack of a strong link between culture and land which is a prerequisite for all great dramatic literature. Consequently there was still no independent organic development of Jewish drama. Every Hebrew or Jewish play was composed under the influence of a certain genre during a specific period in the development of the literature of another nation and the drama does not exhibit the natural developmental stages found in Hebrew literature generally.

In Ferrara (1619) a Purim play entitled *Esther* by Usque and Grazziano was given and five years afterwards some of the most respected Jews of Amsterdam performed a work by Paul de Pinas called *The Dialogues of The Seven Hills* in the synagogue. This was, however, only a dialogue. There are other plays dating from this period and the years immediately following. At first these were no more than allegories on religious or ethical subjects but in 1699 the *Commedia Famosa de Aman y Mordechai* by the "Jewish Calderón", Antonio Enrico de Gamus, appeared and comparable plays for Purim were given in Prague and Breslau. The Purim plays written and produced in Germany in the seventeenth and eighteenth centuries inspired the introduction of Purim drama in Eastern Europe and were linked to the foundation of the Yiddish theatre by Avraham Goldfaden.

The start of the eighteenth century saw the works of Moshe Haim Luzzato written in the full bloom of Hebrew thought and poetry, influenced by the European movement of the Enlightenment. Luzzato's characters were symbolic and his drama allegorical, similar in form and intention to Bunyan's dramatic allegory *The Pilgrim's Progress*. Luzzato's plays were weak from the point of view both of content and dramatic form but they expressed the spirit of the period in Europe, the period of Rationalism, when the elevated ethical ideology and aesthetic form of the dialogue were in any case more important than the dramatic form of the play. The possibility of performance of Luzzato's plays was not at all material: he and other Jewish writers did not even consider this aspect of drama, its live performance. In 1724 Luzzato wrote a dramatised version of the story of Samson. In 1727 he composed the second of his allegorical dramas, *The Tower of Strength* based on Tasso's pastoral play, *L'Aminta*. *The Tower of Strength* was an exposition of a national myth based on the mysteries of the Zohar to which Luzzato was strongly drawn. The allegorical plot tells of an honourable young man who finds the secret entrance to a tower and gains the love of an innocent maiden imprisoned within it while a dishonourable youth fails in his own quest due to his attempts to break into the tower by force. 1743 saw the composition of *Le'yesharim Tehillah*, an allegory which has survived as a theatrical play and which describes, in symbolic form, the battle between forces of good and evil.

Luzzato was well acquainted with Italian literature and temperamentally he was attracted to the pastoral idyll. And this is precisely what he introduced into Hebrew literature, in superb poetic style: an appreciation of the beauties of nature, a zest for living and the natural acceptance and presentation of human emotions. Not only that but he called for an interest in and appreciation of scientific principles. His allegories particularly had a direct and powerful influence on the Hebrew literature of the Enlightenment. His success caused such excessive popularity of Jewish allegorical drama that it tended to stunt the growth of other types of dramatic composition which could have been more significant. Contemporary Jewish allegorical plays covered everything: social criticism, tracts for Enlightenment, against Enlightenment, some were even allegorical criticism of Luzzato himself.

After Luzzato there followed a long period in which playwrights continued to imitate him and produce Biblical plays about Joseph, Esther, Saul and others and a series of allegorical plays dealing mainly with the love of labour, work on the land and the simple life. The conflict of ideas in allegory was an expression of the new dramatists who "fought the war of wisdom against its enemies".[3] Whatever

[3] "The Hebrew Drama" by G.Hanoch. *Zion* no. 3, November 1949.

derived naturally from the cultural milieu it was supposed to represent. His characters were stock, or personifications of ideas which were not realised into fully developed *dramatis personae*.

The major dramatic figure of the period was Mattatiyahu Shoham who composed four Biblical plays in verse which, because of their original style and structure and imaginative concept of historical events, are landmarks in the history of Hebrew drama. Shoham was born in 1893 and died in 1937. His first play *Jericho* has for its main characters Achan and Rahab, whose love for each other is symbolic of the attraction between the decadent culture of Jericho and the rigorous vital Hebrew culture of the desert. In the second play *Balaam* (1925) the tension between Balaam and Moses embodies the dramatic theme of conflict between the forces of darkness (Balaam) and the forces of light (Moses). *Tyre and Jerusalem*, written in 1933, presents the idea of polarities of culture shown through the characterisation of Jezebel, Elijah and Elisha. In *You Will Not Make Iron Gods* (1937) Gog, who personifies Aryanism and Nazism, and Abraham, representing Judaism, are locked in a relentless struggle. Through the power of his poetry Shoham was able to endow language with a dimension of its own and this is precisely why his plays failed as theatre: because his literary, idiosyncratic diction is completely unsuited to the stage. In fact Habimah wanted to stage *Tyre and Jerusalem* a few years ago and Tyrone Guthrie, then the visiting director, refused to do so because of the monumental task of overcoming Shoham's monumental language.

The vital fact about Shoham's approach to his subject matter is that he did not see in the Bible sublime material which was to be avoided at all costs. He regarded it rather as a challenge. To him the Bible was the primary source of human and Jewish archetypes. He accordingly took Biblical events and changed them around, juxtaposed them, anachronised them to a certain extent but the tradition and consecration of the source remained a stable and fundamental background. Shoham's new combination of events which in themselves were familiar to the audiences attained something of the power of metaphor. He tried both to remain faithful to the Biblical world and at the same time to go beyond it. He piled up exotically oriental and Biblical place names, like Jericho, Egypt, Moab, Midian, Lebanon and Arabia to appeal to the historical consciousness of the audience while freeing him from confinement to one historical place. Another method he used to provide his world with both local authenticity and a sense of universality was his detailed enumeration of materials, colours, smells, clothes and ornaments which were

S.An-ski (Solomon Rappoport), the creator of *The Dybbuk*. This is one of the immortal plays in all of theatrical and dramatic literature. Despite the paucity of Jewish drama, despite its slow and painful development through centuries of the greatest theatrical and dramatic activity in practically every country in Europe, it was still able to give the world *The Dybbuk*: one man of genius redeemed the rarity of others in his field. Instead of dying through lack of sustenance the few meagre shoots of Jewish drama consolidated to become the flowering of a masterpiece.

The play was produced by the young Habimah group under the direction of Stanislavski's most promising pupil, Evgeny Vachtangov. Due to his ill health production of *The Dybbuk* was delayed until 1922 when it was first presented in Moscow. Besides the playwright, the director and the actors, three other great artists participated in its staging: the painter Nathan Altman, the composer Yoel Engel and Bialik who translated it into Hebrew.

Like the English miracle plays *The Dybbuk* was not intended only to be a realistic reproduction of life but a moral tale whose symbolism attempts to explain mystic truth concealed from human apprehension. The total effect of the play, still always seen as a copy of the original production, unchanged, exactly as it was over fifty years ago, is that of a religious ritual. The point of the play is that the force of human love ultimately triumphs. The secondary, Hassidic, message is that a religion of law, Orthodox Judaism, is incapable of dealing with the essential emotions of life, but Hassidism, which believes that man can through love and joy achieve personal and total union with God, is able to achieve the highest kind of human experience.

Not only was *The Dybbuk* a milestone in the history of Hebrew drama but the founding and subsequent success of the Moscow-based Habimah Studio was an extraordinary process which culminated in the establishment of Israel's National Theatre. Mendel Kohansky describes it: "Habimah was a phenomenon unique in the entire history of theatre. Founded in the midst of a revolution in an environment which could not provide an audience understanding Hebrew and was moreover hostile to the language, which was officially branded a tool of reactionary clerical elements, the Habimah Studio absorbed so much that was to be derived from one of the great periods of the history of theatre art through some of the greatest teachers that ever lived. It emerged an international sensation with phenomenal success in the capitals of the world, as well as the most cherished cultural possession of the Jewish people . . ."[4]

[4]Mendel Kohansky. *The Hebrew Drama – its First Fifty Years*. Ktav Publishing House, N.Y., 1969.

2 Hascalah

Mention must be made, during any consideration of the history of Hebrew drama, of the Jewish cultural renaissance called the Hascalah which aimed to introduce the Jew to the language, literature and science of other nations, while stimulating a revival of his own culture. For generations the Jews had been enclosed in a restricted circle of religious and moral education and now, for the first time, they were presented with other criteria for their consideration. The Hascalah movement, which swept the areas of Jewish settlement in Eastern Europe in the late nineteenth century, was reflected in and affected all existing literary forms; even the drama underwent a renaissance under the influence of the new humanistic, liberal thinking, for it was during this period that the Yiddish theatre reached a peak of excellence. There was also a growing body of drama written in Hebrew but it had never been functionally theatrical and while it had the value of faithfully reflecting the new cultural philosophy it did not even now exhibit any promising innovations in form.

The eighteenth-century plays of Moshe Haim Luzzato had exerted direct influence upon all subsequent Hebrew dramaturgy, not least of all that of the nineteenth century. His didacticism was particularly suited to the spirit of the Hascalah and deeply affected authors caught up in the movement as it moved rapidly from Western to Eastern Europe. Early nineteenth-century Hebrew drama in any case tended towards didacticism mainly because it had for a long time been customary to teach through the medium of literature and writers had adapted themselves to utilising this method; secondly, by giving their works a strongly moral tone they could still justify their choice of a "forbidden" form by showing that drama, like the other literature, was able to serve as a vehicle for the promotion of moral standards. Their plays were consequently "literary", lacking real characters and convincing plots, but they were nevertheless a means of initiating the Hebrew writer – to whom dramatic art was still foreign – into attempting good dialogue.

There were a few noteworthy trends common to the Hebrew playwriting of this period: the first was a change in the manner of utilising Biblical stories as a basis for the dramatic situation. What the nineteenth-century Hebrew playwrights sought was not so much a concretely historical background, that is, something definite and restricted in time and place, but a vaguely historical milieu which could easily be developed by the writer's imagination. They did not see their source as pure history or as something to be reproduced with historical precision but rather as a kind of legendary or saga material which left room for a free play of creative ideas. Many of them advocated renovating Biblical sources by giving them a modern interpretation; others pointed out the impossibility of theatrically realising the greatest Biblical characters and maintained that the only way open to the Biblical dramatists was to use secondary characters who were not likely to clash with the archetypal figures spectators knew and revered. Still another possibility was to create fictional characters and inject them into the Biblical world, in other words, to use a Biblical background for the presentation of a contemporary melodrama. Similar controversies around the Biblical plays, their nature, structure and purpose, are continuing up to the present day.

Another trend of Hascalah drama was the translation and adaptation of European plays, many on Biblical themes. During the earliest phase of the movement Hebrew writers were not yet capable of producing a viable Biblical drama, for psychological as well as technical reasons. The old taboos were not to be shaken off in so short a time and so suddenly; the Bible was still not to be tampered with. It was far safer at first to translate and present someone else's work on a holy subject. As time passed they did not confine themselves only to Biblical material but translated other plays as well, for example, a dramatist called Meir Ha-Levi Letteris translated and adapted Goethe's *Faust* in his own original manner: he Judaised the text and re-named the characters, at the same time radically altering their personalities. Letteris cast the rebellious third-century sage Elisha ben Avuyah as his Jewish Faust.

Some of the trends of the Hascalah continued through the period of national renaissance in Palestine in the early years of the twentieth century. The most common feature of that period was the historical melodrama which had evolved from the Biblical plays of the Hascalah. Among significant playwrights in this genre was Judah Loeb Landau who was the founder of the Hebrew Department at the Witwatersrand University in Johannesburg and one of the foremost Jewish playwrights of his time, not least of all because his plays were actually staged. His poetic dramas which developed Hascalah themes were written in an ornate and eloquent style and dealt either with the relationships of gentiles and Jews during crises in Jewish history or the ideology of the love of Zion. His style and structure were generally unsuited for the theatre, for his drama, in conformity with the Hebrew historical play of the period, was very much a melodrama of ideas. Landau, in common with his contemporary Hebrew playwrights, was unable to create dramatic action that derived naturally from the cultural milieu it was supposed to represent. His characters were stock, or personifications of ideas which were not realised into fully developed *dramatis personae*.

The major dramatic figure of the period was Mattatiyahu Shoham who composed four Biblical plays in verse which, because of their original style and structure and imaginative concept of historical events, are landmarks in the history of Hebrew drama. Shoham was born in 1893 and died in 1937. His first play *Jericho* has for its main characters Achan and Rahab, whose love for each other is symbolic of the attraction between the decadent culture of Jericho and the rigorous vital Hebrew culture of the desert. In the second play *Balaam* (1925) the tension between Balaam and Moses embodies the dramatic theme of conflict between the forces of darkness (Balaam) and the forces of light (Moses). *Tyre and Jerusalem*, written in 1933, presents the idea of polarities of culture shown through the characterisation of Jezebel, Elijah and Elisha. In *You Will Not Make Iron Gods* (1937) Gog, who personifies Aryanism and Nazism, and Abraham, representing Judaism, are locked in a relentless struggle. Through the power of his poetry Shoham was able to endow language with a dimension of its own and this is precisely why his plays failed as theatre: because his literary, idiosyncratic diction is completely unsuited to the stage. In fact Habimah wanted to stage *Tyre and Jerusalem* a few years ago and Tyrone Guthrie, then the visiting director, refused to do so because of the monumental task of overcoming Shoham's monumental language.

The vital fact about Shoham's approach to his subject matter is that he did not see in the Bible sublime material which was to be avoided at all costs. He regarded it rather as a challenge. To him the Bible was the primary source of human and Jewish archetypes. He accordingly took Biblical events and changed them around, juxtaposed them, anachronised them to a certain extent but the tradition and consecration of the source remained a stable and fundamental background. Shoham's new combination of events which in themselves were familiar to the audiences attained something of the power of metaphor. He tried both to remain faithful to the Biblical world and at the same time to go beyond it. He piled up exotically oriental and Biblical place names, like Jericho, Egypt, Moab, Midian, Lebanon and Arabia to appeal to the historical consciousness of the audience while freeing him from confinement to one historical place. Another method he used to provide his world with both local authenticity and a sense of universality was his detailed enumeration of materials, colours, smells, clothes and ornaments which were characteristic of the period and the area. Images like burnished brass, hewn stone, marble, purple silk, mandrake, balm, incense and so on gave his works the sensuous flavour of eastern exoticism.

His plays were not theatre, primarily because of the predominance in them of inner interpretation over dramatic action. Expository monologues, dialogues, poetic images and characters whose primary function is symbolic or allegorical were more important to Shoham than dramatic action. There is a structural disproportion to his plays which accounts for their atheatrical nature. They are in three acts but are more suited to a five-act structure. The scenes are not organically linked, the characters take turns in coming out to present their points of view. Each offers himself and his ideology to the audience. The dramatic situation is not exhibited on the stage until well into the play, sometimes only at the end of the first act. Throughout the plays the real drama, the encounters and conflicts, all the components of the plot, happen off-stage and only the second act carries a certain amount of action which even then is little more than a dialogue revealing hidden identity, or a love scene which consists very definitely of dialogue only. Characteristic of Shoham's method is the disproportion between the "anticipating motives" (to use Goethe's phrase) and their realisation. The dénouement in the third act is primarily an evaluation of the action that had taken place in the previous act.

Shoham tends to present his characters as dialectical pairs representing opposing ideas but he neither develops the dialectical contrasts nor does he transform them into central threads in the plot. His imagery, vivid as it is, creates a unity that is literary rather than theatrical, a poetic process independent of the dramatic involvement. Yet despite the shortcomings of his drama as theatre Shoham made a positive contribution to the developing Hebrew dramaturgy by supplying Jewish writers with a paradigm for a mythic past and by drawing his characters away from the inviolate framework of the Biblical text.

Hascalah Hebrew drama was profound, philosophical, linguistically innovating and above all intensely serious. Yiddish drama of the same period might not have been any of these things but it was undoubtedly theatre. Yet it functioned only as an expression of a confined and restricted environment and when the need for it had passed it gradually became a theatrical curiosity and has remained so to the present day. Hebrew drama, however, moved forward with the development of the people in the country that was to become their own.

3 The Theatres of Israel

1 The Yishuv

Throughout the period in which Habimah was making momentous progress in Russia and then touring Europe and the United States, attempts to create a Hebrew theatre were already being made in the settlements in Palestine where shortly after the First World War streams of immigrants were pouring in from all over the world. They were in the main young and idealistic and through their diverse backgrounds served as representatives of the culture and language of practically every European country. There was of course no professional theatre as yet in Palestine, there were hardly any dramatists, no professional companies, only dramatic societies consisting of teachers, amateur actors and writers. Many among the older generation opposed the idea of theatre in principle, bound as they were to the totalitarian authority of the rabbis and even some of the young people considered it an unnecessary frivolity. Most of the settlers, however, saw it as a vital aspect of their growing Hebrew culture. In the beginning audiences had been content to see plays in Russian or Yiddish translation but now in the midst of national fervour the decision was taken to stimulate Hebrew as a spoken, living language and the theatre was seen as a superb means of doing so. The young settlers decided also that the theatre could serve as a general educational institution for adults, in fact it was in this aspect that the founders saw its most important function. Because of this rather one-sided attitude they were not particularly concerned with technicalities of theatrecraft for their main interest lay in presenting the new and living language for their fellow pioneers. The Yishuv (Settlement) in Palestine was small, few of the immigrant-pioneers spoke a passable Hebrew and moreover they were scattered throughout the area, sometimes living on remote and unwelcoming tracts of land. Only a few were gathered in the two small towns, Tel-Aviv-Jaffo and Jerusalem. In these difficult conditions "The Hebrew Theatre" – for that was its name – was founded under the management of the producer David Davidoff, and his first theatrical offering in November 1920 was a programme of three one-act plays (including one by Chekhov) translated of course into Hebrew. After this, many translations were presented, Ibsen, Chekhov and Strindberg being the most popular European playwrights. An early offering by this theatre was *A Doll's House* which received the same antagonistic press in Palestine as it had all over the world. It must be one of the incongruities of theatrical history to have had

Ibsen's stifling northern parlours and raging passions fettered under the precise actions of the characters, presented in Hebrew in the desert to Jewish farmers whose world was at present light years away from Ibsen's. And yet they loved him – perhaps because they were not so far removed: the tendency has been for later generations to imagine those days in Palestine exclusively in terms of the swamps and the arid land and shirt-sleeved pioneers wringing sustenance from the soil. These were indeed the major preoccupations of the Yishuv but among its immigrants were also writers, artists and philosophers who had experienced the European theatre, with Ibsen, Strindberg and Chekhov, among others, an inseparable part of their cultural lives in their countries of origin, and they subsequently brought this acquaintance with them to Palestine. The majority of pioneers were, however, not sophisticated theatregoers and while they might have enjoyed Ibsen and the others as a curiosity they preferred to see the native Hebrew drama which expressed an environment more immediately familiar to them. There was still too little of this and faint hope of much more in the years to come. A serious blow to the theatre movement was the splitting of "The Hebrew Theatre", with some of its members remaining in Palestine and the rest moving to Berlin where they joined Menachem Gnessin's Habimah group. Those who remained in the Yishuv reorganised themselves into another company but its character had altered. It could no longer afford to ignore the demands of the theatre as an art or to be careless with the text of a play: generally it had to impose greater self-discipline and then to discipline its audience which had grown accustomed to frequent delays and breakdowns during the course of a performance and was becoming conditioned to taking every theatrical production lightly and frivolously. The group had to concentrate on achieving absolute purity of language as an example to its multilingual audience who were attempting to learn Hebrew as quickly as possible. Translations of foreign texts had to be exact and artistically truthful. Under Davidoff, who had remained, the company persevered but could still not attain a standard high enough to satisfy the few serious critics who had been educated in theatre and drama. Constant criticism, although for the most part constructive, undermined the company's spirit and swayed audiences who were themselves imperfect, comprised, as they were, of some whose theatrical standards were high and others who were ignorant of any kind of theatrical enterprise. A change was inevitable. When the Habimah company arrived from Berlin in 1926 Davidoff joined it as an actor and "The Hebrew Theatre" was split once again.

By 1931 three permanent companies were functioning in Palestine: Habimah, which had come to settle permanently after extensive travels in Europe and the United States, the Ohel and Matateh, a theatre devoted to humour and satire.

The first Hebrew plays produced in Palestine were those written in Europe expressing the powerful impression the national awakening had made on Jews everywhere. The first Hebrew drama about life in the Yishuv was Orloff's "אללה כרים" and many similar plays followed, notably those of Nathan Bistritzski, Aharon Aschman and Sh.Shalom. They were local, regional plays, dealing with topics relevant to the time and the people, mirroring and discussing the hardships of life around them. Their heroes still did not exist as individuals but now they had become representatives of classes and groups. The central and most idealised character-type was the settler-pioneer with his problems of adjustment, the constant battle with harsh government and the stubborn soil. The plays did no more than describe these problems and the people involved in creating or solving them: the Arabs and their employers, young intellectuals, courageous women, the weaklings and failures. Representative of all the plays of the period was Aharon Aschman's *This Earth* (Habimah, 1942) which offered a description of the settlers' lives in Palestine through presentation of the familiar archetypes: the religious Jew who sees settlement in the Promised Land as the only salvation; the Zionist youth, the labourers, pioneers, builders, the intellectual, assimilated in Europe and unwilling to compromise his identity and remain in Israel, and finally the seeker after profit and financial gain. This play and others, in which the only differences are the character-types that changed with the times, are typical of the early development of drama in Israel. What critics and audiences enjoyed most about them was the faithful realism of setting and event, the reproduction of a world familiar to all of them and the living, colloquial language.

In the years following, these topics disappeared from the drama and others, more immediate, took their place. Translations of classical and well-known modern works continued to appear. The Biblical-historical drama had by this time progressed further; its characters were portrayed as living beings, not heroic archetypal figures, yet the plays still did not dare entirely to reduce the massive personalities of the Bible to the proportions of ordinary human life.

2 *The Theatres*

Drama and theatre was of vital importance in the lives of the pioneers in Palestine. They lived in a hostile country at the most hostile time in the history of the modern world. They had to draw fruitfulness from uncompromising, rocky land. They suffered from deprivation and epidemic diseases while the enmity of the forces in control of the country made their enormous task almost hopeless. Yet they wanted an artistic drama representative of themselves and their lives. After a day's work they came off the land and into the makeshift hut that served as a theatre and under the most primitive conditions acted out and watched not only scenes from their own long and tortured history or the drama of their everday life, but also the greatest works in the dramatic repertoire of the world.

From these simple beginnings grew the theatres of modern-day Israel and these first, curious spectators were the founders of the theatrical life of the country. Today the theatre fills a central position in the cultural life of Israel. Attendance of performances is one of the highest in the world, the number of tickets sold in a year being greater than the number of inhabitants in the country. Serious theatre exercises the strongest drawing power; despite competition from companies specialising in light entertainment, the advent of musical comedy, which has recently found a permanent place on the theatrical scene, and numerous productions of satirical plays, the repertory theatre remains the most popular.

In Tel Aviv, a city of slightly less than half a million inhabitants, there are on any given night at the present time plays by Shakespeare, Ibsen, Ionesco, Brecht and two or more Israeli writers in addition to experimental plays offered by young theatre groups. Of the entire Jewish population of Israel (just over three million) almost half this number are new immigrants who have arrived within the last two decades and whose knowledge of Hebrew is still superficial. The ratio of theatre attendance to total population is about eight times higher in Israel than in the USA. In certain European countries the proportion is higher than that of the USA but not as high as in Israel. The percentage of theatregoers is 20 per cent of the entire Israeli population as against 5 per cent in England, this latter figure including tourists, who are to a large extent debarred from Israeli theatre attendance because of the language. There is also a difference in the social constituency of the Israeli theatregoing public. In other western countries theatre-lovers are drawn mainly from the upper middle classes, primarily the professional strata and university students. This is true, for example, of the USA and England, except that the proportion of non-professionals is higher in England than in America, and Western Germany has yet a higher percentage of workers and farmers in theatre audiences. In Israel there is no exclusiveness at all: audiences are comprised of a high percentage of non-professionals, labourers, farmers and immigrants from less developed countries, in addition to the professionals and students.[1]

[1] Statistical material from "The Israeli Theatrophilia" by Isaiah Weinberg. *Bamah* 40, Winter 1969.

Theatrical activity is not confined solely to urban areas. All the Israeli theatres bring their plays to the villages and settlements, however remote they may be. The repertory theatres of Tel Aviv and Haifa give from 30 to 40 per cent of their performances outside their cities, under the auspices and with the help of the Histadrut, the Israel Federation of Labour. The theatrical season in Israel lasts for eleven months of the year. During each season about thirty plays are produced and this figure does not include musicals and light entertainment.

Public controversy rages around almost every aspect of theatre and drama. For example critics and audiences dispute the fact that managements frequently include in a season's offerings musical comedy and light satirical entertainment which their companies are not, according to the experts, equipped to undertake. Until recently managements and officials were engaged in disputes about subsidies and public support of theatres with a view to establishing a consistent identity. There is endless controversy about the value of the original play, about the establishment of a permanent children's theatre and about the ideal form of theatre management. This constant interest in the problems of the theatre and the fact that the number of theatregoers in Israel increases year by year bears witness not only to the popularity drama has attained but also to the influence it exerts on the forging of a cultural image and the cultural standards of the State. This influence is perhaps more important in Israel than in any other country for Israel's initial difficulty in this sphere is the blending of a host of backgrounds and languages from all parts of the world into a homogeneous cultural unity.

The nucleus of Israel's theatrical life is formed by the Habimah Theatre, the Cameri and the Haifa Municipal Theatre. These bear the responsibility of moulding the image that the Israeli theatre and the Hebrew drama is ultimately going to have. The largest and most venerable of these theatres is the official National Theatre, called Habimah, situated in Tel Aviv. Like the history of the development of Israel generally that of Habimah is one of dedication and determination. From Goldfaden's time Jewish troupes in Eastern Europe had battled against harsh official restrictions placed on performances of plays in Yiddish and German. The Habimah troupe had in addition to contend with Jewish socialists who refused to tolerate the separatist idea of cultivating Zionism or the Hebrew language. Attempts to organise Hebrew theatrical groups had been made several years previously in Lodz, Warsaw and Bialystok but they had failed. Nevertheless the concept of Habimah as a Jewish theatre proved to be irresistible for it was growing in a period in which the struggle for freedom was the primary inspiration of life and art, and which saw the renaissance of the Jews as a nation. There had already been migrations to Palestine where pioneers were busy resurrecting the Hebrew language and its vast literature.

The founder of Habimah, Nahum Zemach, a lover of Hebrew and a staunch advocate of its modern revival, was at that time a wealthy merchant in Moscow. For an entire year he personally financed the training of artists he had selected until they were ready to appear before the public. There were thirteen people in the original group when Zemach approached Stanislavski to seek his advice. The famous director grew enthusiastic at the idea of creating a theatre in the ancient Hebrew language and he delegated his brilliant pupil, Evgeny Vachtangov, to teach the group until, with his help, the Habimah Studio was founded, later to be affiliated to the Moscow Arts Theatre. Under Vachtangov's skilled and methodical guidance the group had, within a year, rehearsed four one-act plays by Jewish dramatists which then had their world premiere under the inclusive title of *Genesis* in October 1918. It won instant recognition from the public and in official circles. The production which established Habimah's fame for all time was that of *The Dybbuk* and due to its immense success the studio was accepted as a national academic institution to be subsidised by the Government, despite the continuing objections of the Jewish socialists.

The founders were aware that repertoire was vital in the shaping of a theatre's character; if Habimah were to be a national Hebrew theatre it had to utilise themes relating to the Jewish past in order to give itself a concrete identity. Accordingly they produced *Israel's Dream* by R.B.Hoffman and *The Deluge* by H.Berger. Later, dramatic material relating to subsequent periods in Jewish history would be added. In 1926 Habimah left Russia for the first of its tours of Europe and the United States, including in its repertoire Jewish historical and Biblical plays. In the USA in 1927 the company divided, the smaller group under Zemach remaining in New York where Zemach later died, and the larger group, after a series of tours during which they presented about fifteen hundred performances in one hundred and twenty-five cities, finally settled in Palestine in 1931.

Gradually the company began to deviate from the narrow path of presenting exclusively "Jewish" plays. On their arrival in Palestine they resolved to experiment with foreign works especially those they felt contained greater universal content. They featured Greek tragedy, Shakespeare and the best of classical and contemporary playwrights without, however, losing sight of their original aim which was to cultivate the Biblical-historical drama of the Jews. The years 1932–39 marked a synthesis in the repertoire, a kind of compromise between the "Jewish" and "general" themes and from the end of the thirties a new trend became noticeable: the move to develop original Hebrew dramaturgy and the encouragement of indigenous plays, both Biblical-historical and temporal, for example *Michal, The Daughter of Saul* and *This Earth* by Aharon Aschman, *The Love of Zion* by Avraham Mapu and *At the End of Days* by Haim Hazaz (which has remained a popular feature of the Israeli repertoire).

The group was, however, handicapped by the lack of a permanent theatre. The municipality of Tel Aviv decided to erect a building for them but this project was interrupted by the Second World War and completed only after the war, when Habimah celebrated its silver jubilee with the opening of the new auditorium *Beit Habimah* in Tel Aviv. In 1948 Habimah took the odd decision to tour the United States at the most critical time in their nation's long struggle for survival. It is not surprising that this plan failed to meet with public approval and, to make matters worse, the tour itself was not a success. When the company returned, its membership was divided by the worst crisis of its existence but it was not dissolved and continued to function after certain important internal reforms, one of which abolished the totalitarian rule of the established collective and set up instead a board of management which was more representative of the company as a whole.

In 1954 Habimah was invited to participate in the first international theatre festival in Paris and it visited France again for a similar purpose three years later. In 1958 it was officially accredited by the Government as the National Theatre with an annual subsidy of 100,000 Israeli lira.

Until then its internal structure had been a modified collective which adopted additional regulations concerning both the artistic and administrative aspects of the theatre and gradually evolved with the passage of time from the rigid cooperative of its earliest days. Generally the collective structure of many of Israel's theatres has presented tremendous problems. It was originally established in order to give everyone in the group an equal chance to appear on the stage and an equal voice in all matters of policy, and one of its better consequences was that it successfully prevented the growth of a "star" system. The theatre collective was the fruit of a revolutionary period in history, a time when all accepted values were traumatically changed, and Israel's young and idealistic socialists gladly adopted this system which seemed to suit them better than all others. Its original intention had been to create a superb company in which an actor who played Hamlet would not feel a loss of prestige if in another play he had to say "Dinner is served". But in practice it did not work, for the man who was capable only of announcing dinner demanded to be allowed to play Hamlet and there are few who are equipped artistically or temperamentally consistently to do both. Leah Goldberg describes the system: "Majority decision is of no help to art. In the rest of the world it is customary for an actor who for years has never played two decent parts, whom the public no longer wishes to see, and to whom the critics point as being unable to take two steps without infringing good taste – to leave the theatre and take up some other form of life where he will be more successful. In our country under the collective system, the actor remains on the stage until the day of his death by virtue of his belonging to the company."[2] These frequently useless members were an enormous financial drain on theatres whose artistic existence was in any case plagued by financial worry. The collective still employed until recently in some of Israel's theatres was based on majority opinion but it became clear that democracy cannot function within the framework of an artistic group. In 1968 Habimah's need for a collective fell away. After more than half a century of existence as a cooperative it became a public trusteeship with the trustees and General Manager appointed by the Minister of Education and Culture.

In 1962 its "Little Theatre", having a seating capacity of three hundred, was opened. This has since been instrumental in bringing before the public many works by unknown young authors although constant financial difficulties do not allow it to undertake the independent experimentation that the growing drama of Israel demands. In 1970, after reconstruction lasting almost two years and costing over seven million lira, the new, renovated Habimah was opened. What had been intended to be no more than a repaired structure had eventually grown into a new, modern and highly technological theatre seating nine hundred, with electronically-controlled stage equipment, two revolving stages, one of them fourteen metres in diameter, and forty-five flies able to raise sets to a height of twenty-five metres.

[2] "Aspects of the Israeli Theatre" by Leah Goldberg. *Jewish Affairs* (South Africa), July 1952.

[3]"The New Habimah Theatre" by Dora Sowden. *South African Jewish Chronicle New Year Annual*, September 25th 1970.

The plays chosen to celebrate its opening season were all foreign, by Brecht, Chekhov and Dekker. The reason given by Habimah's artistic director[3] for this selection was that "there was unhappily no Israeli play of international standard for us to start with. To make well-meaning gestures is useless . . ." Unfortunately this attitude – to which no better term than snobbishness can truthfully be applied – is representative of other managements apart from Habimah's when, faced with a choice of repertoire and with the greatest respect to Israel's artistic directors, it is indefensible. Milestones in the development of Israel's theatre must be marked by the presentation of at least one native play in a celebratory or festive season, and a "well-meaning gesture" in this respect is essential to the pride and confidence of Israeli dramaturgy. The gesture need not even be well-meaning for Hebrew drama is not so faulty that it has to be hidden away, like an ugly and backward child, from the eyes of important visitors. There is indeed a narrow line dividing certain priorities on an occasion such as that represented by the opening of the New Habimah in 1970: the priority of emotionalism, typified by pride – and Habimah has in the past rarely lacked a sense of occasion – and the priority of art, typified by the selection of plays for a season. Habimah has never shown itself deficient in its encouragement of young Israeli playwrights and in order to be justifiably regarded as Israel's National Theatre it should unequivocally support its own national drama.

While Habimah was touring America and Europe after having left Russia, one of its founders arrived in Palestine. Moshe Halevi was a young man of vision, a pupil of the great Vachtangov, an actor and director. In 1925 he founded a drama studio together with the cultural committee of the Histadrut. Conditions that year were far from suitable for any kind of theatrical venture: European theatre was enduring a time of crisis, it had lost its direction and was experimenting with form and content, rebelliously rejecting all the traditions of the nineteenth century. In Palestine the Jewish population was struggling for its daily existence. Immigration was increasing and absorption of the new pioneers presented many problems; people from all over the world were arriving, speaking their native languages, finding Hebrew difficult and learning it slowly. This did not deter Moshe Halevi: his dream was to found a Hebrew workers' theatre which, in addition to achieving the stated aim of bringing Hebrew language and culture to the new settlers in the new land, would also serve the ideals of the revolution. He called his theatre Ohel, meaning tent or tabernacle. Its drama studio began to teach speech, movement, deportment, music and the theoretical principles of art, following the Stanislavski-Vachtangov method. Classes were held in the evenings when the workers came off the land. Thirty-six men and women had been selected from among those who showed particular interest in the project. They studied Hebrew together with methods of stagecraft and they built a small house in Tel Aviv which rapidly became the cultural centre of the community.

At the end of its first year, on the stage of the Herzlia Secondary School in Tel Aviv, the new company presented scenes from dramatised stories of Y.L.Peretz. This production was enthusiastically received and the theatre was launched with much public approval. However, the choice of repertoire presented a serious problem from the beginning. The Ohel as a workers' theatre had to analyse, on the one hand, the desire for general social justice, for the establishment of a unique form of society and, on the other, the renaissance of a *specific* nation in its homeland. Nor could the new nation neglect its cultural heritage, so the Bible was not to be ignored. Halevi used to say: "The Bible is our folklore; it is so to this day; it is not bare history." He clearly grasped the important implications of the Biblical text as the mainspring of Hebrew dramatic classicism. The Ohel accordingly returned to Biblical source material, at the same time seeking original methods of staging it. Its actors would, for example, actively participate in the people's celebrations that took place throughout the country, such as revivals of harvest festival rites (Shavuot) or the Purim carnivals, and incorporate elements of these festivities in their productions. While they were rehearsing *Jacob and Rachel* by the Russian playwright Kroschennikov, translated and altered by the Hebrew poet Avraham Shlonsky, the entire company went to visit Bedouin encampments in the Negev desert, to familiarise themselves with the life of the nomad before mounting the play. Throughout their training Halevi put into practice the ideas and methods learned from his mentors Stanislavski and Vachtangov. Later Ohel presented Stefan Zweig's *Jeremiah* which had been rehearsed among the ruins in Jerusalem and which was relevant to the nineteen-twenties, after the First World War. Because of Ohel's initial success directors began to visit its centre and some of them produced plays for it, including Brecht's *The Threepenny Opera*. Immigration from Germany, due to the rise of Nazism to power in 1933, injected into the new theatre a permanent nucleus of talented artists, including the director Friedrich Lobbe, who guided it away from its rigid programme of Biblical themes, Jewish socialist dramatisations and Russian-Jewish folklore and introduced contemporary works from every European country. The Ohel theatre began to be worthy of evaluation by artistic criteria, no longer only as a studio but as a professional body gradually crystallising into a popular Hebrew theatre in principle and style, working towards a specific national image, still socialist in outlook. At the same time Halevi continued producing plays with Jewish historical appeal, including original Hebrew plays such as *Batya* (1940) by Zvi Shatz, about the workers in the Yishuv, *In the Alleys of Jerusalem* (1941) by Yeshua Bar-Yosef, about the Jewish community in the old city of Jerusalem and Sami Groneman's *The King and the Cobbler* (1943) the first Biblical musical comedy to be performed in Israel.

In 1948 the entire country was plunged into turmoil and theatres were not unaffected, except Habimah which undertook its tour of the United States at that particularly inopportune time. Actors from all theatre companies and studios joined the army and there was certainly no money to spare for ambitious theatrical ventures. After the war masses of immigrants arrived in Israel and theatre was very far from their immediate needs. The Ohel's collective structure disintegrated; at the same time new little companies began to develop, providing immense competition for the established groups. The Ohel's theatrical knowledge was proved insufficient, its means were dwindling. The company disbanded but later reorganised, with certain changes in its character and formation. Its greatest success at that time was a revival of *The Good Soldier Schweik* which ran for over seven hundred performances. Yet the theatre had lost its definite direction and its unique identity.

In 1954 Ohel broke away from the Histadrut which had been calling for its closure after withdrawing its subsidies; the theatre continued, however, to produce plays with a social message, including a number of original Hebrew plays which described life factually as it was lived in the new State. It then attempted to reorganise as a cooperative-collective but in 1963 this structure was again modified, the theatre then being run by an executive composed of three actors and headed by an administrative and an artistic manager. The major problem facing Ohel was one which until recently had plagued every professional theatre in Israel: choice of repertoire being dependent on financial means; the forging of a specific personality with only limited funds at its disposal; the inability to remain free of external problems as long as it was insufficiently subsidised by official institutions. The Ohel had finally to surrender after struggling on as a repertory theatre until 1969, when it was liquidated. "True to its decision to limit the number of subsidised theatres the Government did not rush to the stricken company's rescue. The public accepted this without protest . . ."[4] A bitter ending to a valiant theatrical endeavour.

[4]"Structural Changes in the Israel Theatre" by Isaiah Weinberg. *Israel Theatre 69/70*. Published by the Israel Centre of the ITI, 1971.

With the end of the Second World War all the latent forces among the Jewish population of Palestine and among the youth in particular suddenly burst loose onto the political, social, economic and cultural scenes. It was a critical time for the country with the Yishuv – among its other problems – bitterly resentful of the Mandatory Government. Nevertheless a group of five young actors, all Israel-born, who had left Habimah, joined Czechoslovakian Joseph Milo who had resigned from the "Matateh" company to found the youngest and to date the most dynamic of Israel's theatres: the Cameri or Chamber Theatre. This theatre was to express methods of presentation radically different from anything customary in the country; it would forge a distinct Israeli art by altering, inter alia, acting techniques which were still stilted and stylised, by using only the Hebrew vernacular with its richness of colloquialism and slang and above all by promoting the original Hebrew play. "The fact that promoters of the Cameri all belonged in the circle of the young Israeli generation is one of the determining and characteristic features of this theatre to this day . . ."[5]

[5]"The Cameri Theatre" by Moshe Shamir. *World Theatre*, May–June 1965.

Milo directed the early performances and constituted the dynamic force behind the new theatre's activities. He was the first Israeli director blessed with fresh and independent ideas. "Everything centred around him. It was he who decided on the plays we would do. He had new ideas, unheard of on the Hebrew stage. The manner of directing was all his own. His personality permeated everything we did."[6] Milo's aim was to depart from the many little copies of the original *Dybbuk* and to prove that the theatre was not a place of prayer on the one hand nor boredom on the other, but enjoyment, which need not be provided solely by American comedy or British farce but also by Shakespeare and O'Neill and, above all, by contemporary original Hebrew plays.

[6]Hannah Meron, quoted in "The Cameri" by Sraya Shapiro. *Jerusalem Post*, December 26th 1969.

His company chose four one-act plays for their debut and later, in October 1945, their production of *The Servant of Two Masters* by Goldoni made a tremendous impression on what was largely an apathetic public. It was played in the style of the *commedia dell'arte* utilising free and colloquial language. Only a few professionals took part, the rest were apprentice actors who were talented, young and enthusiastic. It was something completely novel in the country's theatre. During the first few years of its existence the young company encountered characteristic obstacles: it realised, as have all the Israeli theatres, that where survival depends on public patronage and box-office returns it cannot afford to perform only "good" experimental drama which is unknown and likely to be unpopular, no matter how youthful and adventurous the theatre's spirit may be. At the same time Cameri recognised that its cast was not technically equipped to handle foreign plays and its standard of performance was dropping. With an eye to front office returns it then mounted plays like *I Remember Mama* and *Charley's Aunt* which revealed a great deal about its public's taste, for their immediate success saved the theatre and allowed it to introduce a selection of contemporary American drama: Miller, Odets, O'Neill and Williams, in addition to revivals of well-loved classics.

1948 brought the War of Independence. The Cameri performed in the field and was the first company to reach Jerusalem after the siege. And it was the Cameri that provided what was to be the turning-point in the history and development of contemporary Hebrew drama: the first performance of Moshe Shamir's play *He Walked in the Fields* under the direction of Joseph Milo. It proved a theatrical sensation. Moshe Shamir himself says: "This play represented the response of the Cameri Theatre to the spirit of the time; by reason of its outstanding success it exerted a profound influence on this and on other theatres as well as on the younger generation of writers, and promoted them to evolve new paths in Israeli dramaturgy . . ."[7] The immediate results were the Cameri's productions of *They Will Arrive Tomorrow* by Nathan Shaham, *Casablan* by Yigal Mossinzon, later *The Chatelaine* by Leah Goldberg, *The War of the Sons of Light* by Shamir – and later still, two plays by the noted poet Nathan Alterman.

[7]Moshe Shamir, *op. cit.*

In 1955 the Cameri moved to a permanent theatre in Tel Aviv and with better technical equipment could stage more ambitious plays, those by Brecht and Kafka, among others. It ceased to be a Chamber theatre in its repertoire and the scope of its performance, but still continued to play at the old Mograbi theatre and in various provincial towns. The company was giving three performances simultaneously almost every night of the week. During a period of three years it offered nearly thirty new works and made a trip to the Theatre of the Nations in Paris. But in 1958, when the State was ten years old, the adverse effects of rapid over-expansion became apparent. Quality of the plays was sacrificed for quantity as the Cameri attempted to draw the masses. Their standard both of production and repertoire dropped. Box-office takings dwindled as the theatre continued to stage spectacular shows which it was technically ill-equipped to handle, all for the purpose of attracting large audiences. The company was near bankruptcy. There was a tremendous crisis, and Joseph Milo resigned as the theatre's director, to become the director of the Haifa Municipal Theatre. Finally a group of eleven artists took the Cameri in hand, dismissed more than a third of the personnel connected with it and reorganised its management. The repertoire changed, included plays with smaller casts, and performances were confined to Tel Aviv only. Their financial recovery began at the end of the fifties. In 1961 a committee of supporters was formed in conjunction with the municipality, and this gave the Cameri a new permanent theatre seating 900; it was inaugurated with the first performance of Nathan Alterman's *Kinneret, Kinneret*.

Since then the Cameri has gone from strength to strength, certainly one of the most enterprising and progressive of Israel's theatres. It has become the Tel Aviv Municipal Theatre and a public trusteeship. It maintains a permanent dramatic studio of about seventy pupils and a special children's theatre. Its repertoire in any given season shows a perfect balance between classical, contemporary European and contemporary Israeli works. Its standard is consistently high. Until the establishment of the Haifa Municipal Theatre it seemed clear that of all the existing theatres the Cameri was the most likely to make the major contribution to the continued development of original Hebrew drama and to theatre generally in Israel. Now it must share this distinction with one of the youngest and most vital of all the larger theatres in the country.

Israel's first Municipal Theatre was opened in Haifa in 1961. For the first time in Israel a public body had taken upon itself responsibility for the establishment and maintenance of a theatre. This type of administrative structure is not without problems, the largest being independent choice of repertoire without interference from the administrative bodies representing the municipality by which, in effect, the theatre is owned. The company must be sure that there will be no censorship, no objection to repertoire on subjective moral or ideological grounds: it must have complete freedom in the artistic sphere . . . "Subsidised theatres as institutions of local government are liable to suffer from a multitude of related faults. They tend to develop a rigidity, a bureaucratic attitude of their own. They have a tendency to fossilise."[8]

Problems notwithstanding, the Haifa Theatre met with instant

[8] "View from the Gods" by Martin Esslin. *Plays & Players*, March 1967.

popularity in its own city. Until 1961 Haifa audiences had had to rely on short visits from Tel Aviv companies, limiting performances of any one play to less than fifty so that comparatively few people were able to see them. Now a fresh and interested public has been attracted to the theatre leading to their becoming aware of performances given by visiting companies in other venues in the city. The Haifa Theatre seats 854 and has a small adjoining hall which can be used for experimental productions. Further, it has initiated a system of subscriptions and, by 1965, had over thirteen thousand subscribers, which is an amazing number for a small and rather provincial city. The theatre is affiliated to the Histadrut for the purpose of organising special performances for workers preceded by explanatory evenings, and also to the Department of Education in order to provide visits by scholars. An affiliated children's theatre has been established. Furthermore the theatre organises introductory sessions before the opening of new plays, given by those associated with the productions who, together with writers and artists, meet informally to discuss the plays with members of the public. The repertoire is based on a synthesis of the old and the new – including contemporary Hebrew plays, although this theatre in particular was at first accused of showing insufficient interest in indigenous works, a deficiency which it has since remedied. In its first season it featured plays by Shakespeare, Frisch, Kenan, Ionesco and Shamir; since then it has presented a wide selection of contemporary European drama in addition to established classical works. In its earliest years it made important connections, for example during the Shakespeare quatercentenary it acted as host to the Bristol Old Vic; early in 1965 it was visited by the Zurich Schauspielhaus; the Haifa company visited Venice in 1963 to participate in its drama festival and it has since received invitations from theatres and festivals throughout Europe.

Israel has reason to be proud of one of its youngest theatrical children who, with its vital new ideas, its courage and incentive, may well influence the future of Hebrew drama.

Not long after the establishment of the Haifa Municipal Theatre the foundation stone of the new Jerusalem Municipal Theatre was laid. This is without doubt the most luxurious and also the most beautifully constructed of Israel's theatres. It was built at a cost of twelve million Israeli lira, a portion of this sum being provided by a private sponsor. It seats about 960 and has a stage large enough to accommodate a full-scale *Aida*. It offers similar educational facilities to those of the Haifa Municipal Theatre in respect of the drama:

discussions, poetry readings, drama classes, lectures presented in the main auditorium and activities coordinated with the accompanying productions presented by the theatre.[9] The capital has long been a problem in respect of theatre for it apparently could not provide an audience sufficiently large to justify the establishment of its own permanent theatrical company and therefore has been dependent on offerings by visiting groups. Avital Mossinzon, manager of the Jerusalem Theatre in 1973, explained this deficiency by saying that first of all Jerusalem is not sufficiently close to villages and towns housing potential theatregoers; secondly, a large percentage of the city's population is rigidly orthodox and to them the theatre is still an abomination; a further percentage are immigrants who are not orientated towards theatregoing. The magnificent Jerusalem Theatre has consequently been called a white elephant by more than one journalist for its exact purpose seems to be in question. It serves as a ballet and concert hall, a theatre, a cinema, a conference hall, a place for general entertainment and the yearly musical marathon; it is too vast for experimental plays or chamber theatre but is suitable, in fact, only for the large presentations brought to the capital by Habimah or the Cameri or the Haifa Municipal Theatre. Construction of a small 400-seat additional hall has been delayed due to lack of funds.

The Khan company, on the other hand, is a successful permanent repertory company based in Jerusalem utilising the Khan theatre complex and sharing it with other groups. It is subsidised in part by various state bodies and its aim is to present only plays "which have a particularly Israeli relevance".[10] This fact has caused some controversy for its material is often radical, leading to the general accusation of political bias wholly unacceptable to the Establishment.

The "Little Theatres", some of which have claimed several years of uninterrupted activity, are indispensable to the theatrical life of Israel. Most of them attempt to concentrate on a repertoire which the larger theatres do not or cannot handle.[11] Existence for all of them, however, is not easy. They have very few actors and necessarily a limited choice of repertoire; all suffer continuous financial problems. One of the oldest of these groups was the Zuta, established in 1955 and managed by the Polish actor Zigmund Turkov who began acting in Hebrew when he was already a veteran of the Yiddish stage. The unique feature of this company was that it presented only original Hebrew plays and was therefore of invaluable aid to unknown playwrights who were refused recognition by established theatres. The Zuta travelled throughout the country but

[9] "The Jerusalem Sherover Theatre" Pamphlet, October 1971.

[10] Naomi Sheldon. *Jerusalem Post*, August 3rd 1973.

[11] Some have, for example, specialised in humour and satire, revues and musical shows.

in 1969 it ceased to exist due partly to competition and partly to a change in governmental approach to theatre structuring. The Zavit Theatre shared a similar fate; it too had travelled throughout Israel presenting serious drama and examples of the European avant-garde, and it was responsible for staging Yehuda Amichai's first play. Unlike most of the "little" theatres it had a permanent cast. The youngest of the smaller theatres and boasting the greatest vitality was the Onot (the "Theatre of the Seasons"), founded by one of the most talented playwrights in Israel, Nissim Aloni. With this company he produced his experimental play *The American Princess*, which met with only partial success, and he followed this with a novel adaptation of a *commedia dell'arte* play which he called *Arlecchino*. The Onot had noble aims but was unable always to fulfil its ideal of a purely artistic repertoire and was forced to close in 1964. The most notable among the present-day "little" theatres is the Tzavta, maintained by the left-wing Mapam party. It designates itself a progressive theatre and is dedicated to the production of original plays and those allowing the public the opportunity of seeing the kind of drama which established theatres for one reason or another cannot offer. A remarkable "little" theatre is the Inbal Dance Group consisting of a company of dancers, singers and actors of Yemenite origin whose work is a combination of Western technique and oriental theme. Its presentations are a kind of drama in dance and song, based on elements of Yemenite-Jewish folklore both religious and secular. Its importance lies in the fact that it interprets its special themes in its own stylised manner. Each programme deals with a specific topic: Yemenite dances, imaginative Biblical scenes, shepherd dances and folk songs, or more modern and topical subjects humorously treated. The achievement of the Inbal group is amazing considering that without any artistic tradition at all its evolution of form, style and individual abilities has been remarkably rapid.

There is practically no single aspect of life in Israel – economic, social or cultural – that can be considered without taking into account the part played by the kibbutzim, particularly during the fifties when the cities were not yet claiming so many young people from the land. Almost every kibbutz has a choir, a dance company, study groups learning every possible subject, courses in foreign languages and an amateur theatre group. The structure of the kibbutz makes dramatic expression a necessary part of life for many festivals and festive occasions are celebrated by dramatic pageants or concerts, for example, the *mesibot* which include minor dramatic sketches, often ad-lib, reading aloud, playlets, the festival pageants such as that of Shavuot requiring large-scale rehearsal and the occasional presentation of a full-scale play.

The main purpose of kibbutz drama is self-expression. For years there has been a need for the representation of kibbutz life as it is with its special problems and conflicts. At the end of 1963 the first collectively organised Kibbutz Theatre was instituted and its purpose was clearly to fulfil the need for formal theatre on the kibbutzim. It was created by an entire network of active amateur groups and it has become obvious through the activity of members of these groups that the kibbutzim shelter enormous talent which has not been sufficiently exploited.

The Kibbutz Theatre was inaugurated with a production of a play by the noted playwright Nathan Shaham, himself a member of Beit Alfa. It was called *The Bicycle* and it dealt with problems specific to kibbutz life; its form was abstract and experimental, an unusual departure for the author of one of Israel's first great representational war dramas, *They Will Arrive Tomorow*.

The immigrants have not been neglected by the theatre. It is obvious that they still present an enormous problem because of their diversity of background and multitude of languages. Some of them have never been to a theatre. For them especially a group sponsored by the Histadrut was formed in 1950 and it began its activities by staging programmes of one-act plays describing the life of the country and that of the immigrants in particular.

Aviva Geli, once the theatre correspondent of the journal *Orot*, describes a typical visit to country areas by the theatrical group: "The small company arrives at the Yishuv early in the evening. Generally the hall in which the play is to be presented is still empty. Immediately the company begins to arrange the chairs and benches and they select one end of the hall as a 'stage' . . . There is no decor, only tables and chairs. When this preparation has been completed the accordionist goes outside and begins to play. The children immediately cluster around him and they are dispatched to gather the adults. In about an hour the hall is filled . . . only then does the company begin.

"At the end of the programme the audience does not move from its place, cries of 'More!' are heard . . . It has not been easy to accustom this kind of audience to plays. They prefer to go to the cinema, the miracle of film charms them more . . . but the repeated appearances of small companies have taught them to love the theatre, albeit a primitive form of the theatre . . ."[12]

These are but a few of the theatrical companies, past and present,

[12] "The Theatre on Immigrant Settlements" by Aviva Geli. *Orot*, November 1961.

which have constituted Israel's virile and dynamic theatrical life. Theatre groups come and go and experimentation continues, especially in the direction of the native Hebrew play which must be the focal point of every new theatrical venture.

Part II. The State of Israel

. . . artists who are not searching, not reaching out for anything, but working comfortably within their established resources, and who are completely lacking in daring, who never "cock a snoot", "take a crack" at anything, "stick their necks out" – for them should be reserved the harshest adjective in the critical vocabulary: innocuous.

1 1948 and After

National theatre cannot function only as a testing ground for the products of other countries, no matter how excellent its technical resources and ability to do these foreign plays the finest justice. A theatregoing public is not content to study the manners and norms of foreign society alone or to be conditioned into observing a strange way of life with its unfamiliar crises, particular despairs or triumphs. It wants also to see its own, to recognise its own environment and to use its theatre as a personal forum in which it can identify its characteristic patterns of existence. On the other hand a national theatre cannot isolate itself to become a provincial and self-centred home of dramatic newsreels drawn only from the daily life of the country and its people. The ideal is a combination of both and in Israel this synthesis has been attempted from the earliest days of its theatres' existence: masterpieces of foreign drama have been seen side by side with the fruit of the local playwrights. Plays born of brilliant writers with centuries of theatrical tradition behind them have alternated with those written by Hebrew poets and authors whose experience in the living theatre was non-existent, who themselves had never actively participated in the theatre in any way.

Again and again it has been proved that the true distinction of a nation's theatre is determined not by the standard of acting, the number of theatres, the size of audiences but by the quality of the country's original drama. In Israel the indigenous drama is constantly under fire and criticism of it, by Israel's own critics, is frequently unfair particularly when one considers that the State has not yet entered its fourth decade, and when taking into account the essential nature of this art form: it demands a very special type of acquaintanceship on the part of creator, director and audience alike. Yet the crisis of dramatic structure is not limited only to contemporary Hebrew drama for drama generally has been faltering for the past forty years or so. According to Gershon Shaked[1] some of the reasons for this are to be found in the fields of sociology and psychology: man has come face to face with his loss of value to himself, consequently the significance of his existence is being diminished – all of which is robbing the dramatic artist of every impetus towards the creation of true tragedy. The spiritual revolution confounding this generation is causing an internal undermining of dramatic form just as loss of contact between human beings leads to the destruction of true dialogue and the need for total social interdependence is breaking down man's autonomy which is a

[1] "In the Paths of the Hebrew Play" by Gershon Shaked. *Bamah* 6, July 1960.

vital condition for the shaping of every dramatic situation. This prolonged crisis has brought about much experimentation in drama, from Maeterlinck's symbolism, the introverted, subjective drama of Strindberg, German Expressionism, the Epic Realism of Piscator and Brecht, the Absurd and the excesses of the Americans' "third" theatre.

Naturally the crisis of dramatic form in Europe and America has an entirely different cause and character from that in Israel. Because of the development of Jewish nationalism and the events leading from it playwrights could not "represent a Jewish man simply, without this man carrying on his weak shoulders all the problems of his nation"[2] and his environment. The excesses of nationalistic preoccupation in Hebrew drama appear in the drama for the very reason that it is more socially orientated than any other literary form. But it appears, according to Professor Shaked, that the only way the Hebrew drama can succeed in achieving a play which is the ideal synthesis between the perfect literary and the perfect theatrical work is "to go the way of humanism", to represent the man, the Jew as an individual.

[2] *Ibid.*

The course of development from the nationalistic, social play to the subjective and humanistic play has been a difficult one and has paralleled similar developments in Hebrew poetry. The great dividing line in the history of Hebrew drama was the establishment of the State. The War of Liberation constituted a turning point in Israel's cultural life which, for the first time, rested with the country's youth who had previously had little share or participation in creative artistic work. Now that the past and all its ugly connotations was being slowly expunged a new generation of artists had to take the place of those who were identified with obsolete cultural forms and themes. Among the *sabras* arose writers, playwrights, producers and actors who displayed great talent – while still being handicapped by a lack of concrete experience. The lack of a theatrical tradition naturally went hand in hand with the lack of drama as a literary genre and the rare instances of drama written in Hebrew, scattered through the history of Hebrew literature did not help the Hebrew theatre of the new State. In any case its new artistic generation consciously broke away from the heritage which Eastern European Jewry had offered them. They associated these communities with abject acquiescence to the hardships of ghetto life and the degradation of Judaism generally. They wanted no reminder of it – of the *Dybbuk* and the *Golem* which spoke of a tradition that was becoming totally alien to them. They wanted rather to create a theatre reflecting the reality of Israel, representing the living, spoken Hebrew language to a public which, in the main, understood what was being said on the stage; a theatre and drama that would dig its roots deep down into the present life of the country.

[3]"Aspects of the Israel Theatre" by Leah Goldberg. *Jewish Affairs* (South Africa), July 1952.

However, as Leah Goldberg pointed out,[3] the excellent conditions under which the early Hebrew theatre in Moscow worked were absent in the State of Israel: the atmosphere of a theatrical tradition and culture on the one hand and of artistic daring on the other; the measuring up against good theatres and the guiding force of a great director; the common background of the actors and the homogeneous public; the exact knowledge of the kind of language the actors should speak on the stage, the knowledge of the style that could express both themselves and their world. In Israel there were no dramatists as such, people with a basic knowledge of the technicalities of the theatre who could create specifically for the theatre. The result was that most of the early Israeli plays were adaptations of novels and short stories which had been written as circumstances demanded them, works that were a reflection of the turbulent events of the time. Consequently the plays constructed from them also stuck fast to the sphere of contemporary events, rendering the drama a kind of newspaper columnists' commentary on a problem specific to a time and place. Also the new inexperienced Israeli playwrights considered it their duty to write only about daily life in their own community in the conviction that that was the way to create a native school of playwriting, for they were aware that the future of the theatre as a medium of art and culture was largely dependent on the development of original Israeli drama. Their greatest failing, however, was not so much their choice of subject matter – although in the early years it was repetitive and narrow enough – but in their style, their lack of experimentation with forms that would raise the play above the level of merely 'acting out' events, to make it a drama that had greater artistic and universal merit.

The first topic dealt with by the new dramatic writing was, naturally, the War of Independence. The plays written on this subject were condemned by the critics even at the time for having no universal dramatic value, but they were unquestionably acceptable to their audiences because they dealt vividly with relevant events so close to the experience of every individual watching the play. The plays placed the struggle for independence factually in an arena for all to see but without commenting on it, in this way creating a virtual dramatic newsreel. Like the factual plays of the Yishuv, in most of the plays of this type and belonging to this period the characters were stock-symbolic. There was little attempt to give them human depth and reality or individual characterisation. They represented types with which the audience was well acquainted: the soldier, the pioneer, the idealist and so on.

The vexing problem of "universalism" in drama as opposed to nationalism (as an artistic form) has troubled many of the critics of Israel's young theatre. Neither of these terms can be strictly defined in relation to art. "A theatre that wishes to stay alive," says John Arden, "needs passion and contemporary relevance (sometimes known sneeringly as 'ephemeral journalism'). Elegance, good taste and verbal mellifluence, though excellent qualities in themselves, are inadequate substitutes . . ."[4] A play cannot easily be dismissed as "too national"; it can be placed in a unique and specific setting, deal with a unique and vital national event and still have a certain universal value as is the case, despite the critics' views to the contrary, of many of Israel's early plays, those dealing with the war and the years immediately following it. The Event, which was a war of a specific people for a specific reason against other specific people, was still based on a universal ideal, one which any other people at any other time can comprehend: the ideal of freedom from oppression. No play dealing, however narrowly, with such a subject can be accused of having no universal value whatsoever, although, according to Eric Bentley, man, not any event, is the centre of the universe of drama. In the case of the Jews fighting in Israel the real oppressor was history and not a concrete enemy; this was indeed a unique situation, but now its symbols were the British and the Arabs, actual antagonists who reduced the national idealistic struggle to terms that anyone could understand. The setting – for example that of a kibbutz – is remote and unfamiliar to most people outside of Israel but the picture of a small, tightly-knit community united in a common struggle but divided by individual conflicts is unfamiliar to no one. And art "becomes universal if it is specific, but if it attempts universality it becomes merely specious".[5] When, for example, O'Casey writes about the little house in Dublin, he is writing about every little house in the world and so, Ibsen, Miller, Pinter with their drawing-rooms, family conflicts, tramps and beggars.

Of the three major and representative plays dealing with the 1948 war, two were set in a kibbutz and the third on a lonely hill under enemy siege. In each of these plays the larger conflict – the war – is the major theme, and in each of them a small community, thrust together and forced to remain together, struggles with its own problem on a lesser battlefield.

[4] "Pinter and Wesker" by G.W.Brandt. *Contemporary Theatre no. 4.*, ed. Clifford Leech.

[5] "The Israel Theatre" by Bernard Kops. *Ariel*, July 1962.

In Moshe Shamir's "הוא הלך בשדות" (*He Walked in the Fields*) produced by Joseph Milo in 1948, the setting is a kibbutz and the major protagonists perhaps the most totally "universal" group of all: the family. This was the first Hebrew play to abandon the framework of the establishment of the Yishuv and to move into the contemporary scene. It was the first Hebrew play in which there was some attempt, although unsuccessful, to individualise the characters and lift them above their setting, to endow them with some kind of universal value by giving them universal problems, and it is true that one of the most important methods of universalising a dramatic work is by endowing it with human emotions and problems that human beings of all cultures, races and creeds will understand, no matter what the setting or the circumstances. In this early play the problems were universal only to a certain extent while remaining dramatically naive. It tells of a woman who cannot fit into the framework of her husband's life, who is searching for love and understanding; of her husband's striving for external fulfilment partly in order to compensate for the unhappy relationship with his wife; of the son who is unable to understand his parents; of the isolation of one person who has suffered almost unimaginable horrors in Europe during the Second World War. While the setting and the unique set of circumstances – the "plot" encompassing the characters' lives – determine the outcome of the individual problems, these are not necessarily confined to a kibbutz nor solely to Israel; the struggle for independence is not, especially in our time, confined to a kibbutz or to Israel. Therefore thematically this play cannot be categorically denounced, as it has been, as being devoid entirely of universal dramatic value.

Nevertheless it is not a great play in purely dramatic terms or in any respect other than its novelty for Israel in 1948. Its hero, Uri, is a young kibbutznik. As the play opens he has recently returned to the kibbutz from an agricultural school and he learns that his parents have separated and his mother is living with another man. He is very troubled and finds consolation with a Polish girl called Mika who is a refugee and who has suffered a great deal, almost too much in the framework of the play to prevent her from becoming melodramatic. They decide to marry but on the eve of their marriage Gingy, an old schoolfriend, invites Uri to join the Palmach (the elite force of the Haganah, responsible for the more spectacular acts of bravery and daring – and subsequently the name given to an entire Israeli literary movement). Uri agrees and decides also to leave immediately. He goes to inform Mika. This is the major human confrontation of the play. He is unmoved by her anguish, in fact he exhibits the rather single-minded insensitivity incorrectly regarded as a characteristic of the *sabra*. Mika, on her part, has not told him that she is pregnant nor does she do so on the only other occasion that they again meet.

Uri is in camp when he receives the news that a group of "illegal" immigrants is about to be landed and the British Army has set a trap to intercept them. The order comes to blow up a bridge which the British forces have to cross. One of the soldiers in Uri's unit volunteers for the mission despite the fact that he has a sick wife and several children. Uri's comrades tell him that as commanding officer he should go; he agrees and is killed. The play ends when Mika is persuaded not to commit suicide but to bear the child who will be one of the first-born citizens of the independent State.

The audience of young people watching this play saw themselves truthfully represented on the stage. The older generation were perhaps also able to understand why their traditions had so suddenly been rejected. The play exhibited the immediate problems of the war; it also for the first time presented the Hebrew language in all its colloquial richness, its slang expressions and army jargon. Milo's staging was direct and uncluttered. The kibbutz was presented as a place of work and the actors in fact shifted scenery as if they were doing their normal chores. A narrator wandered on and off the stage, commenting on the action, representing a kind of satirical chorus. The setting was understaged and casual with landscapes projected onto a screen. It was an emotional play given at an emotional time. What was shown on the stage was happening all around the actors and the audience – it was almost like a replay of the day's events, day after day. Gunfire and mortars often drowned out the voices of the actors. Performances were given on the evenings after battles. It was not by any means the first play to have been given in wartime but this was the first truly Hebrew play after all those centuries of scarcely any drama at all and it was, moreover, given in Israel at so extraordinary a time in Jewish history. After the first performance one member of the audience wrote: "Outside it was very dark – but inside (the Mograbi Theatre) it was like a festival, like a premiere, when on this evening young people came to see a young play in a young theatre with its drama and direction and acting." About seven hundred soldiers took advantage of the brief truce being maintained at the time and attended this festive opening night. At the end of the play there was dead silence; then the audience broke into a kind of hysteria. The play subsequently moved into Jerusalem shortly after the long and deadly siege, when the Israelis had broken through on the Latrun road.

The lack of profound characterisation in *He Walked in the Fields* is a typical deficiency of early Israeli drama. Uri, the hero, is a symbol and a stereotype. However, despite near-sentimentality of theme the characters are not sentimentalised, in fact they have obeyed Uri's own injunction in the play that "it's wrong to be emotional" – which the Israelis seem to have absorbed into their personalities. Shamir did not analyse motivation or purpose or conflict. The entire situation was too immediate to allow any historical perspective and too close for analysis or, indeed, for comment. The play was not expository but descriptive. The conflicts are not explained, the attitudes are puzzling and the audience has to supply the answers. Only when the situation had stabilised was the period of the War of Independence analysed in the drama. Later plays on the subject attempted to view it with a measure of objectivity.

One of the main elements of *He Walked in the Fields* is the character of the "Palmachnik", that is, the young Palmach fighter like Uri and even more like Gingy. He is an idealised character: unsentimental to the point almost of cruelty, rigidly just, dedicated, capable, unostentatious and possessing, with all this, a lively sense of humour. This is what every Palmachnik yearned to be, this was his model. Yet he wanted to be devoid of conflict, unlike Uri, who was shown as having to bear personal problems. His own conflict is not simply between his father and himself – in fact his antagonism to his parents is not clearly or overtly explained in the play, other than as a kind of pique at their marital difficulties. Or perhaps it is, as Mendel Kohansky says, representative of "the gap of understanding between the two generations [which] had by then become a painful problem of the new nation. The immigrant parents with their European ghetto-bred mentality looked with a mixture of pride and pain at the offspring who were handsome, strong, crude, brave, speaking a Biblical Hebrew, disdaining parental authority, looking down on all that smacked of the ghetto. It was a generation that suffered from being thrown on its own, having to find its own way without any guidance, hiding its insecurity under a mask of deliberate rudeness."[6] This was undoubtedly the truth, but in the play it was symbolised far more by the contrasting characters of Uri and Mika than by Uri and his parents.

[6] Mendel Kohansky. *The Hebrew Theatre – its First Fifty Years*. Ktav Publishing House, N.Y., 1969.

The second conflict in which Uri has a part is a more subtle one: his wife is neurotic, uncertain of herself and her environment, a girl who has suffered. She is unable to identify with the overall purpose of the soldiers as easily as she should or as the character called Dinah'le, who represents a foil to Mika and who is the "perfect" female *sabra*, succeeds in doing. Mika's presence in the play serves to highlight or to throw into relief by contrast the mental and physical health of the ideal warrior. Uri becomes purged of his emotional problem through his participation in the larger conflict, the war; he throws off Mika, emerging as the ideal hero, even to the point of his death which is inevitable in this kind of characterisation. Mika and Uri therefore represent the preoccupation of the *sabra* at that time: the breach between the past in the diaspora, with its heritage of cruelty and suffering, and the present redemption and rebirth. Shamir concedes that the past may give rise to the promised Israel of the future, in the fact of Mika's pregnancy. He is also saying that the perfect *sabra* should have the perfect wife, in his clear contrasting of the characters of Mika and Dinah'le.

The play also serves to give the audience an interesting picture of kibbutz life. Shamir described to perfection the collective, the life of the kibbutz with its communal showers, communal clothes, job rotation, the committee and its decisions, the submerging of all individuality for the whole, the idea of moving from a single to a double hut as the only outward manifestation of marriage. Shamir even has Mika say: "The whole kibbutz has to love me before they can agree that one of their boys should love me." She is the antagonist to the kibbutz and its ideology. She is disliked by the characters in the play and almost certainly by the audience of the day whose rejection of her was their rejection of a stereotype that had become uncomfortable to them.

Most critics denounced *He Walked in the Fields* as having no literary or dramatic value, merely validity for the time. They declared that it showed no attempt to delve beneath the surface, to discover the essence of the period or to analyse the prevailing emotions and aspirations of the time. They dismissed it as having no "universal" dramatic value. Perhaps they were right; but the play is no less a part of Israel's dramatic literature than so much of Sheridan, for example, dealing as it does with vanished and outdated problems and people and classes, is part of England's dramatic tradition.

He Walked in the Fields was given again, in a slightly revised form, by the Cameri in 1956 and it was then as relevant as it had originally been because of the recent eruption of the Sinai campaign. In the same year it went, still with the Cameri, to Paris. In 1966, to celebrate the twenty-fifth anniversary of the Palmach, the play was again produced in Haifa, once more in a revised version but this time it was not as successful for the audience had changed: the typical Palmachnik of 1948 who was at that moment sitting in the audience was already middle-aged and a little disillusioned. The 1967 war was yet to come.

"בערבות הנגב" (*In the Wastes of the Negev*) by Yigal Mossinzon, produced by Habimah in 1949 was also set on a kibbutz and presented more of the problems that were prevalent in Israel at that time. It tells of a community on a kibbutz undergoing an Egyptian siege which is impossible to withstand. The situation is intolerable and the only alternative is to retreat. Conflict arises between two groups – the first which advocates retaliation and a fight to probable annihilation and the second which calls for an objective appraisal of the situation, and consequently a withdrawal while this is still possible. The youth of the kibbutz wants to stay and fight for as usual it is arrogant and unafraid. The play ends tragically with the death of one of the young men of the *meshek* and a subsequent reconciliation between the leaders of the opposing factions. This play, even more than *He Walked in the Fields*, is "national"; its problems relate far more specifically to the circumstances of the time yet, like the former, the encompassing theme is a national struggle for freedom in which are involved conflicts of courage and cowardice, moderation and aggression, love and hatred, youth and maturity. It is seldom staged now for it is undoubtedly anachronistic and in its own time received a similar press to that of Shamir's play for the same reason: lack of "universal" appeal.

The third play representative of this period was one which achieved enormous success, Nathan Shaham's "הם יגיעו מחר" (*They Will Arrive Tomorrow*, 1950, Cameri). Its theme, like that of the others, was the War of Independence, its setting a hill under enemy siege and its characters a small detachment of soldiers. This was the war seen from the inside, exhibited on the stage without any extraneous problems or characters. The atmosphere of the play is tense, its purpose is to show the reaction of individuals under unbearable stress. The area of the hill has been dotted with twelve landmines; their location is unknown because the man detailed to bury them had been killed and his map destroyed with him. This is the first of the war plays possessing ingredients of powerful drama, not an ideological conflict or a family struggle but a contemporary picture of individual characters in a compelling situation on the one hand and an exploitation of a popular dramatic device on the other. There is no hero in the play. The major protagonists are two commanding officers, antithetical personalities who seem to represent Shaham's criticism of the ideological literary stereotypes of his time. One by one the audience's certainties are broken down in the battle between these two men. Jonah is the typical, brash *sabra* whose only purpose is to lead his men to victory at whatever sacrifice. But Shaham suggests that he may be a coward and a man of brutal insensitivity. Avi is his foil, a gentle and intelligent person, terribly concerned for the welfare of his men. But he is weak and indecisive, too theoretical for the ugly facts of war and a failure as a leader of men. This discursive and intellectual play explores moral problems seen through the personalities of the two officers. The war outside is subjugated to their fierce moral battle in which not only men's lives are at stake but also the contemporary ideals of honour and loyalty.

The play explores as well the behaviour of soldiers in wartime, not as cinematic heroes but ordinary young men in a situation of unbearable stress. The situation is not that of battle in which fear is accepted as inescapable but it deals with an emotion of a different kind: the men fear sudden, violent, unexpected death which is waiting to pounce without warning. Instead of remaining a fighting group united against the common and known enemy the men become spiritually isolated and hate one another because they see in each other's obsession for self-preservation their own moral disintegration. Each mine exploded and therefore each man killed is one less menace to those who remain and wait. In battle they would sacrifice their lives for their companions, now no man will find peace until the twelfth man dies; they are ready to rejoice when he falls before them, releasing them from the last mine.

In 1948 the Jewish soldier-pioneer in Israel was a heroic figure. He was courageous and intense and fanatical and he was able to fashion the solid mass of his people's history into an effective sword. He lived by action instead of the slogans which had fed the Jews for generations and his action was desperate. He did not sail into battle with a holy light in his eyes while mouthing verses from the Bible. He fought and killed and bled; he was fighting foremost for an ideal but he was also fighting for his life. Not very much of the true emotion of the period, except the celebrated idealism, ever intruded on the formal superficiality of most of the State's early plays. There was no mention, for example, of the frustration the people felt at international intolerance and indifference, or their own fear of failure, or the hatred they felt for the enemy – the Arabs and the British. All around, a war which had been delayed for two thousand years was being fought and a destiny, prophesied in the Bible, was being met and fulfilled. Young Jews from everywhere in the world were arriving and fighting, flying primitive aircraft, sailing on unseaworthy boats, shooting, sniping, dying for the *practical* application of an ideal in a world which had just lived through the Second World War.

Perhaps the reason for these plays having failed to entrench themselves in Israel's tradition of dramatic literature is that so little of the desperation and exaltation of the time appears in them. The plays lack a pervading philosophy or "dynamic schema" which is Eric Bentley's term for the all-embracing unity of a play, the unifying philosophy which has given it life. They present incidents in a vacuum. They express a period but fail to analyse it. They remain examples of dramatic reportage, a static description of reality in the most familiar of terms, a continued pandering to a public that wanted everything to be devoted to them, a kind of parading of their achievements. Not one of the plays gives the impression that its author was compelled to write through the need to express something powerful, specific and personal, that he had a point of view, a grudge, a problem, that the play was an emotional expression of some kind, not a dramatic exercise. Or perhaps this had all originally been expressed in the novels and stories from which the plays were adapted and then lost in the formal structure of the drama because of the author's inexperience with this vastly different and difficult medium.

2 Early Social Realism

Once the soldier-pioneer had established his country's independence he settled down in the hope of living a normal life. He had invited and welcomed hundreds of thousands of people from a host of countries to the new home he had made for them and it had received with joy their vastly differing experience and background, their varied talents and all their aspirations and ambitions. Gradually the long process of consolidation began. The original idealism was somewhat diminished for the war was won and the State, for the moment, ensured. Its inhabitants chose a continental European way of life and became a western democracy, no better and no worse than any other. And being so it began to manifest the customary social ills of our time: pettiness, corruption and hypocrisy, opportunism and crime. The situations and emotions that had characterised the pioneer fighting for and then establishing his national homeland faded over the years and others less worthy took their place, slowly blurring the once sharply-defined outline of the Israeli Jew into something more flaccid.

These were problems of which the nation's thinkers were very much aware and which they began to discuss in novels, in poetry and in the drama. Audiences settled back to view them presented on the stage, shown to them from every conceivable point of view. Every local problem, every facet of the life of the community as a whole, every major issue or petty annoyance was aired and commented upon. Yet, for the most part – with only a few notable exceptions – the drama was still one of situation and locale, in form still bound to a mixture of romanticism and nineteenth-century realism and cast in the mould of the well-made play. Very little said was new, certainly very little that can be regarded as an artistic creation representative of a unique nation and one which, by virtue of the elements constituting it, could be the most brilliant.

One of the major problems faced by Israel during its entire existence and particularly in the early years is that of the absorption of immigrants and the interrelationship of their communities. Many plays have been written around this subject, providing an adequate forum for debating its every point of view and one which reveals the shifting sympathies of a number of playwrights each with his own standpoint or approach. Many of them deal specifically with the problems of the immigrants themselves and others present the viewpoint of the "old" settlers in their relationship with the immigrants.

The two most notable and representative plays of this type were written some years apart – "שש כנפים לאחד" (*Each Had Six Wings*) by Hanoch Bar-Tov, produced by Habimah in 1958, and *Tura* by Joseph Bar-Joseph, produced by Cameri in 1963. The first, *Each Had Six Wings*, says much of all there is to say about the arrival, attitude, hardships and ultimate triumph of immigrant communities in the new State of Israel. They come, filled with hope after having suffered through years of unimaginable horror and now, justifiably, they expect to find a haven, a kind of Utopia which has suddenly become feasible for them while to their ancestors it was only a wistful dream. Instead they discover themselves once again to be strangers in a strange land. Instead of being welcomed and aided they meet intolerance and hostility. Life is hard and competitive, their houses are derelict in an abandoned quarter, the language is unfamiliar, the *sabras* are aloof and the government officials appointed to aid them are revealed to be unsympathetic bureaucrats.

The purpose of the play is to show how these people readjust, eventually coming to terms with each other and their new surroundings. The playwright, in his introduction to the play, says: "When I tried to plumb the heart of the immigrants I realised suddenly that I am not telling the story merely of their life but of my life too, that as a matter of fact I myself, although I am a *sabra*, am not so distant and foreign to them. I, too, have been, in my childhood, the son of new immigrants.

"The 'Other Israel', I thought, is not so distant from the veteran Israel as it would seem at a superficial glance. I wanted to emphasise how similar we all are, that we are simply human beings . . . I realised that I wanted to describe how people who have found themselves suddenly, almost by accident, in a strange, abandoned place, had struck roots, until they came to feel that again they have a home, that they are no strangers to each other, that again they are a unified Jewish community."[1]

[1] From the programme notes.

The characters in this play are symbols representing aspects of Bar-Tov's ideology. They are prototypes without depth, created to express his rather naive view of what immigrants should do about their situation and how they should behave. Despite enormous disappointment, hardship, bewilderment and above all the lack of sympathy they encounter almost everywhere, the immigrants are able to find security and a growing peace and contentment; they forget their diverse origins to become a united, altruistic community. To symbolise this victory a child is born to the young wife of an elderly baker and they give it a Hebrew name – that of the young schoolteacher who was the only *sabra* to help and understand them.

Despite its obvious weaknesses the play is an important one because it demonstrated that the Israeli drama could express a point of view and become the instrument for a personal expression of the playwright, in this case his very definite message of hope to the immigrants he knew and loved so well. This play could – and should – become a classic in the repertoire of the Hebrew theatre for despite its static form and structural deficiencies it reflects, more than any other of its time, the prevailing atmosphere of a period in the history of Israel. It contains in microcosm the varied experiences of diverse groups of immigrants and the situations that typified their arrival in Israel, but because of Bar-Tov's idealism and optimism it transcends the dreaded label of "reportage" which has arbitrarily and contemptuously been stuck onto so many plays. The structural weakness of *Each Had Six Wings* does not, therefore, diminish its thematic appeal and it could quite appropriately be called the first Israeli folk-play because it has successfully bridged the gap between the "other" and the "real" Israel, the Jews of the past and the Israelis of the present.

Some immigrants were able to undergo successfully the painful process of adjustment to alien surroundings; others found it impossible to sacrifice their most cherished customs and traditions. Such is the case with Abraham Tura in Bar-Joseph's play – and perhaps his symbolic struggle has greater "universal" validity than that of Bar-Tov's characters. *Tura* presents a dramatic conflict between the world of the primitive Middle-Eastern Jews, still cleaving fast to the uncompromising legal and ritual traditions of the Bible, and the present in the new State of Israel. An organic part of the old tradition is that the father is undisputed ruler of the family, possessing totalitarian power of life and death over his children.

The disintegration of the family as an inviolable and cohesive unit was slower and more evolutionary among Western European Jews than among the Middle-Eastern communities. For the latter the collapse happened traumatically when they arrived in Israel and encountered a way of life totally different from what they had been accustomed to for countless generations. They came into contact with an external legal system which overrode the absolute power of the father-judge, for he was suddenly responsible to the State for his actions; moreover the State failed to understand his unquestioning subordination to ancient doctrine which, to the primitive Jew, is the encompassing credo of his life: reward for virtue and punishment for sin. Murderous anger, which enlightened man is permitted to express only through words, becomes translated into tragic action in primitive man. His reaction is impulsive, spontaneous and dangerous and he consequently becomes an archetype for primitive tragedy.

In a drama similar in spirit to the Spanish plays of the sixteenth and seventeenth centuries Tura kills his daughter because she has betrayed the honour of the family by carrying an illegitimate child. Because Tura is motivated by forces beyond his control – the ancient laws and customs of the Jews in this case in place of the gods of the Greeks or the Spanish doctrine of *pundonor* – he becomes a figure of tragic stature, driven to self-degradation and a denial of everything that once constituted dignity in his life. This is the basic theme of the play. The tragic atmosphere is further heightened by Bar-Joseph's use of a type of chorus in the form of a woman who has the dual role of neighbour to the Tura family and of providing a lyrical commentary to the action of the play. Unfortunately, however, the play fails to develop its tragic theme; it becomes complicated by mitigating sub-plots and rationalisations which slow down the action and deflect it from its inevitable climax. In addition to this the essential atmosphere of Middle-Eastern community life and spirit is spoiled by "modern" symbolism and pseudo-psychoanalysis or by Bar-Joseph's attempt to put too much into a drama which could have remained a nearly perfect example of classical tragedy in form and theme, made doubly impressive by its unusual setting. Dr Haim Gamzu states that it might have been better as a one-act play which would then have been capable of sustaining the extraordinary tension of its first few minutes, instead of "endangering the entire dramatic structure by the addition of unnecessary storeys . . ."[2] Mendel Kohansky says: "The basic fault is the structure of the play, which clusters most of its climaxes near the beginning, leaving for the rest of it nothing but the predictable."[3] The critics were unanimous in their praise of Bar-Joseph's dialogue which was partly halting and inarticulate, entirely appropriate to the tension of the characters in their dark, bewildering circumstances, and partly lyrical, attaining the level of superb dramatic prose. They applauded Bar-Joseph's experimentation with form and his obvious attempt to create drama instead of the dreaded reportage. Since the bulk of their adverse criticism dealt in detail with the play's serious structural flaws it can be summarised quite simply: once again a talented young playwright's major fault or deficiency was his lack of *theatrical* experience. This became more frequently the case as Hebrew drama developed; playwrights startled and delighted audiences and critics

[2] *Haaretz*, April 26th 1963.

[3] *Jerusalem Post*, April 19th 1963.

with thematic experimentation and variation of every kind but still could not make significant progress because of their ignorance of dramatic structure.

Most of the plays on the subject of immigrant communities dealt with problems similar to those appearing in these two most representative dramas, but their dramatic and literary value was slight and they were quickly forgotten. A typical situation was that considered by Shamir's "גם זו לטובה" *This Too Is For The Best* (1957, Ohel), the story of two disputing immigrant villages, North African and Rumanian, eventually united by a Romeo-and-Juliet situation between two of their children. Only one immigrant group was totally ignored by Hebrew drama: the English-speaking settlers; while representatives of every other immigrant group and its problems appeared in some play or other during this period, the Anglo-Saxon (as he was called in Israel in the fifties) was forgotten or deliberately ignored.

Gradually individual playwrights, like Bar-Joseph and Bar-Tov, attempted to lift Hebrew drama out of the imprisonment of reportage into something vaster and more expressive of the national consciousness. As the years passed and the country stabilised the immigrants were absorbed and the pioneers grew older. Playwrights turned their attention to the other problems, those which were threatening the basic morality of Israeli society. It took many of them a long time to come to terms with the reality of the present which revealed a growing emptiness of spirit and a lessening of the vital idealism that had brought the State into being. They were faced with the shattered dream of the fighters – the dream of a beautiful country, a united nation without political intrigues and governmental corruption. The realisation that this could not be achieved filled many of them with nostalgia for the past and an idealisation of it which appeared in many of the plays they wrote. At the same time they were not afraid to portray contemporary reality in their work: they dealt with Israel's growing bureaucracy, the movement of the youth from the kibbutz to the city, the widening gap between generations, the intrusion of progress into traditional life, juvenile delinquency, the veneration of money and growing materialism. Plots were taken from the daily life of the country describing incidents and situations from various points of view. But there was still no hint of an Israeli drama in terms of structure *as well as* content. The public at that time came to the theatre seeking repose, relaxation and a certain amount of encouragement and support, for it saw itself as the hero of the historic drama shown on the stage. "Israeli society," writes Ezra Zussman, "that was always, in a certain sense, mobilised for action, 'ordered' a theatre that would serve it, defend it, strengthen it in its struggle for independence whether it be by a play of heroism and strife or one of merriment and fun. And the Hebrew play responded to this demand. Hence the committed, engagé character of Hebrew drama, particularly in this early period."[4] One of Israel's dramatic critics and playwrights, Joseph Lapid, has given another reason for the lack of originality and experimentation in the plays of this period and that is that the Israeli playwright "is on the defensive, he is playing safe, instead of entering a rather hopeless competition on a universal level he prefers to use the one advantage he has: the knowledge of contemporary Israeli life and problems".[5] There is no doubt that this is so and yet confining the subject matter to the life of the country is not necessarily a fault; on the contrary, drama does right to cultivate its own national personality. Whether it should do so exclusively by means of documentary drama is the question to be resolved.

[4]"The Hebrew Drama" by Ezra Zussman. *World Theatre*, May–June 1965.

[5]Taken from a letter. Quoted with permission.

At the start of the fifties there was no consideration of technique because the task of the playwright was still more social and political than artistic. The "regional" play dealing with problems of time and place was being well received by managements and audiences. The subject of Man, that is, the so-called Universal Question was thrust far away in favour of the theatrical necessity to portray the problems of the moment. The theatre became a kind of political platform offering social comedies or political melodramas in which the style of expression did not perturb authors because they were too preoccupied with content – the "what" not the "how". "From the moment political problems ceased to suffice," writes Gershon Shaked, "the problem of expression arose."[6] What could be called real conflict, the kind of contention that arouses audiences, was absent from the plays. The playwright and his viewers were always in accord, there was agreement on all sides and therefore no more to be said. But, on the other hand, a writer must not be contentious purely for effect like some of the later pseudo-Absurdists who became active in Israel or the radical writers whose fundamental task is to shock even at the expense of the play itself.

[6]From a letter. Quoted with permission.

The major fault was above all the playwright's unfailing use of static dramatic structure that did nothing but retard any dramatically viable potential in the plays. The proof of this lies in the fact that even at this later stage so many of the dramas were adaptations of novels and stories – for example *Hedva and I* or *The Street of Steps* – indicating that the authors had not yet conceived their stories in dramatic terms because they did not know how to do so and therefore found the dramatic medium unsatisfactory as a primary means of expression. Consequently the plays lacked poetic daring. Apart from a few exceptions, *Tura* for one, playwrights did not experiment with verse or prose, with song or even the linguistic devices of Brechtian Epic Realism which would have suited their material, but used only the most prosaic diction, unrelieved colloquialism and jargon. The innovation introduced by the Yishuv generation of writers, the use of Hebrew as a living, spoken language on the stage, had rebounded.

The Refusal by Yehuda Haezrachi is a characteristic example of the Hebrew drama of the fifties. It was written in 1959, presented by Ohel in 1962 and contains most of the themes topical in the writing of the time, primarily the guilt besetting the ex-kibbutznik ten or fifteen years later when he is moving towards settled middle-age. Its story is told through a series of flashbacks which apparently take place in the mind of the protagonist. His dead comrade appears and talks to him, his wife and a friend in younger incarnations move in and out of his life while he struggles to take stock and reach a decision. Like many of the plays of the time such "plot" as there is is vested entirely in the characters who still represent types immediately and pleasurably familiar to the audience. The story is a simple one: Dr Ariel Ravina, a thirty-year-old scientist, has been offered an important managerial position in the Ministry of Planning and Production. He is contented in his scientific research, about to reach an important chemical breakthrough when the offer is made, hence his hesitation in reaching a decision. His wife, Dorit, a contemptuously-drawn portrait of a grasping middle-class wife eager for the status the important job will bring, urges him to accept. In the short period before Ariel telephones his acceptance or refusal he relives the vital moments of his life which have shaped his present situation. His past is represented by four people who carry the movement of the play backwards and forwards through time and space, from Ariel's adolescence to his present maturity and from the kibbutz to the city. The major themes of guilt and disillusionment are personified by each of the characters and linked together by the mind of Ariel himself.

Ariel is an ex-kibbutznik who paints in his spare time, a pastime which once would have been admired in terms of the romantic idealism of the period of his youth but which now prompts Mr Sharon, the Minister, to comment: ". . . a scientist who dabbles in art. Very nice, but I hope he doesn't have the characteristics of an artist, for example that he isn't scatterbrained or a dreamer. A man holding a State position must fight these traits otherwise he won't be able to carry the responsibility . . ." At first Ariel wants nothing to do with Sharon's proposition; he is a chemist, working quietly in his laboratory, happy to be isolated in his work. He shuns the responsibility of supervising others' activities and he opposes his wife's ambition towards what she terms a "career" and their "social status". She, on the other hand, pushes him towards acceptance because of the implied wealth and position the job will bring. Ariel calls upon his memories in an attempt to make up his mind. We learn, by seeing his past enacted for us on the stage, that with his friends, Ehud, Naṭhan and Dorit (now his wife) he graduated from high school, went on a training course and joined a kibbutz as part of the *garin* or nucleus. His first imaginary encounter is with the now-dead poet, Ehud, who in death has remained eternally young while Ariel "ages, day by day . . ." Ehud's poetry is in some ways a contradiction to his personality: by nature he is troubled and unsure, hiding his insecurity beneath a charming and happy-go-lucky cynicism which purports to take life as it comes and to leave questions to the "philosophers". His verse is reminiscent of the romanticism of the Palmach writers, Haim Guri in particular, in its evocation of the young men, ". . . us, my companion like a brother to me/the eternal dreamers . . ." These lines constitute a cheerful mockery of the poetic conventions of the young Palmachniks but Ehud's more representative although flippant verse strikes deeply into the reality of Ariel's present state by referring to the necessity to make a new hole in his belt to accommodate the weight gain of prosperity. Ehud is something of a misfit: a realist with a gaze that pierces all idealism and an emotional makeup that rejects theorising, something of a prophet in his ability to predict future disappointments. He accepts without questioning, aware of life's difficulties and the impracticability of singlemindedness. "Ideals on this side, a career on that. Work on the land on the one hand, studies in science on the other. Spiritual invalids! Utter nonsense! In life dilemmas like these don't exist. In life, everything is more complicated, or maybe simpler but not so theoretical." Predictably Ehud, the cynic whose verses outrage the entire community, is killed while defending the kibbutz singlehanded with one rifle and ten shells against five or more enemy infiltrators. His heroic death is a logical dramatic outcome of his irreverent attitude to life, so much so that Dorit accuses him of having committed suicide. It is unlikely that the playwright killed him because of his lack of dedication –

there are too many levels of uncertainty in Haezrachi's own thinking, although cynicism, in the context of the play, is almost the worst crime a young man can commit.

Ariel: You're exaggerating! Our Ehud was always a great big clown.

Nathan: That isn't clowning. It's cynicism. (*To Ehud*) It's a kind of black gloom you have in your heart. And it's liable to poison the whole kibbutz.

Nathan is a more complex character, one who embodies a compelling sense of familiarity. The playwright has taken greater care with his realisation and he consequently has certain depth and believability. As a young man he led a training group with speeches echoing those that have since become part of Israel's folklore:

> "To those who still have any doubts I can say only one thing: the way of actual realisation – is the only way. It's the only way because only on a kibbutz and only on the land can every one of us find himself... I'm speaking about inner satisfaction... on the kibbutz we'll be given the opportunity to achieve inner fulfilment on the background of social right... this is the legacy of a man who is close to the soil, to nature..."

Nathan is the uncompromising idealist who has grown the most disillusioned of them all. His way of life permits no conflict, he has put aside every thought of a career without hesitation or doubt. He talks, then acts; he is pragmatic and practical, the perfect conformist who has succeeded in submerging his selfhood in the group identity, a living symbol of an ideal that led to the woeful unhappiness expressed in the Hebrew literature of the fifties and sixties. "I am a person," he says, "who knows how to see reality face to face, who can live without illusions and without self doubt." Compared to his two companions he is endowed with awesome spiritual health. But Haezrachi does not leave him at that, a static, two-dimensional over-romanticised figure sure to be loved deeply then forgotten by his audience: he adds an element of self-mockery, lending the characterisation of Nathan a depth of pathos which brings him closer to the truth than is the customary kibbutz-figure so often encountered in early Israeli drama. Nathan says: "My importance was that of simplicity and practicality, as a person who is simple and practical like me should be." And: "Of course I had personal considerations – as far as I was given to personal considerations at that time..." His fate at the age of thirty is pathetic for due to lack of personnel and the consequent multitude of official duties imposed on him as kibbutz veteran he has no time for the work he loves or for contact with his fellows. He is reduced to a few moments of digging in his little garden after a day's work, a fact prompting his wry statement: "... my gardening is ... let's call it: ideological. Through it I keep my contact with the soil." Then Ariel says to him: "What a long way we have come, Nathan, to end up in the same place: working in the garden – twice a week." Nathan speaks for the perfect idealist ("... perhaps you won't believe me – I'm still faithful to my old-fashioned ideals ...") who has failed in an environment which places social process and order above the aspirations of the individual dedicated to the good of the same society by the most ideal means. Youth is no longer attracted to the land; those who do remain on the kibbutzim have to fill a number of necessary functions at the expense of their own gifts and the result is "... correspondence. Papers, papers, papers". From the start Nathan has been thwarted at every turn by the bureaucracy represented in the play by Sharon, formerly Sharshevski the controller of supplies, whose failure to authorise sufficient arms for the defence of the kibbutz led to Ehud's death. Nathan, the man of infinite patience and love, the perfect *sabra*, the kibbutznik, the repository and evangelist of social ideals is left, at the age of thirty, tired and disillusioned through a system become distorted and unworkable. He has nowhere to go whereas Ariel, the tortured thinker, the artist, the scholar, the alienated kibbutz dropout, traitor and possibly coward is given the opportunity, by the very factor that destroyed Nathan, to recreate his life. The audience's sympathy must, at the time, have been very clear.

Ariel most closely foreshadows the modern anti-hero, a personality with no place in the spiritual atmosphere of the forties in Israel. The antithesis of Nathan and Shamir's archetypal Uri (*He Walked in the Fields*), Ariel's life has been composed by uncertainty; he wanted above all to become a scholar but guilt at these individualistic aspirations compelled him to join the kibbutz. He is ageing but would like to have remained young like Ehud, recently summoned (by Ariel) from the grave. He lives a comfortable life in a pleasantly furnished flat with carpets, books and pictures – while longing for a life-style which he has already once rejected in the past. He and Ehud are "brothers for eternity" yet Ariel left his "brother" to defend the kibbutz without ever knowing whether he himself ran away or went in search of aid. He cannot decide whether to accept the new post for he scorns affluence – but still he hesitates. Nathan convinces him that his elevation – despite the fact that he will be no more than a cog in a wheel – will be of use to the kibbutz and Ariel assents to this opinion, it being the closest to what he would like to believe. He accepts the appointment. The true reason for his agreement is never clarified. Anyone in the audience still retaining a measure of classical idealism would attribute the acceptance to Ariel's desire to serve the community at the expense of self. But Haezrachi's attitudes are always equivocal and Ariel's decision, however motivated, is not a worthy one. It may be due to his lack of self-confidence as a scientist, to a want of courage to pursue his research alone, to Dorit's blandishments which amount to blackmail or to Nathan's weary advice. The true reason lies in rationalisation: he has convinced himself that he can repair his treachery to the kibbutz by serving it indirectly from his new height. This is a salve to his conscience despite Ehud's accurate accusation of self-deceit, lies and self-betrayal.

Ariel: Who knows: maybe in the agreement there is the refusal. We accept appointments, progress from achievement to achievement. But perhaps we refuse – ourselves, the truth inside us.

Indeed in his acceptance he negates the death of Ehud and Nathan's lifelong sacrifice and his refusal of his own truth is no more than an unhappy compromise and a refuge. If he once rejected the kibbutz as interfering with his personal ambition he justified that decision by being happy and successful in chemical research; now he nullifies even that. Haezrachi has repudiated the philosophical dreamer who, like certain characters of Nissim Aloni, is blind to all but what he wants to see. The playwright is clearly more partisan to Ehud who functions instinctively and to Nathan who acts without any vestige of selfishness. Although all three men perish in their own manner Haezrachi has made his priorities clear.

Dorit is Ariel's beautiful wife, once loved by Nathan and possibly also by Ehud, although he rejected her advances without being sure of his own motive for doing so. She is certainly responsible for having sown discord in the formerly united group of three young men. She is an unlikable character seen, at first, in her attempts to push the weaker Ariel towards fulfilment of her own desire for money and power, then in her younger incarnation, as a sulky and rejected lover, playing each man off against the other. It is difficult to find, in the context of the play, a reason for her desirability to the three men. Her presence, on another level, causes the greatest structural deficiency in the play in that the second act, which is almost entirely devoted to her relationships with the men, is protracted and repetitive. The author has already said almost all there is to say. But Dorit serves the important purpose of exemplifying the author's indictment of what he surely sees as the modern Israeli housewife:

Ariel: A wonderful wife. A model housewife, energetic, a good cook. A good hostess to my friends. Always encourages me in my work, to improving my career, plays the piano. A clever, humorous woman. And tasteful in matters of furnishing. Happy when there is cause and worries when she has to . . .

She has been incapable of conformity to any way of life, she is perpetually discontented, she has mocked the kibbutz, Nathan's idealism, even the *hora* – and now she barters her love for Ariel's promotion. It is an unattractive fate for an unattractive character.

Sharon, the arch-bureaucrat, is similarly created with dislike. He is pompous, verbose, mulish and self-righteous:

> ". . . I have never been able to stand little rebels and grumblers like you. They always rush in to accuse the commander of every single soldier's death. A lot of people have been killed in this country in the last ten, twenty, fifty years. National heroes, sacred people. And who knows why they were killed? And who knows that their death wasn't caused by negligence . . ."

And so on. One can almost hear the Russian accent in his diction which is in any case different from that of the young men, littered as it is with long words and convoluted sentences.

Sharshevski-Sharon is filled with resentment of the youth, with aggressive and prolix self-justification; he is a pawn of order and authority and has obviously had no difficulty in raising himself to the rank of Minister. Sharon is Haezrachi's dislike and distrust of bureaucracy and the people constituting it.

The play's twin themes are disillusionment and guilt. The first is self-evident and realised essentially through the character of Nathan. The second is more subtle and represented by Ariel, caused primarily by his having deserted the kibbutz, then by his abandonment of Ehud, then by his acceptance of the job from Sharon, the archetypal bureaucrat. It is the guilt of a generation that has changed (Nathan says: "Listen, Ehud, it's altogether difficult for me to explain to you. After all, you were killed ten years ago. A great many things have changed") and which will never overcome its guilt at either having caused or submitted to a new situation and surrendered to a way of life alien to every youthful dream. This guilt was not easy to expunge for it recurs in the drama as late as 1970 in Arieh Chen's prize-winning play *Virgo* where, once again, the ex-Palmachniks are revealed mourning their past and their treachery to the ideal. *The*

Refusal is permeated with a feeling of melancholy and sadness and a sense of waste. The joy of recognising well-known and beloved characters such as Nathan and Ehud, the staple types of Hebrew drama and folk-heroes in every sense, is tempered by sadness at the predictability of their fate, the inevitability of a social process out of the control of the people who served to initiate it.

The major fault of this play is its structure. It is formless, meandering from one situation to the next without logical unity. Once again a potentially strong story is dissipated by weak dramatic construction. The play appears to have been conceived in cinematic terms relying, as it does, on flashbacks and the rapid movement of the characters through time. It would be simple to realise Haezrachi's idea if the stage could approximate the film's fades and mixes and easy distortions of time. As it stands it is clumsy, with characters wandering on and off or standing in upstage darkness interjecting lines, wearing, in turn, their youthful or modern apparel, flitting into the action for a few moments at a time. Offstage voices suddenly interrupt the dialogue to intensify or explain a point. The play is not divided into scenes yet there is no organic continuity. The majority of the action takes place in Ariel's mind yet there are many dialogues and situations in which he has no part and about which he could not have known unless one assumes that he was told about them. Conversations between Dorit and Nathan, for example, or Dorit and Ehud or between Nathan and Sharon towards the end of the play should have been outside Ariel's experience. Similarly, arguments between the other characters seem to take place on strange levels of reality:

Dorit (to Ehud angrily): Why do you keep coming back to Ariel, keep being killed before his eyes? To take revenge on him?

Ehud (offended): Would I want to take revenge on my childhood friend?

Dorit: Yes, because he is alive and you're dead.

It could be that Ariel's mind has divided its burden among his companions for it is difficult to accept that Dorit and the others act in his own fantasy independently of his will.

However, defective structure cannot spoil the essential beauty and vitality of this play. It may be naive and simple, perhaps too predictable, yet it speaks for its time and to a certain extent beyond it, for the gentle characterisation of Nathan transcends the setting and the period. What the play lacks in real dramatic conflict it gains in sincerity, unlike many of the dramatic exercises of the time in Israel. Its humour, the depiction of the strong spiritual bond between

Ehud and Ariel, even the rather overdone villainy of Sharon constitute an unforgettable portrait of a period, one which may not have been to everyone's liking. Haezrachi has taken certain conventional character-types and penetrated beyond their surface to reveal flaws in the old idols; in this way he invests them with a humanity rare in the Hebrew drama of the time.

The following plays were also representative of the "problem" drama of this period in structure and subject-matter:
Call Me Siomka by Nathan Shaham. Produced in 1950 by Cameri. The theme of this play is corruption in government and civil departments and the exploitation of older settlers and immigrants by the new bureaucracy. The past is represented by Siomka, an honest man who is wrongly and maliciously accused of fraud. Siomka's world is that of the past and its traditions. He is unwilling to come to terms with the present he fails to understand. This is a common situation in all literature, no less in Hebrew drama because in Israel the transition between past and present had come too suddenly for most members of the older generation to comprehend.

The brutal present is represented by Eiberland, an official in a government department, a symbol of petty power, corruption and ruthlessness. He states cynically that the days of romanticism are over, that one must strive for one's own advantage even if it means destroying one's fellows along the way.

Mooli, Siomka's son, represents an unusual view of the new generation, educated in Israel and having absorbed echoes of the basic morality of the past. He tries to escape reality because he too is unable to come to terms with it. He is a weak, constantly daydreaming youth who exhibits none of the toughness of the young men of the war.

Hedva and I by Aharon Meged. Produced in 1954 by Habimah. This play is similar to the former in its subject. It considers the problem of those who leave the kibbutz in order to settle – and prosper – in the city. Hedva wants comfort and a home of her own so in order to keep the peace her husband Shlomik agrees and they leave the kibbutz. He is dominated by his young wife and her worldly parents who insist on his going into commerce instead of becoming an artisan which he would prefer to do. He enters the civil service and becomes a soulless clerk. The characters in this play are once again representative of certain sections of the society with which Hedva and Shlomik come into contact: the avaricious parents who indulge in illegal trade; the girl from the kibbutz; Shlomik's city friends, many of whom have become cynical opportunists. All idealism is forgotten and the past no longer exists for them. Their moral values are disappearing, their exalted standards have been lost. Shlomik, still a kibbutznik at heart, believes that he can transcend all this but he fails and loses his identity like all the others.

Meged avoided any real involvement with his subject by structuring the play as a flashback so that from the start the audience knows that Shlomik has returned to the kibbutz with the result that the story loses a good deal of its impact, unlike *The Refusal* in which the vital decision is taken at the end of the play.

Eldorado by Yigal Mossinzon. Produced in 1955 by Ohel.
The problem in this play is that of the criminal element in the slums of Jaffa. Sherman, ex-smuggler and thief, is released from prison and tries to escape his dismal environment firstly by refusing to resume his old participation in criminal activities, then by attempting to aid the police despite their suspicion of him and ultimately by marrying a "nice" girl. This play was like hundreds of others being produced at that time throughout Europe but it was distinguished by a few individually local touches: the character of Kohelet, the old man, and the atmosphere of Jaffa.

Mahazeh Ragil by Yoram Matmor. Produced in 1956 by Cameri.
Once again the theme is loss of idealism and futility in a society that once offered so much to its youth. The setting is unusual: a rehearsal of a play in a theatre. The cast is arguing with the playwright regarding the content and meaning of his play. From their discussions emerge pictures of the war generation which performed its immense task and then sank into careerism, immorality and cynicism. One of their number, the leading actor in their play, leaves the company and returns to the kibbutz where he is subsequently killed by border infiltrators. *Mahazeh Ragil* is by definition a psychological drama and Matmor has attempted a measure of symbolism both in the setting and in the dialogue.

I Like Mike by Aharon Meged. Produced in 1956 by Habimah.
This play deals with the provincialism and narrow-mindedness of civil servants. Ambitious wives scheme for their husbands' advancement and are unwavering social climbers. The story of the play is the exploitation by an Israeli family of a naive American tourist. The parents want him to marry their daughter in order to exempt her from army training and to send her to America, also

because they themselves would like to have some share in his money. Their plan almost succeeds but not quite for Mike decides to settle in Eilat. The daughter refuses to follow him there and he leaves her with her father who has embezzled money on the strength of the wealth to come.

Throw Him to the Dogs by Yigal Mossinzon. Produced in 1958 by Habimah.
Discusses the "yellow" press which causes inestimable harm through sensationalism and irresponsibility. It deals also with the corruption of certain merchants – in this case building contractors – who will do anything for money even if people dependent on them are endangered.

The Street of Steps by Yehudit Handel. Produced in 1958 by Habimah. One of the most important plays of the period. *Rehov Hamadregot* is a narrow alley in Haifa whose inhabitants are drawn from impoverished Eastern communities. Above them looms Mt Carmel the symbol, in this play, of wealth and status. Living on the alley, side by side with the immigrants, are ex-heroes of the War of Independence who are now older and consider themselves useless. Chasms of class had been bridged during the war but now that there is no common motivation uniting every section of the community the gaps between them are widening and a new social structure, based on class, is beginning to appear. The youth too is bewildered – the war had unified them, now something as intangible as status divides them. They are impatient with their elders who are still living in the days of *Haluziut* and the Second *Aliyah*; they attempt to escape the cloying atmosphere of the past and to improve their situation but they are prevented from doing so by intolerance and bureaucracy. The older generation has discovered a new and distressing kind of anti-semitism in their promised land: class distinction. However, because of their emotional ties with the past they are content to remain in the alley and struggle with the physical degradations of poverty and hardship. Like Siomka they cannot come to terms with the present and its loss of romanticism and idealism. They are unable to accept the new Israel.

The story of the play is simple: the son of one of the alley's families falls in love with a girl who lives in prosperity on the Carmel. Predictable problems arise. The basic plot expresses clearly the essential purpose of the play: to acquaint its audiences with the growing and intolerable spectre of class-consciousness and discrimination in the country which had served as an ideal for countless generations of oppressed Jews.

A House in Good Order by Moshe Shamir. Produced in 1961 by Zavit. The setting is a familiar one: the Tel Aviv apartment of a contemporary young married couple. The wife, Ruth, is an attractive, petulant, spoiled and self-centred woman with no inner resources and nothing to fill the long empty hours of her days. Her husband, Dov, is no less shallow than she although he cloaks his petty ambitions with talk of great ideals and honesty. He is as prepared as she to compromise his principles in order to remain in the good graces of his superiors. Once again this is a play about the loss of idealism and the negation of values fought for in the war. Its irony lies in the fact that its hero, Dov, is a colonel in the Permanent Force.

The Price of Credit by Nathan Shaham (Zuta, 1962).
This deals with the problems of opportunism, materialism, a lack of moral values, corruption and the loss of idealism with its accompanying reduction of the individual to a cog in a relentless machine.

The Quarry by Ehud ben Ezer (Zuta, 1964) again discusses corruption, this time in political parties and emphasises the political exploitation of unwary immigrants. These plays and many others like them draw a clear picture of Israel's urban society and its continuing deterioration over the years. Idealism has gone because there is nothing more to strive for. The Promised Land is hastening to remould its historic image for not by a hint must it be distinguishable from its neighbours. The scourge of our time is conformity and the State of Israel, say the playwrights, is consciously conforming, politically and socially, to the accepted and false image of the enlightened post-war democracy.

Despite the clear awareness of everything happening around them it appears that no playwright dared to deal with one of the most pervasive and constantly developing problems of the State: the relationship between Arabs and Jews. Similarly the problem of religion and specifically the growing anti-clericism of the youth was totally ignored. These subjects were too complicated and dangerous in the touchy, explosive atmosphere of the time and, unrealistically, they were avoided in the theatre. The plays were, for the most part, still non-controversial. They each stated a fact not a conflict and this was a weakness of the drama. Great drama has been a drama of ideas from the very first. The accomplished dramatist not only projects a strongly-held subjective viewpoint onto his drama but also provides a complete image of his milieu, even his age as a whole. He must not, in the words of Eric Bentley, "be a propagandist who passes over any good points the other side may have in order to make his own side the stronger". He must certainly not pass over the very points which have the potential for creating the dramatic situation! The dramatist seeks conflict and suppression of any other's case suppresses the possibility of conflict; deliberate avoidance of contention suppresses the possibility of drama.

Even after many years of theatrical activity the Israeli critics still deplored the "lack of universal appeal" of the indigenous plays. They still avoided what Giora Manor calls a "soldering force" – which is a twofold concept: the philosophical unity and emotional or psychological motivation which gives life to any work of art.[7]

In 1953 Harold Clurman visited Israel and made the following comment: "Israelis complain that they have not produced a native drama worth mentioning. In fact, they complain about everything in their theatre. It becomes a visitor's duty therefore to point out to them that these complaints are themselves a sign of their country's youthful ferment and that, putting aside all social and material considerations, Israel has good reason to be proud of its theatrical accomplishments. Perhaps when Israel is more developed it will learn to make an artistic virtue of its primitive crudeness . . ."[8]

[7] "Seventy Original Plays" by Giora Manor. *Theatron*, April–May 1965.

[8] "Theatre" by Harold Clurman. *The Nation*, June 1953.

3 Israel and the World

Three plays, written a number of years apart, express certain attitudes towards relations between Israel and the diaspora during the early sixties. The first was *Go Home, Jonathan* by Hanoch Bar-Tov (Zuta, 1963) a comedy that met with great local success. It describes the world of international diplomacy in New York with emphasis on the Israeli diplomatic service. An old *moshavnik* from Kfar Shaul travels to New York in order to persuade his diplomat son and his family to return to the *moshav* where they belong. He finds that although his son regularly packs his suitcase for the journey back to Israel something has always arisen to prevent his departure and in the meanwhile he has settled down well with his American family. The old man confronts the slick and sophisticated world of international diplomacy and he is not found wanting: his exhortations are impressive but in relation to Israel of 1963 he is speaking in outdated terms, employing the terminology of an earlier decade, and as a character he does not represent, any more than does his son, the reality of modern Israel. The play is, however, an entertaining and pleasant comedy without serious undertones. Not so the second play considering Israelis and Jews in the diaspora, *A Happy Evening on Park Avenue* (Haifa Municipal Theatre, 1965) by Yigal Mossinzon which has an undercurrent of contempt, almost hatred, for the people it describes and embodies the attitude of disdain for diaspora Jews that seemed during the sixties to be a characteristic of many young Israelis. There is no doubt that there are Jews in America like the family the playwright describes but his generalisations are too wild to be effectual and we are not convinced that his stage family is representative of all American Jewish families.

The play portrays certain kinds of Jew, all smothered in the subjective veneer the author has given them. Marshall Cowan (né Cohen) is the rich, sophisticated Jewish businessman who celebrates Christmas and has a butler; there are two *sabras*, one of whom, Josh, is arrogant, brusque, honest and contemptuous of all Jews outside of Israel, particularly "Anglo-Saxons". His is a naive characterisation, the picture of Young Israel prominent in the social drama of the fifties. On the other hand there is the emancipated Israeli, Dani, who can admit to new values without abandoning his own. Both are idealised stock types. The only figure with any life of its own is the daughter, Helen, who, through Josh and her visit to Israel, is able to perceive how far her father has come along the road to assimilation. Her bitterness has a valid source since she had married an artist and lived in Greenwich Village until his death but her wealthy father, Marshall, would not give them any money because the young man was a gentile. That he should celebrate Christmas with a tree and gifts and the ritual dinner and support the Arab states instead of Israel yet not allow his daughter to marry a "goy" is, according to Helen, contemptible hypocrisy and one of the sounder points in the play.

Marshall himself is the cliché of cheap American fiction: the rich businessman to whom money is the only deity. He is urbane and controlled and represents a catalyst in the play, a peg on which the playwright hangs every grievance. He is totally behind the American Way of Life, quite unequivocal in his approach to it, devoid of dual allegiance or guilt. His partner is a gentile called Donald McClaren, an ingenuous stage portrait of a Scotsman who drinks whisky and served as a captain during the war. His opposition to Marshall stems from his condemnation of Marshall's intention to do business with the Arabs. He appears personally to accept responsibility for all Jewish persecutions. It seems incredible that in the quasi-realistic American society that Mossinzon has created there should be a gentile who is prepared to resign his position in a large national concern for the idealistic reason that his superior, his boss, a Jew, would rather support Nasser than Israel!

The play attacks numerous aspects of Jewish social life. Assimilation is the first, symbolised by the Jew who becomes rich and forgets his allegiance to Judaism and Israel, maintaining only what suits him. It attacks wealth as a means to every end, the totalitarian power of money. It also clearly demonstrates the author's attitude towards the Jews in the United States, his dislike of their television, apartments and participation in the daily rat race. Mossinzon obviously believes that no Jew has the right to be anywhere but in Israel for there lies his salvation.

Although written some years later, *Virgo* by Arieh Chen (Habimah, 1972) must be mentioned here for it belongs in every way to the drama of an earlier period. Like the previous play it demonstrates an artless misconception about Jewish life in America, focussing on the clichéd aspects of the American Way of Life, drink, drugs and sex. Despite the prominence of these factors in daily television melodrama and in American films, Israeli playwrights cannot be so naive as to believe that this is a competent portrait of every level of life in the United States. Mendel Kohansky writes: "Everything about 'Virgo' – the characters, the situations, the dialogue – is second-hand. The author seems never to have come closer to his characters and to his situations than newspaper articles on Americans in America and has used every worn-out cliché ever perpetrated."[1]

[1] *Jerusalem Post*, 29th December 1972.

The focus of attention of this play is, however, not that of the Mossinzon work. It deals in the main with the guilt of Israelis living abroad, having abandoned the idealism of the early days after the war in order to participate in the race for material wealth at the price of the spiritual riches of comradeship and patriotism. This is symbolised by Amnon, the play's "hero", who had originally gone to America in order to study agriculture but turned instead to business and became a millionaire brassiere manufacturer, a clever symbol of one of the United States' most pervasive consumer preoccupations. The couple are visiting Israel on the eve of Independence Day and are called on by a friend of their youth, Shosh (Dinah in the translated English text) who, by drawing them into a discussion of the past, reminds them of the disintegration of their moral values, their decline into self-destructive nihilism, and stresses the contrast between their splendid past and ignoble present.

As in the earlier play America is presented solely in terms of clichés: the couple drink exorbitantly, discuss psychoanalysis, money, blacks and hippies, reducing pills and consumerism.

Yael: Everything's fun, Dinah: remember! Just imagine you could've . . . turned into the wife of a successful New York bra manufacturer . . . a housekeeper with an eight-bedroom house in New Jersey; a farm in Connecticut so that her husband can have fun; a very expensive simple-looking cabin in Florida; two or three cars, I can never remember; stocks and shares; and . . . yes, I almost forgot: a hippie daughter who runs around dirty with the lowest scum . . .

Their guilt at their abandonment of the past is expressed by their defensive contempt for everything Israel represented in the early days. They mock the old idealism:

Yael: There's no time for getting old when one's building one's land, hm?

The past is "finished and forgotten" but there has been no meaningful substitute for it. Yael's neurotic contempt extends to the "unsophisticated" people in Israel, the landscape which appears to her to have "had a face lift", the "old guard" that would sit together eating sunflower seeds, the excess of parades and historical pageants – and perversely they blame all this for their palpable unhappiness in the new land of promise, as if Israel itself were responsible for their defection to it.

These two plays are characterised by an over-subjective and immature attitude on the part of the playwrights to the apparent corruption of Jews in the diaspora, significantly not directed at the wealthy Jews of Europe, the United Kingdom or even South Africa, but America, seen purely in terms of its Madison Avenue image of boobs, booze and boredom. It is an unconvincing picture and one which does a disservice to the audiences for whom the plays are directed due to the implication that they share the playwright's irrational anger at something which is outside his experience. No Israeli can convincingly write about Jewish life in the diaspora unless he himself has been a *yoréd* (emigrant) for a considerable time.

Black Man's Burden by Joseph Lapid (Cameri, 1967) is a satirical comedy based on the foibles of Israeli society and dealing specifically with a problem of our time as yet unexplored further in Hebrew dramaturgy: the relationship between blacks and whites in Israel and the political attitudes relating to Israel and the African countries in the late sixties.

The plays forming this small category may not be any more progressive in theatrical terms than the others already discussed but they have the virtue of contentiousness, they do contain the possibility of arousing a negative response in the viewer and of stimulating some form of argument. They demonstrate an attitude amounting sometimes to an obsession on the part of the playwright and while drama should not serve as an outlet for an author's personal vendetta it has the right to present what is not necessarily the popular view.

In form these plays are still static, suffering from the deficiencies that characterise the other drama of their period. The anomaly is *Virgo*, written almost a decade later, but which has not raised itself above its milieu or created characters other than the identical "types" of one kind or another that peopled the social drama of the fifties and sixties. In this respect it is retrogressive for by the seventies an explosion of experimentation was taking place concerning every aspect of the drama, and social comment, however blatant, was no longer being made in terms as confined as those of *Virgo*.

Part III. Thematic Development

. . . the "serious" modern playwright is, or should be, engaged, along with other modern writers, in the search for the human essence . . .

Artists are disturbing unsettling people, not by what they preach but by what they are, conservatives like Dante and Shakespeare being far more disturbing and unsettling than our little revolutionaries. The greater the artist the greater the upset.

1 The Biblical-Historical Play

Introduction

With the establishment of post-1948 Israeli theatre the Biblical-historical play at last came into its own. After enduring for centuries as a kind of forerunner of Hebrew classical drama it has found its true shape in the talented hands of a few playwrights who know precisely how to work with the original scriptural material.

It has taken a long time to reach this point. Without a heritage of dramatic classicism and a living tradition of the stage, the Hebrew theatre through the ages could utilise only one tried and trusted national reservoir, one which had already proved itself invaluable to poetry and prose: the Bible with its wealth of epic and human material. Many Jewish authors had for centuries used Biblical stories as subject-matter for their plays but for reasons already discussed these plays were not suitable drama and they were certainly not theatre. Drama depends on conflict; it is a study of various levels of encounter with an issue that must be decided one way or the other. There might not always be a clear winner or loser but the outcome in all cases must be in question until resolved by the playwright. The Jewish authors concluded that since the Biblical story rests on the relationship between God and man it cannot fulfil this requirement, for its conflict is necessarily limited. For example, in Job's desperate struggle with God every one of his complaints is destined for rejection because he is questioning the Almighty who cannot lose. In one of his plays Moshe Shamir attempted to make the comforters and Elihu part of Job's own mind, conflicting sides of his character. Israel Eldad in his important article "The Bible as Drama"[1] calls this the "Hamletisation of the Bible" and observes that in this particular case the internal conflict must fail because it is "like a man who plays chess with himself while being determined that the white pieces win". This statement can aptly be applied to all drama that has as its premise an encounter between God and man.

[1] "The Bible as Drama" by Israel Eldad. *Bamah* 8, November–December 1960.

Because of the adherence of the early Jewish dramatists to the monotheistic ideal of God's unquestioned power they did not attempt any true dramatic rendering of Biblical topics, rational explanations of any of the stories or psychological interpretation of character, for any meddling meant blasphemy. The Purim tale had originally been selected because it does not mention God's name and the fact that it continued to be frequently used proves that authors were afraid to involve themselves with larger and more basic and profound issues in the field of religion and faith. Early Biblical dramatists did not do more, therefore, than render sections of the Biblical narrative into dialogue without changing, enlarging or interpreting the text. The scriptural stories did not serve as frameworks or allegories or as background for symbolic or expository dramatic works.

The idea of the Bible as a drama has been discussed by Eldad who sheds new and valuable light on the age-old problem. By implication he affirms the possibility of creating drama from the Biblical text without offence or blasphemy. He does so by comparing the elements of Greek tragedy with the basic philosophy of Biblical religion and by separating the religious elements that constituted tragic thought from the divergent Judaic elements of the Biblical story.

Tragedy as a dramatic genre was not considered in terms of Jewish drama because of the pagan religious philosophy which was its source. The metaphysical basis of tragedy is relentless fate pursuing both men and gods, the *moira* from which there is no escape, which reveals itself in the terrible constancy of nature. The Greek hero is governed by this very constancy but Biblical man is not, for he and his events have been released from its compulsion and, as a creature granted free will by God, he has become the hero of a universal, ethical historical story.

This applies to the Bible as a moral and historical unity. In his article Eldad disputes an author's right to extract material from the Bible in order to compose a drama, for it is his opinion that there are no independent stories, all being parts of the whole. Modern Hebrew writers have not adhered to this condition, however, for they have isolated sections from the text and built totally independent structures upon them. Yet in the main they have understood Eldad's insistence on maintaining the entire Biblical story as a *moral* unity, for each author of Biblical drama has exhibited his awareness of the spirit of the Bible and its ethical framework. Whatever they extract still bears some relationship to the whole and however far they may go in their analysis or exposition they reveal at least their knowledge of the ideological framework of the Bible as a unity.

The King is the Most Cruel

Biblical plays of a comparatively later period (1890–1940) exhibit many novel characteristics when compared with their ancestors of the seventeenth and eighteenth centuries. In 1940 the modern Biblical drama was born, with Aharon Aschman's *Michal, the Daughter of Saul* and *Tamar, the Wife of Er* by Yigal Mossinzon. In these plays the dramatists portrayed the characters as individuals instead of archetypal hero-figures though still not reducing them entirely to normal and understandable human terms. The main fault of these plays lay in their imitation of Biblical diction so that at times the effect was contrived, even rather ludicrous when characters talked of prosaic events in the flowery and exaggerated style of the Bible. However, these playwrights "tried to remain true to the Biblical narrative . . . and its spirit, sought to expand what they could as convincingly as possible, to bestow dramatic form on the epic essence, to fill in the missing details, to cast some light on shaded portions of the picture, to add movement and colour to a plot that was sometimes enclosed in a few short sentences. And above all to interpret and bring to light, as far as possible, the submerged psychological tenor."[2] As these attempts continued there appeared a growing tendency to recreate Biblical themes in terms of modern motives and concepts by reducing the religious dominance of the stories. Dramatists sought to use a more critical approach, along the lines of the contemporary historical novel.

[2]"Hebrew Drama" by Ezra Zussman. *World Theatre*, May–June 1965.

The breakthrough occurred in the fifties. Two Biblical-historical plays written in 1953 and 1955 seemed to be the forerunners of a kind of "new wave" in Hebrew drama. They were *The King is the Most Cruel* by Nissim Aloni (Habimah, 1953) and *The War of the Sons of Light* by Moshe Shamir (Cameri, 1955). They concentrated their attention on moral political problems pertaining directly to Israeli society of the time yet offered a commentary on society and humanity as a whole. They discussed the vital problems of democracy and statesmanship, the relationship of government – in both plays symbolised by a monarch – to society (the king's subjects). This fundamental and truly "universal" subject was expressed in Biblical-historical terms so that the plays are, strictly speaking, still allegories. The characters remain as true as possible to what is known about them as real historical figures but they are interpreted by the playwright in the light of the subject they have been chosen to present and symbolise and emerge as distinctive personalities. Using long-dead but immortal historical personages to state the eternal problems of humanity is an effective way of "universalising" a play by making it suit all peoples, all nations and all times. Also, employing the Bible as source material links modern Hebrew culture with the ancient culture of the nation ensuring the emergence of a drama totally Hebrew in environment and spirit yet general in its examination of human morality in the modern world.

The production of *The King is the Most Cruel* introduced the Israeli public to a brilliant young playwright, Nissim Aloni, the first Israeli dramatist worthy of international recognition. His play was a decisive milestone in Hebrew drama because of its dramatic and intellectual qualities which, apart from anything else, contrasted it strongly with the ephemeral playwriting that had developed during the early years of the State. Aloni had found a powerful motif and a viable symbol to express it: the motif of man as a political animal suffering from the various cruelties inherent in hierarchical rulership; the symbol, as in so many of his subsequent dramas, is the king. Apart from *The King is the Most Cruel* his plays are satirical, often dealing farcically with ideas of control and subservience. His creatures battle against conformism and condemn the dehumanisation of the man who exists as nothing more than a political cipher. Aloni was influenced by Brecht, Ionesco and Alfred Jarry, among others, having spent many of his formative years as a dramatist in France. In the main, however, his style is original, it makes original theatre and some critics see in him "our most important playwright and the hope of the Israeli theatre . . ."[3] "In one literary sweep Aloni discredited the exaggerated artistic praise given to the hollow writing of dramatic reportage in the enthusiastic atmosphere of the years of strife and the War of Independence. Every aspect of *The King is the Most Cruel*, although it was still experimental, revealed the blight in the Palmach plays and those of the wastes of the Negev. His attempts to achieve lyrical, rhythmic and descriptive language attained only partial success, but emphasised unequivocally the bankruptcy of the style that had pretentions towards establishing realistic dramatic language, with the aid of the most stereotyped affectations.

"In his efforts to present the conflicts between man, that are also contrasting points of view, collisions between worlds (Jeroboam, Zeruah, Rehoboam) Aloni laid bare the non-dramatic essence in the majority of the war plays that were coated with an entirely external tension. In the problems that were revealed in *The King is the Most Cruel*, the most basic problems in the life of the small nation pressed between Assyria and Egypt, torn between the choice of religious supremacy and the desire for secular life, between its definition as a messenger of God and its seeing itself as the son of a family of the soil, the great, latent spiritual possibilities were hinted at in this drama.

"In this play the possibility of theatre was immediately perceptible, theatre that epitomises the basic problems of the nation and presents before it the enormous questions that are not visible on the external surface of its life. In this – more than anything else – Aloni exposed the intellectual vacuity of a drama that contained

[3]From a letter. Quoted with permission.

nothing but a kind of narcissistic self-caress . . . we are good, we are heroes . . . always 'we', the voice of bravado . . ."[4]

[4]Dan Meron. *Haaretz*, March 1st 1963.

In *The King is the Most Cruel*, writes Professor Gershon Shaked, "Aloni attempted to approach the world of men. He tried to understand the historiosophic laws of history in its earliest development. He wanted to give form to the personal consciousness of a generation that had succeeded in its social strivings and then become disappointed by the *Golem* it had created. The dream of the wonderful monarchy that overlaid the skin and bones of kingship and kingdom brought Aloni to the point of astonishment about the value and implication of all monarchy, the end of which is always odium and hatred. He left this problem to history but inspired in the characters he created a spirit of life – and they lived and breathed of their own accord. He understood Rehoboam in his inferiority and Jeroboam through his relationship with the two women, Zeruah and Maacah, his mother and his ex-mistress; the characters live, despite the historiosophic background and the references to actuality."[5] Many do not agree with these and other even more lavish views expressed about Aloni and his work but there is no doubt that he burst onto the Israeli stage with a forcefulness that called for notice and appraisal and that his plays are incomparable in structure and content to anything written by any Israeli dramatist up to the present time.

[5]"In the Paths of the Hebrew Play" by Gershon Shaked. *Bamah* 6, July 1960.

For his political allegory Aloni takes the story of Rehoboam, the son of Solomon, King of Israel, and Jeroboam, the son of Nebat, an overseer under Solomon. After incurring the King's suspicion of his role as leader of the popular democratic parties Jeroboam was exiled to Egypt where he spent ten years. He was then recalled by the northern tribes on the refusal of Rehoboam, "the cruellest of all", to accept the constitutional terms offered to him at his accession. Rebellion, led by Jeroboam, was inevitable. At first the ensuing civil war seemed to have gone in favour of the south but the power of Judah was permanently checked by an Egyptian invasion. The nation was finally split into the independent kingdoms of Judah and Israel. On this basis Aloni built a drama of ideas that attempts to demonstrate the futility of revolution, the hypocrisy of democratic idealism, the corruption of the ruler who, as in so many cases throughout history, is all-powerful yet a misfit at war with his own weakness, the smooth expediency of diplomatic advisers – the fate of whom is revealed in this play in unequivocal terms, the ugliness of chauvinistic and religious fanaticism that takes on its eternal disguise of piety and justice resting upon direct orders from God.

These diverse elements in the play are typified by the characters as is the case in much of the earlier Biblical drama but with one vital difference: the *dramatis personae* in *The King is the Most Cruel* have assumed the attributes of objective life through meticulous characterisation, prompting the kind of reaction in the viewer or reader which could not possibly have been evoked by their stylised predecessors, the figures of the nineteenth century, and earlier, Biblical plays.

The widow Zeruah is Jeroboam's mother, a cold, bitter and frustrated woman who is unable to "laugh in the sunlight, to drink from jars of wine, to love without fearing that it is a sin . . ." Her personal hatred has been sublimated into political and religious zeal. She lives only for the rebellion because of her hatred for Rehoboam and her need to avenge her husband, killed in the service of King Solomon, Rehoboam's father. She believes blindly in Ahiah the prophet, himself a political opportunist, because it suits her immediate purpose. She has schemed and plotted for years to turn her son, Jeroboam, into an instrument of rebellion and when he hesitates she transfers her scorn to him: "I have sinned, my son, because I have not fixed greater hatred in your heart . . ." In the end she becomes the victim. Her son, by his sudden change of purpose is, ironically, the cause of her death. Instead of welcoming his change of heart and his decision to do precisely what she had once urged she censures him in the most bitter terms not only because she must be sacrificed but also because Jeroboam has rejected her mentor, Ahiah the prophet. Her vengeful anger proves her utilisation of apparent political and religious idealism as no more than tools for essentially dynastic aspirations. Zeruah is the classical mother-figure who uses a child as an instrument of vengeance and ambition, a combination of Volumnia, Electra and Lady Macbeth in her obsessive purpose. Her portrayal is often a little overdone in the sense of classical projection: she rants a great deal, at times becoming no more than a malicious and irritating old woman. She feels no human emotions save hatred and her compulsive religious zeal. Maternal love is, of course, unknown to her. She detests Maacah above all others for representing what the frigid Zeruah was incapable of ever knowing: life, love, beauty and passion, also because the young woman had once been Jeroboam's mistress, capturing his love and diverting his attention from his mother's intent.

Rehoboam, like Jeroboam, is a complex character representing monarchy although he appears in the play not only as a symbol but as a fully and cleverly realised character, the most original of them all.

He reveals that throughout his youth he suffered humiliation and mockery for being a stupid fat boy or else he was dismissed as an idiot, later a drunkard and a hedonist. He has grown up hiding his innate perceptiveness, acuity, cunning and sharp intelligence, keeping these qualities for his own use when necessary. He becomes the king – ruthless and despotic, sly and quick-witted, ready to inflict on anyone revenge for his lifelong ignominy. His cruelty derives from resentment, a simmering hatred that can be exposed only when he has the power to use it, a dangerous situation for he represents the danger of a weak, frightened man suddenly endowed with limitless power, suddenly able to take by force everything denied him, like Maacah's love. Only to her, in one of the most moving and revealing scenes in the play, does he show his true self – a cringing little man, a lonely man who has to beg – or pay – for love. Then he is transformed into a figure of despair and anguish aware of his own debasement and this self-knowledge elevates his character from the villainous grotesquerie of the Biblical original to one of dramatic nobility. He is conscious not only of his own corruption but that his beautiful and coveted wife loathes him. Moreover he is afraid for his throne, he has no faith in God. "Have you seen God standing with two legs on the institutions of earth, flicking his whip at the faces of all of us, slaves who cannot die because his whip cracks 'live!' and cannot live because life stems from despair and ends in despair."

Politically, however, he is astute and, like a good politician, a pragmatist. He sees directly into the hearts of men due to the clarity of his own self-awareness. All men desire power, this is his credo as it is the playwright's, even Ahiah the prophet who will be king while Rehoboam wears the crown. Peace, he claims can be gained only one way when a nation is squeezed between two voracious giants like Assyria and Egypt: through silver lifted from the people who will pay because the king so demands.

Rehoboam's queen, Maacah, is a woman made only for love. She symbolises the personal level of the conflict between Jeroboam and Rehoboam and her presence adds depth to their political struggle, for she is a bone of contention between them no less than the throne. She had once loved Jeroboam but did not wait for his return from exile in Egypt, marrying the king instead. When Jeroboam comes home her love is reawakened but he rejects her; she takes her revenge by allying herself with Rehoboam in his attempt to destroy her former lover. For once the king and queen are united. Ultimately, however, she falters in her vengeance when she realises that no threats nor any scheming will restore Jeroboam's love to her, even in the face of failure and death. Then she cries: "Hold me, Jeroboam . . . let me kiss the straps of your sandals, the dust your feet tread upon. For what do I need a crown, Jeroboam, a palace and handmaidens? Take me to the fields, Jeroboam, indulge me with your love . . . I love you, Jeroboam . . ." She falls at his feet and clings to his knees but Jeroboam, after accusing her of being a whore and loving a life of idle luxury more than personal purity and social justice, sends her away. This scene, like many others in the play, attains a climax of pure dramatic tension and while this particular situation is not original it reaches in this play a level of intensity that calls for the audience's response. Maacah is a shallow woman who lives for and by her emotions, as incapable of strong sincere feeling as she is of involvement in ideology, in this way thoroughly feminine and also fairly stupid. Yet there is some measure of drama in her self-induced suffering, her emotional fluctuations and what appears to be her hopeless love for Jeroboam.

Jeroboam the son of Nebat is by far the most enigmatic figure in the play for he is not fully resolved and often contradictory. It is possible that Aloni deliberately left him incomplete in order to emphasise the lack of clarity in Jeroboam's own mind, his dilemma and lack of resolution, his Hamlet-like equivocation. He has returned from his ten years' exile in Egypt having gained in maturity and caution and a good deal of disillusionment. At the court of Pharaoh Shishak he had seen power abused. "Pharaoh Shishak was a captain in the Egyptian army and he rebelled against his masters. Much blood was spilt. Today Pharaoh Shishak is the king. In the squares of Egypt's capital many are gathering together secretly, waving their fists at the king's palace." Jeroboam is no longer the ingenuous young man overawed by Ahiah's impressive prophecies, for his own belief in God is in question. He penetrates through the calculated veneer of Ahiah's holiness into the political ambition beneath just as he sees through his ideological vision of holy war into the bloodshed and suffering it must bring. He is aware of the perverting of the rulers' personalities through their power and for this reason initially rejects power for himself because of its end as corruption. Throughout Zeruah's harangues he remains impassive except for the occasion when he makes the rather naive statement that he is a man who cares only about living – and bread. "I am one of those holy men who have been cursed with being unable to forget that they are men. I am an anointed monk who mocks the oil that anointed his head." He no longer considers himself the "monk of God" and shows little confidence in his own abilities as a military leader. His extraordinary clarity of vision relates, however, only to his own idealism for like so many crusaders he is blind to political reality and his rebellion must, therefore, fail.

Rehoboam's assessment of him is keen and possibly accurate: "Jeroboam was a captain over Ephraim in my father's palace and he smelled both the odour of sweat and the aroma of herbs; therefore one half of his heart follows the shout of the populace, and the other half the charms of the palace . . ." Later he confronts Jeroboam: "What do you want? Today we'll talk clearly. You and I both covet a woman and a crown. Therefore the country can't contain us both . . ." After this meeting with Rehoboam, Jeroboam decides to lead the mutiny after all. Despite the fact that he abhors war, that he fears for his followers and that he dreads bloodshed, he resolves to fight the king because of his own basic and misguided idealism, "because I talk of bread". That is his own reason. In a rapidly moving scene involving all the major characters in the play with the exception of Rehoboam all the accusations against Jeroboam, all the theories about his initial hesitation and subsequent decision to fight are brought out into the open and Jeroboam neither confirms nor denies any of them. He himself states only that the rebels have come too far to turn back. He – and they – are committed. Shamai, the king's confidant and adviser, a spy in Jeroboam's camp, accuses him of having involved the nation in his own personal battle – referring to Maacah – instead of involving himself in theirs. Furthermore, accuses Shamai, Jeroboam has made an alliance with Shishak of Egypt to use Israel as a buffer against the might of Assyria.

Maacah, rejecting and rejected, out of the hysteria of a woman scorned, declares that Jeroboam is filled with ambition and covets nothing less than the throne. "He will thrust behind him the most precious of all, his nation and his country, for one throne, one throne in Jerusalem, the throne of David! He is not seeing the nation, only the crown!" His antagonists are convinced that he has been bought by Egypt. One after the other they hurl their spite at him exposing and revealing, in their indictment of him, the savage depths of their own personalities. Finally the young men of his army decide to leave the matter to Ahiah the prophet.

At this point Jeroboam loses patience. After enduring their venom in silence he explodes into anger. His speech, the last and longest in the play, is at the same time his own vindication to his accusers and, more importantly, Aloni's perceptive comment on Israel's modern political policy. A small, poor nation, says Jeroboam, must make some alliance with the surrounding states for it cannot exist alone. In this same outburst Aloni is expressing his opposition to the spiritual exclusivism that Israel has imposed upon herself as the example and messenger of God. By his creative manipulation of the character of Ahiah, Aloni suggests his suspicion of the political opportunism implied in prophecy and reveals his attitude towards religious extremism. Finally Jeroboam's tirade is Aloni's opinion of the nationalistic bravado with which modern Israel insulated herself during the early years of the State and his prophetic comment on her stubborn isolationism: "If the man who closes his eyes not to see the surrounding countries is a Hebrew I am an Egyptian because I see the peace of Jerusalem in Damascus . . . If Ahiah the Shilonite who shouts that we must exist alone is a Hebrew – I, Jeroboam, am an Egyptian because I seek to find allies in other lands . . . Between the hammer of Assyria and the anvil of Egypt we all stand – alone." He ends on an impassioned demand: "Am I an Egyptian because I tell you to seek Damascus and Hamat, that their losses should be ours and our war theirs? Or because I have had enough of all the . . . curses that have been flung at me? The lies . . . the contempt. Soon the trumpets will sound and thousands will watch the platform to know if the rebellion will rise or fall. What shall I reply to them when among us there are only serpents whispering venom? What shall I reply to them when among us, even now, there are traitors?" Jeroboam's rebellion begins in blood. He kills Shamai, and his mother is executed by his men. His conviction that it is impossible to establish a kingdom in Israel or anywhere else without cruelty and bloodshed has again been demonstrated. "Every king erects an altar steeped in blood. I am not yet king but my altar is already erected. Mother, the king is very cruel. The king is the cruellest of all."

Together with the four major characters of the play all of whom represent certain struggling powers appear others whose function it is to typify diverse elements in the life of the State. One of these is Shamai who stands as the personification of political diplomacy, a man who, to quote Rehoboam, "is one of those people who wets his finger to know whence the wind is blowing". He does what he considers expedient and if it is not lawful he changes the law. Aloni treats him with contempt and executes him in the end. A more important and considerably more dangerous figure is Ahiah the Shilonite, the symbol of a theocracy in which every perversion of justice is given the rationale of God's will. Ahiah wears the cloak of prophecy to further his own political ambition to be a kingmaker and consequently the highest power in the State, both religious and temporal.

He supports the one of the two contenders who is most likely to be of use to him by acquiescing to his demands. He and Rehoboam understand one another well but Jeroboam is a danger to him: the idealist who will not tolerate personal ambition in a man of God and who can therefore not be influenced or directed by him. For this reason Ahiah repudiates him. The prophet does not once appear in *The King is the Most Cruel* but his original prophecy concerning Jeroboam is the *raison d'être* of the situation described in the play. His manoeuvring, his powerful hold over the people, his unspoken bargain with Rehoboam pervade every aspect of the story and direct all its events.

Jonathan, one of the young men of Rehoboam's army, is a rebel without a specific cause and none of Jeroboam's conflicts. He represents the youth of the country who are prepared to spill blood for the adventure and danger of it.

Structurally the play is fairly conventional, maintaining the unities throughout three acts and employing a chorus as prologue to supply the historical background of the story. The impact of the play is derived not from the plot or structure but from its poetry. Aloni has the gift of manipulating language, rendering it exciting and earthy, filled with vivid imagery that is explicit without being banal. He uses extraordinary subtleties of phrase and word-play. With this early drama he created a modern prose-poetry that has not yet been equalled in Hebrew dramatic writing.

From the time of its first performance to its successful revival in 1974 critics have debated the nature of the play, whether or not it is a tragedy in the hope, perhaps, that Hebrew drama could recreate classical tragedy with a Judaic foundation. Jeroboam, the protagonist, has some of the qualities of a tragic hero – his moral idealism for one, his fateful lack of political vision or reality, his indecision which consistently reveals a need for justifying any positive action. Instead of the gods directing his steps his mother stands over him like a reproachful deity creating a compulsion for action. But tragedy should end at least in the physical death of the hero; in this play it is Zeruah, the mother, who dies. It is she who ends a predestined and fateful course, it is her obsession that has set the events in motion and fulfilled a prophecy.

The play loosely follows the pattern of tragic rhythm defined by Kenneth Burke as purpose, passion and perception although the perception in *The King is the Most Cruel* is not the Greek *anagnorisis*, a sudden insight into self that spiritually ennobles the tragic hero before his death but the hero's full awareness, from the start, of his inevitable destiny. It has been suggested that Jeroboam's tragedy is his continuing life "... condemned to live in self-despair and in bitter recognition that [his] dreams die the day they are born into actual reality ..."[6]

The spur to present action was the death of King Solomon which allowed Jeroboam to return to Israel. There is no external supernatural directing force save perhaps Ahiah in his guise of prophet of the Lord, except that he cannot in this play be said to represent God's justice and righteousness. No myth underlies the play other than a tenuous link with Oedipus in Jeroboam's desire for the king's death, his emotional subordination to his mother and the conflict between her demands and his own needs, symbolised by Maacah whom, significantly, he rejects. The tragedy implicit in the play is that of the domination of man by his own nature, an evolution of tragedy explored by many great modern dramatists. In this sense the three principal figures are tragic victims, especially Rehoboam who is assailed not only by his moral weakness but also by its effect on the political reality outside of himself. Indeed all tragic heroes are victims of their temporal fate but emerge, after their trials, as spiritual victors. None of the primary characters in Aloni's play achieves this victory.

The King is the Most Cruel was revived at the Haifa Municipal Theatre in 1974. It seemed that the critics were delighted to be able to praise an Aloni play after so many years of encountering his artistic incomprehensibility. There was a spate of new critical writings on the play and new interpretations which in themselves were interesting because of the changed political and social situation in Israel. But Aloni himself had, even by 1964, moved so far away from his initial dramatic realism that he denigrated his youthful achievement, dismissing it as an immature exercise.[7]

[6] "The Tragicomedy of Fulfilment in Nissim Aloni's Plays" by Zephyra Porat. Date and source obliterated on photostatic copy obtained from Genazim.

[7] *Davar*, July 16th 1975.

Genesis

Whereas *The King is the Most Cruel* can be compared in conception, form and treatment to the style of Shakespeare's histories and certain modern historical dramas (for example, Robert Bolt's *A Man for All Seasons*, *Beckett* by Anouilh and even *Murder in the Cathedral* by Eliot), Aharon Meged's *Genesis* (Habimah, 1962) is thoroughly unconventional in its choice of subject matter which is the most basic of all mythic-historical material: the story of the expulsion of Adam and Eve from Eden and their life together thereafter. Meged's most impudent achievement in this play is his treatment of God in the form of the Keeper of the Garden with his amiable adversary, an ingratiatingly charming Serpent.

Meged's play makes few concessions to the accepted moral intention of the Biblical story, relying far more on the mythic for purposes of his own speculation. His play is at once lighthearted and profound, amusing and tragic, philosophical, cynical, pious and blasphemous and yet with all these diverse and contradictory elements it remains uncommitted, a fault derived from its lack of philosophical purpose. It is an entertainment with isolated pieces of sombre reason but it has no fundamental point of view with the result that the story is engaging but sadly devoid of ideological unity. Still, Meged presents a few outrageous theories regarding man's eternal enigmas. It is the lightheartedness of *Genesis* that charms the reader or audience where a dogmatic statement or studied hypothesis would probably not have done, for lightheartedness in this case attempts to conceal some disturbing undercurrents of bewilderment about the problems of man's own psyche and the terrifying primeval world around him.

The essential thing about the myths and stories of the Old Testament is that they are "paradigms of the continuing situation; we are involved in them. Adam and Eve, characters in an ancient tale, are at the same time Man and Woman in general, we are all expelled from our Edens and sacrifice our happiness to the ambitions of our intellects. All of us metaphorically flee our Egypts, receive our revelation and trek through our deserts to a promised land which only our children or our children's children may eventually enjoy. In every generation God fights the Dragon and David fells Goliath. We all wrestle with angels through a dark night."[8] Meged has added yet another layer to his paradigm embodied in the Book of Genesis, having allegorised the allegory in the creation of his own particular aetiology. His family in the play, the family of Adam and Eve and their sons are, so to speak, Everyfamily. Its members have Biblical names, it is the first and only family in the world, its external environment is that of the Genesis story in time and place but the characters are given "universal" and metaphorical value by a clever device of the playwright's: constant use of anachronism that raises them out of their confinement in time. They speak a modern, colloquial language using the most contemporary expressions, they live in a B.C.E. dwelling presented as a primitive parody of a staple of modern society – a flat with all mod. cons. They coyly mention subsequent books of the Bible: "Stop teaching me the Ten Commandments all the time!" They speak of later historical events,

[8]Theodore H.Gaster. *Myth, Legend and Custom in the Old Testament*. Harper and Row, 1969.

they self-consciously and theatrically refer to things that in their ancient environment do not exist, for example Eve asks Adam whether they will have a telephone in their new house:

Adam: As you know, Madam, this is not the twentieth century. This is the thirtieth century B.C. Even electricity hasn't been invented yet.

Eve: I was confused. So – am I then to understand that I won't even have a radio?

Adam: No – no radio, no electric range, no electric oven, no fridge. I can't jump 5,000 years forward.

They refer to themselves as Biblical figures:

Eve: Don't keep talking in Biblical style.

Abel: Aren't we Biblical characters?

and . . .

Adam: Adam, Eve, Cain and Abel – this is the entire society of the world, as it is written in black and white in the Book of Genesis.

Hand in hand with the simple story of a family told in allegorical form is a satire on modern marriage. Every cliché in the Marriage Guidance manual, every trivial situation of glossy romantic films, every problem to be found in the agony columns of women's magazines, every housewife's complaint about her husband, every well-aired issue pertaining to marriage, superficial and serious, appears somewhere in *Genesis*. Eve is the eternal woman growing bored when her husband stops behaving as he did "when we were first married". He is no longer interested in courtship, he does not talk to her as he used to. She is jealous of his devotion to the Keeper, accusing Adam of a stronger allegiance to him than to her. She is immature and romantic, discontented and disillusioned, in every way a modern suburban wife full of complaints: they live too far away from social activity, from the fruit trees where she daily gathers their food. She wants to see and be seen, to experience excitement and adventure and she comes to sense all the possibilities in the person of the Serpent – the eternal tempter. Adam, also according to disparaging modern western standards, is the typical husband, stolid, practical, unimaginative, loyal, desiring nothing more than peace and quiet, his food on time and his routine undisturbed.

The story proceeds. Eve succumbs to the Serpent's charming wiles and returns to Adam a little older and much wiser after recognising that the kind of love the Serpent has offered her is not what she is seeking. Self-knowledge has taught her tenderness and the maturity to be able to accept her husband's nature for what it is.

She had wanted to learn, to know (the apple), now she has learned and is content. "We know many things now that we didn't know before – sin and the strength to withstand it. And also love – and also good and evil . . ."

The couple are banished from the Garden by an affectionate Keeper who is acting for their own good and who has to set history in motion. Later two sons are born, and grow to manhood and the marriage enters its second and more problematical phase: discontented middle-age. The "typical" marriage has developed along "typical" lines. Adam is out working all day. Where does he go? Why does he come home so late? Adam's dour reply to her accusation of infidelity is that he could not make love to another woman even if he wanted to since Eve is the only woman in the world. This remark and others very similar are burlesques of frequently reiterated modern clichés, the principal components of popular television melodrama and the romantic novel, in this case: "You are the only woman in the world for me."

They quarrel about "typical" matters satirically listed by the playwright. Wayward Eve regrets her conventionally chaste life, she remembers the Serpent with growing regret and affection. He appears to her in a dream, still young, handsome, the eternal gigolo wooing a safely-married ageing ex-mistress. Yet now that Eve is older she wants what she once rejected in her youth: peace and emotional stability. Then she longed for adventure, now she knows that none exists, but what she had when young was definite and ordered: Paradise. Now her life has neither one nor the other.

One feels that had this been presented in its appropriate setting, our modern social environment, it would have been specious and unoriginal, in fact of no more value than a soap opera. It is the unusual setting of *Genesis* that validates the re-examination of the hoary old problems for by implication these were the world's first marital troubles and Adam and Eve acted as paradigms for their solution. And while there is scarcely any evocation of primordial rite, of the elemental mysteries of myth with its fearful primal response, Meged's stories still rest on the basic impulses of humanity translated into the tamer terminology of twentieth-century sensibility.

Adam grows old; he is always tired, surly, still resentful of Eve's infidelity, never allowing her to forget it. All his actions are "for your sake and the sake of the children". The play moves on towards the preordained tragedy with the introduction of the two sons and a novel hypothesis about the first murder. Abel (*hevel:* vanity, a most suitable name as he himself explains) the herdsman is the pampered young son, irresponsible, sly, charming and artistically talented. Both parents adore and over-protect him. His older brother Cain is, like his father, dependable and responsible, always loyally concealing Abel's misdemeanours even though he himself is their victim. Adam in particular is the doting fatuous parent, a rather stupid bourgeois father who regards an artist in the family as an awesome honour. The situation between the brothers is a literary commonplace, with Cain misunderstood by his parents yet doggedly devoted to both, particularly his insensitive father, and Abel, the adored baby of the family with no thought for anyone but himself, very like the insufferable youngest son of the fairy-tales. His murder is a direct result of Adam's unfairness: Cain has served him cabbage which has been spoilt by the sheep that Abel had allowed to wander free while he sat dreaming. Adam complains about the cabbage and Abel, without malice or guile brings him some meat. Then he plays his flute. He basks in the limelight of his parents' fondness. Cain, misjudged and impotent, says nothing but storms outside to chop wood. At his mother's bidding Abel follows to call him in. An accident occurs and Abel is slain.

The story continues: Eve dies after bearing a third son. Cain disappears only to return, when Adam is old and ill, with a young and beautiful fiancée whose name is Astarte. The girl is again a stereotype: promiscuous, gay, vain, selfish, symbolising both illicit sex and the gulf between generations. Cain is enchanted by her, Adam distressed because of her empty-headedness and because she originates from the "wrong background" for Adam's is the "first family" in the world while Astarte is a daughter of the Nefilim, those strange newcomers to earth, described in Genesis 6.4. The ever-present Serpent recognises her for what she is but, being the element of evil, allows her to proceed. Adam has developed in compassion with old age. He loves his son and apologises to him, having for years lived with the realisation of his own injustice thus raising yet another item in the long list of familial problems: the guilt of the parents in the sins of the children, a neat illustration of the Biblical maxim. Adam dies and is taken by the Keeper back to the Garden of Eden, protesting all the while that he would rather remain on earth.

The characters of the Keeper and the Serpent, unlike the mortals, bring the play into a secondary, metaphysical realm that is closer in intent to the Genesis story than to twentieth-century social problems. The family remains the family of man but the issues raised are profound and Meged treats his hypotheses seriously. He is on this mythic level presenting the vulnerable family unit, surrounded on all sides by immense supernatural and primeval forces which battle for supremacy on a Jobian level incomprehensible to mortals who are all the while blindly moving towards some ultimate outcome over which they have no control. In the first act the Keeper appears as a capricious and rather selfish being, although benign. Eve complains that because he has given them life he uses them as he wishes and she would rather not have been created in such circumstances:

> "What are you thinking of, that because you have inspired breath in us you are permitted to play with us as you wish? To send us here and there, command what is allowed and what is forbidden? If this is the price that I must pay – take back your breath!"

The view of the Deity in *Genesis* conforms to the pagan primitive concept of Good pitted against Evil, sometimes outwitted by it, and represents the God of the early Book of Job. The Keeper is corporeal and confined to a particular area, not omnipresent, which is a later concept than that of the personified God of the Biblical Genesis. Like the prophet Jonah, Eve wants to escape, even to suffer outside of Eden as long as she is away from the Keeper's all-seeing and all-knowing eyes in the Garden. In Eve's objection to the Keeper Meged illustrates the Biblical case of free will. God has created his first humans free and able to have withstood temptation, beings of unshackled and unhindered decision. Yet Eve complains that in Eden everything is given and decided for them and man has no will of his own; the only way the Keeper is able to maintain his supremacy is by keeping one thing away from man-in-his-image: the tree. She exercises her will and eats of the tree, with the immediate and necessary result of the acquisition of forbidden knowledge leading to banishment. At the end of the play the question is approached once more.

Adam: [in reply to the Keeper's query as to whether he had regretted leaving Eden]: No . . . not for one moment. I was only sorry that you abandoned us. That you didn't intervene at all. That you did not prevent what you could have prevented.

Keeper: I gave you the *choice*. A gift that no other creature has achieved. There, in the garden, everything is measured and control is not given. You got the *control*!

Adam: Control over what?

Keeper: To love, to hate, to sin, to forgive . . .

Meged's sympathetic characterisation of the Serpent who can hardly be called evil in this play offers paradoxically a more frightening concept than the traditional fire-and-brimstone Devil whose essence is destruction and suffering. Meged's is closer to Milton's Satan, the fallen angel who still loves God and longs to be back in favour but who is now destined to fulfil the task assigned to him: to be the obverse implementation of man's free will. He is the temptation to sin, whereas God is the temptation to virtue but neither of them uses compulsion in their battle over mankind. In *Genesis* the Keeper and the Serpent are like old sparring partners, fond of each other despite their differences, regretful that they have always to fight yet aware that there are compensations for this too. It is a frightening theory that Meged proposes in what the Keeper declares: that the Serpent relieves his boredom for he becomes bored indeed with all the perfection of Eden: "Your venom," he says, "is the only balm here for boredom." The thought of God using evil capriciously as a plaything to make his eternity more interesting is a terrifying one, and one of Meged's most cynical ideas in a cynical play.

The Serpent in *Genesis* appears from time to time, himself maturing and growing bitter, driven on by his destiny, at times very much like an ageing playboy who has nothing left but new attempts and old memories. He symbolises one-half of man's will but does not much like his task because he is capable of compassion, surely an original gift to one of a long line of literary Devils. His part is that of a catalyst which leaves men to their own destruction. He does not incite but plays on mortals' weaknesses. He is there to pour another glass of brandy, to seduce another willing girl . . . The cause of all psychological complexity and negative human emotions, of all the things found outside of Paradise, he had only to set everything in motion, and Man, in his folly, would take care of the rest. "Don't worry, Adam," he says, "I am not dangerous, as you know. I only dance in the middle . . ." He is, then, not evil, because man is not evil, man is nothing but petty and silly, lacking nobility and emotional breadth.

At the end of the play Meged comes to certain conclusions about the human condition and the reasons for man's suffering. Why, asks Adam, was man created at all?

Keeper: Had I not created *him*, who would have known me?
Why must man suffer? – Adam asks.
Keeper: Without sorrow you would not know what joy is.
Why does God not restrain evil? – Adam asks.
Keeper: In order that you may *fight* it.
Adam: Have you given us the power to overcome it?

Keeper: There is no victory in this conflict.
Adam: Why? Why?
Keeper: Because if you were to overcome him [the Serpent] the world would return to Eden. If he were to overcome you the world would return to chaos. The war between you – *this* is life.

Yet despite Adam's bewildered despair, particularly when the Keeper tells him (and one cannot help feeling that he does so in this play with a certain satisfaction) that he, Adam, has been standing only on the threshold of suffering and that his descendants will "break their heads" over all of life's contradictions without ever solving any of them, the play ends with a restrained message of hope. The Keeper appears to Adam and tells him that he is returning him to Eden; Adam protests desperately with his last breath but submits finally for he has no more strength with which to struggle. It seems, therefore, that in spite of everything man would sooner remain mortal and possess the gift of life with all its complexities than bow before the eternal peace of Eden.

Genesis differs from *Paradise Lost* in every possible way – thematically, stylistically, structurally, in genre, in intent, in profundity but the greatest difference is that Milton created his epic from *faith*, as a reaffirmation of his love of God at a time when he had good cause to despair. He kept the Biblical story within the scheme of religion. Meged's play is the opposite. He has used the story as a means of expressing his doubts concerning faith in general and his final message is a rather precarious compromise.

Structurally *Genesis* is conventional, overlong and often unnecessarily repetitive. It was extended into a full-length drama from a one-act playlet based on the first section called *Original Sin* which met with enormous success when first performed at Beit Lessin in 1960. The longer play was first presented at Habimah's Little Theatre in 1962 and is based on the Biblical story, Talmudic commentary and other classical sources. Each act is a self-contained play on its own with only the leitmotif of sin and the Serpent common to them all. The greater originality of structure found in *The King is the Most Cruel* was not developed by Meged in *Genesis* and there is in his play no formal experimentation to complement his thematic novelty.

Journey to Nineveh

Yehuda Amichai's plays may be structurally flawed but they present a consistent world-view (as do Nissim Aloni's) which attains the controlling power of metaphor. Amichai's people are trapped in lives that twist around them like cages being paradoxically both a trap and a refuge from the commitment-demanding world outside. This is partly Amichai's view of Israel – the nameless Institution in *No-Man's-Land* is the country as a whole, the prophet Jonah's travels in *Journey to Nineveh* lead him to encounters that are uncomfortably familiar to his audience. Yet Amichai does not merely reiterate in allegorical form the regional "problem" topics of the Israeli social realists. His world and its inhabitants assume an existential breadth, occupying the no-exit, unbounded wastelands of Beckett and Kafka.

His plays introduced the Israeli public to the malady of alienation, the fragmentation of the individual wherever he may be by the need for role-play in the fulfilment of unwanted social duty. Amichai has been the first Israeli dramatist to offer a portrait of twentieth-century man in all his spiritual darkness and sickness, the Jonah both resisting his confinement in the fish and yearning to remain enclosed by it. In his *Journey to Nineveh* (Habimah, 1964) the Biblical play lost its primary scriptural or canonic significance but clearly exhibited the force of the Bible and Biblical stories as inspiration for the modern playwright. It remained Biblical only in its choice of theme not in its setting, unlike Aloni's *The King is the Most Cruel* or Meged's *Genesis* and became an exposition on this theme rather than merely an interpretation, following the outline of the original story but with its significance moulded to suit the playwright's subjective purpose. *Journey to Nineveh* with all its faults is one of the milestones in the history of Hebrew drama, a modern dramatic allegory which, like Meged's *Genesis*, "puts onto the stage abstractions or generalisations in the place of autonomous characters".[9] It expresses one of Amichai's most consistent attitudes towards society and a theme recurring throughout his poetry: the existence of an undefined "them" – government or society or God or the nation – who are forcing a man out of his "house" onto the "road" which represents war and social or national duty while his house has meant love, privacy and security. This is expressed in a psychological drama which "... springs from fear of the other, of society, of the world and from preoccupation with the self"[10] In Amichai's world there is no place for the life of the individual, for all men have been driven to fulfil a preordained but incomprehensible function. They are rootless and homeless, they long to enter their safe houses but are compelled to remain outside. Amichai's Jonah, like his Biblical predecessor, attempts always to escape his missions. He finds it good in the great fish for there he has the peace and privacy of home:

[9] "Wesker and Pinter" by G.W.Brandt. *Contemporary Theatre* no. 4, ed. Clifford Leech.

[10] Eric Bentley. *The Dramatic Event*. Methuen, 1954.

"Once I ran away, I don't recall when and from which god. And so I shall journey through my life like Jonah in his gloomy fish. We have agreed, I and my fish, for we are both in the bowels of the earth. I shall not leave him. He will not consume me."[11]

[11] "Quatrain no. 3." *Poems 1948–1962*. Schocken, 1967.

"I shall not leave him" – this is the essence of Jonah-Amichai who yearns only to hide away from the probing needs of "them" and "their" world. The author describes his own attitude and relationship to Jonah:

"It began at school, in my youth. I studied at a religious high school. We had to write an essay about Jonah, and of course we were told to dwell on the idea of Jonah's escape from God – and I remember well what I wrote – it was at the end of the 30's. I wrote that Jonah's attempt to escape from God was only an expression of the nature of the bourgeois. We were all against bourgeois values and I wrote that the bourgeois is one who runs from his responsibility and that God is the 'Haganah' or the Party or something else – the public duty . . . actually I see all of us, the whole world, as a world of escapers."

The central motif of the play is, then, the attempt of the little man who has been summoned to fulfil certain tasks to insulate himself within his own experience of being, without reference or recourse to the world outside. Numerous secondary themes appear: the failure of men to communicate with each other, their fear of social pressures, their inability to reach God, the ultimate barrenness and futility of any social mission. Amichai said of this play, "There are two things I wanted to say here; one is on the level of social criticism: man escapes from any kind of mission; he prefers to remain closeted in his 'four *amot*' in the apparent security of his home and on the other side society which, however it is organised – and it doesn't matter whether it is in the east or the west – becomes a kind of Nineveh, that is to say: hypocrisy, treachery, the cynicism of the intellectual . . . I think that one of the characteristic things about post-war literature and that following the War of Independence, is a continuation of the deterioration that still existed before the First World War when people had no exact values . . . an outcome of the weakening of religion on the one hand and the revolutionary movements on the other."[12]

[12] "Monologue". *Maariv*, August 28th 1964.

The curtain rises on the house of Jonah, the ordinary man secure within himself and his home. He is passive, apathetic, uncertain of what he wants from life, a man who will never take the initiative, who ". . . over many years has built a ship made of matches inside a bottle; so, too, has he built his life and, after many years, the man will be seen – and behold! a small ship inside a bottle!" He lives happily with his wife in a delusion of love, a negative companionship; in a brittle scene Amichai emphasises their utter failure to communicate with each other, a failure of which they are quite unaware. "In the Tower of Babel," says a character known only as the Strange Woman, "the languages were muddled. One can learn other foreign languages at school but what can people who speak the same language do when they don't understand each other, when words have no value other than their sounds?"

Fate or Amichai's "them" or duty, in the form of the Strange Woman, brings to Jonah news of his mission to the sinful city of Nineveh. Jonah refuses, clinging to his privilege to remain in his house but the woman who is not sure herself exactly what his mission implies finally compels him to leave. However, Jonah's attitude is not at all clear: he shows conflict in his wanting to hide and at the same time participate in whatever awaits him, later symbolised in a scene where he only partially climbs out of a large box, one leg remaining inside as he straddles the "in" and the "out". He describes how he has at times attempted to change his life: "Here are the cards; from above and below the same image: queen, king and in this manner I wanted to change my life. I turned my life over, I turned it on its head and yet – the same Jonah from above and below" – and after each such endeavour he has returned to the security of his "square", his house. On this occasion in the play it is simply his desire for the tantalising woman that finally sways him and which plucks him from his shelter. He is confused and bewildered but he is prepared to obey her if only to be able to possess her. In terms of Amichai's imagery it is logical that the next scene should open in a harbour, for "dark ships" have consistently symbolised sexual desire in his poetry.

Even after he has almost been seduced by the Strange Woman Jonah protests that he does not know what to do in Nineveh and requests details of his task. Then the voice from the radio, the voice of God or conscience, commands: "You must find your way by yourself," prompting Jonah to remark on his failure to control his own life: ". . . As always, I wait. I won't take the plunge; I wait to be pushed. Hands have raised me; hands will push me . . ." and: ". . . A man must be able to burn his bridges behind him . . ." – to meet new challenges, face new situations. Later in the play the author remarks again on the refusal of most men to judge for themselves: "I don't want to see what is happening outside," declares an inhabitant of Nineveh, "the newspapers give us all we need" – a sharp comment on our failure to think for ourselves without being directed.

Jonah finds himself at the port waiting for his ship. He is still vigorously protesting and attempts to be taken to Tarshish rather than Nineveh which he fears without knowing why. Eventually he is hidden in a box and put aboard a boat bound for Tarshish. A storm rises and Jonah, like the Jonah of the Bible, is thrown overboard and swallowed by a great fish, but here the resemblance to the prophet ends. When the time comes for the modern Jonah to leave the fish's belly he resists for it suggests the illusion of home as did the box, his shelter on the ship which symbolised a house, the four walls that shut each man off from his fellows. "It is good to sit in a box; I have returned to the box of my four-sided life." In the fish he meets two other Jonahs, each portraying an extension of himself as well as being his predecessor on a similar mission. Jonah 1 (the hero) wants to be imprisoned, Jonah 2 is imprisoned, yet does not like it but when given the opportunity to escape he hesitates and literally "misses the train" (a railway line runs through the fish's interior). Jonah 3 is always industriously making the prison ready and habitable by cleaning and sweeping. These are all facets of the same personality and a distinct fragmentation of the individual into the self who will not face his situation, another one who is satisfied with it and the third who would change it if he had the courage to initiate any action. Later in the play Jonah says, "I have no ties with the past; I have burnt all the bridges behind me." The woman observes: "But the smell of burning has remained with you . . . and the smoke is bringing tears to your eyes." This is also possibly a comment on the dilemma of those Jews who hesitated about leaving Germany during the early thirties, deciding rather to remain and take the consequences. Amichai, as a child, did not understand why departure from his beloved native German city was suddenly so imperative. In the play it is Jonah 3 who attempts a definite choice and sets about making his life as comfortable as possible within its restrictions. Despite himself Jonah 1 is compelled to seek the truth about himself and his world, to discover why "a sigh without a body is seeking the body it has lost; blood without a body flows in the world; weeping seeks the pain that fits it . . ." His bridges have been burnt for him and he cannot return to his past. The other Jonahs tell him that there is in any case no point to his mission as there was no point to theirs, due to his own weakness and to the futility of the mission itself. Jonah 1 begs to be allowed to remain in the fish but God's voice calls him, as always through the radio, and accuses him of being "fixed to every place". The inescapable voice at the same time makes a wry comment on the spiritual condition of modern man: "You have invented for yourselves a pretty slogan: 'To find yourselves' and so you don't have to bother, like your forefathers, to find me. But," adds the voice, "if you find me – that is the end of me."

So there is no escape for Jonah and he arrives in Nineveh to the reality from which he has attempted to hide. What is Nineveh? Not merely a distant city as is the enigmatic Nineveh of the Bible but many things, symbols of the author's subjective view of the world. It is the reality of the world outside Jonah's door, the place where on the one hand all is laughter and freedom and on the other everything is judged according to its value to the Government: "The love of truth is not for the good of the government in this city," says the mysterious barber, representative of opportunism and conformism. In the view of Ben-Ami Feingold,[13] this barber's discussion of Nineveh contains satirical allusions to contemporary events, forsaking the existential allegory to touch on the actuality of modern Israel. Everything in Nineveh, declares Feingold, is pretence, emptiness, temporariness in which the chastisement of a "prophet" is received as propaganda; it is, after all, a place where people are tired of war, where air-raid alarm sirens have been a daily occurrence. In the words of the barber Amichai states his own despair at useless war and demonstrates how Nineveh expresses this despair in a life of frenzied hedonism.

[13]"Journey to Nineveh". *Bamah* 20, Winter 1964.

Amichai's Nineveh means different things to different people. To God it is a place of sin that must be destroyed, to Jonah the modern prophet it is the world of unknown duty outside of his home. According to the sailors whom he meets at the port Nineveh is an adolescent's dream of sexual pleasure, of willing and passionate women, fun and enjoyment without commitment, offering a life of satisfaction for all men's desires but it is in the end fantasy – vanishing at the moment of fulfilment. "It is all an illusion, all pretence; even the woman that you hold in your arms crumbles like a cake." It is therefore a dream world, enticing men but offering no lasting satisfaction, the chimerical reveries that flit through the lives of most people without being realised or if they do materialise they end in disappointment. Nineveh could also symbolise Jonah's own yearning, that of a little man set in his ways but like everyone else saved by dreams. Near the beginning of the play his unexpected visitor, the strange, desirable woman, says to him: "Perhaps you did not see me, but I sat on the steps when you passed to go to work every day . . . Perhaps you did not see me, but you sensed that I was there and your heart beat more strongly, and all your intentions rose at once and then sank, like papers lifted by a sudden wind; echoes of paper in the ear; traces of the red heart in your face." Therefore to Jonah the man Nineveh constitutes the world of his own most secret fantasies and his escape is from this element of his own nature, a resistance to facing this Nineveh, the deepest, most hidden, most inadmissible part of himself.

Having reached the material Nineveh Jonah again seeks the shelter of a house, this time through the love of a third woman who, like all the other characters, has no name. Again he is unable to find it. "Don't think," he says to the people of Nineveh, "that you are returning home. The house is not your house; the walls are barricaded, the door is stuck, the windows are drawings." "Go out, go out of the delusion of your houses; don't rely on the walls and the electric light, don't believe in doors . . ." "Your house," Jonah 3 had told him in the fish, "does not exist." Then "they" arrive in the form of three surgeons or orderlies dressed and equipped to perform a surgical operation. Again appears the trinity without face or character, this time representing cold humanity and the impersonal forces of government whose duty it is to remain in power at all costs. They interrogate Jonah, find him guilty of treason and imprison him. This is an interpolated satire on the methods of contriving the guilt of an individual plotting against the State. The "operators"[14] discuss their intended brainwashing of the prophet into a conformism that suits their rule – the weapon of totalitarianism. The woman, Jonah's new friend, is *forcibly* freed:

[14] מנתחים

First "operator":	Take her out immediately – to freedom.
Jonah:	You say that as if you commanded that she be taken out and executed.

Freedom in Nineveh means imprisonment in political and social conformity and she would rather remain with Jonah, the prophet-revolutionary.

Jonah's fourth attempt to settle in his own world and escape from social duty has failed and so does his fifth and most desperate effort to return to his original home after his useless forays into prophecy. He reaches his house, only to find a group of soldiers guarding his door. For the last time he is given the opportunity to destroy Nineveh but still he finds himself unable to be the final, ultimate judge. He is suddenly filled with anger at God's weakness, His leniency and His readiness to allow a mortal prophet the awesome responsibility of punishing a corrupt city simply by pressing a lever, exploding and erasing it from the face of the earth. All Jonah's own impotence is revealed to him together with his mercy and inability to destroy life.

The entire cycle begins again. "At this moment," says the general, "another Jonah has already left his house on the mission that you failed to accomplish." He adds – another totalitarian dictum: "Whoever is not prepared to destroy will not be able to build. Whoever is not prepared to beat will not be able to pity."

Jonah: Are you from God?

General: That is a question that can occupy your mind until the end of your days.

The play ends on a note of futility and despair. Once again Jonah is forced out of his house, begging for a little time, a little longer, as he did in the box and in the fish. Only a small and dubious note of hope is offered by the woman – that love may be the only salvation. "Come," she says, "let us go to another place . . . a third place. There is always a third place for two lovers . . . Come . . . There is no love in this place." To Amichai the poet love is an entity existing on its own which, like faith, may not be questioned or analysed only accepted and used. It is a predestined condition which must be acted out, as if bestowed like a blessing on selected people whose identities or natures are not important. It is similar to Rilke's view of a love from which "everything transitive has been removed" having no object and existing "purely in self-sufficiency". It is the only hope remaining to alienated individuals, all the Jonahs and their nameless women.

In his criticism of *Journey to Nineveh* Dr Haim Gamzu[15] commented that the play could have been a successful "broadening of the fabric of the original, a kind of poetic licence wrapped in the mantle of the drama. But Amichai was not satisfied with this, he wanted 'Journey to Nineveh' to be the height of modernism . . ." With respect to this brilliant and controversial critic, this desire of Amichai's is in itself not unfeasible for the play could have demonstrated the best possible combination in Hebrew drama, that of "modernism" in form and treatment woven around Jewish classical source material.

[15] *Haaretz*, July 31st 1964.

Journey to Nineveh almost succeeds in this aim. It is expressionist in its portrayal of a nameless "non-hero" – for "Jonah" is an image – rushing from one encounter to another in an effort to escape some or other form of imprisonment. Amichai's desperate little man is, however, not a prey to specific social injustice as is, for example, Kaiser's character in *From Morn to Midnight*, rather a victim of his own inability to form any relationship whatsoever with any material representative of his society. *Journey to Nineveh* is composed within a far wider framework than that of inter-war German Expressionism although it employs most of the dramatic devices characteristic of the movement including its violence of symbolism. Whether the play is at all a social protest is in question, for the focus of attention is not the anomalous society but the man himself. The play may be better defined as Absurd in form and particularly in theme. Edward Albee defines the Theatre of the Absurd as being: "an absorption-in-art of certain existentialist and post-existentialist philosophical concepts, having to do, in the main, with man's attempts to make sense for himself out of his senseless position in a world which makes no sense – which makes no sense because the moral, religious, political and social structures man has erected to 'illusion' himself have collapsed. Ultimately a phenomenon like the Theatre of the Absurd does not reflect despair or a return to dark, irrational forces but expresses modern man's endeavour to come to terms with the world in which he lives. It attempts to make him face up to the human condition as it really is, to free him from illusions that are bound to cause constant maladjustment and disappointment . . . For the dignity of man lies in his ability to face reality in all its senselessness; to accept it freely, without fear, without illusions and to laugh at it." Albee concludes, "I would submit that the Theatre of the Absurd, in the sense that it is truly the contemporary theatre, facing as it does man's condition as it is, is the realistic theatre of our time; and that the supposed realistic theatre – the term used here to mean most of what is done on Broadway – in the sense that it panders to the public need for self-congratulation and reassurance, and presents a false picture of ourselves to ourselves is, with an occasional very lovely exception, really and truly the Theatre of the Absurd."[16]

[16]John Gassner. *Directions in Modern Theatre and Drama*. Holt, Rinehart, and Winston, 1966.

Journey to Nineveh does indeed reflect the despair of a man who is unable to come to terms with the world he lives in, at first he refuses to "face up to the human condition as it really is", he shelters in illusion but he does ultimately attempt, although unsuccessfully, to make sense for himself out of his position in the world. Like other early Absurd dramas it aroused a flurry of speculative theorising, since Amichai's approach is too subjective to allow any one categorical interpretation. It requires the audience to react subjectively, to Feingold a paradoxical situation, being the result of "the desire to express the little man by the literary means of a great poet that the little man in the audience can't grasp".[17] But a play as an entity must be understood as well as the playwright and *Journey to Nineveh* is too much an extension of Amichai's poetic existentialism to be completely grasped in its own right. It crystallises every theme his poetry has explored and analysed; it discusses the role of fate in

[17]Feingold, *op. cit.*

man's existence, the fact that human life is not ordered, that it is at the mercy of circumstances. Amichai stresses this in no uncertain terms with his almost refrain-like repetition of "Let a coin decide" which is also the title of a poem:

Let a coin decide
Kings have done this; do not decide anything
Let the clouds express
everything you wanted to say.

He advises a distortion of reality for one's own self-preservation: let the roads lead wherever they will, leave every man to himself without even enquiring his name for, he says, all of life is as arbitrary as the decision of the spinning coin. Jonah's commitment is curtailed by the knowledge that the outcome of whatever he does will be unaccountable and that he is barred from exercising control: "The paths on which my life is ordered are fixed and no-one can take me off them." Opportunity is given to him many times by the Voice on the radio and even by the army officer at the end of the play: "You still have free will, and don't say oppressive fate, a tyrannic God. You can still turn the wheel back but you don't want to turn the wheel back . . ." Jonah's is not so much an inability to act as the lack of motivation, of desire to act for he is convinced that from the start any action is futile, consequently he will continue to hide and reject any need for change.

Fragmentation is an all-pervading theme in every part of Amichai's work. In this play he sees Jonah as the prototype of modern metropolitan man, suffering "the progressive fragmenting of the individual self into routinised roles and a blunting first of recognition of others, then of one's own self . . . The same factors that lead to a regimentation of the mind and a blunting of its sense of individuality lead also to a withdrawal from the outer world, a retreat into apathy."[18] This is alienation and there is no character in Amichai's literature more alienated than his prophet Jonah who, in his own words, is "scattered throughout the world". His alienation is further illustrated by his negative response to the possibility of love for despite the existence of a "third place" for lovers Jonah is not destined to find it. The desire for erotic adventure lured him away from his home but its promise remained unfulfilled. When offered a final refuge by the woman in Nineveh he hesitates until she is taken away from him. A prostitute in the play complains that Jonah does not listen to what she has to say and sings a song which Amichai has, in one form or another, sung in his poetry many times:

[18] "The Sociology of Georg Simmel" by Kurt H. Wolff. Trans. and ed. New York Free Press of Glencoe, 1908.

He did not hear anything
He did not arrange anything
He only said that I would be there
That he would be there
And I was there
And he was not.

What is the nature of Jonah's prophecy? According to the Biblical narrative Jonah was forced to warn Nineveh of its impending destruction. In this play, too, Nineveh is about to be destroyed but Jonah's intrinsic mission is to bring the truth, the voice of reason, of the individual, to the attention of the mass: to prevent the Many from turning their backs on what concerns them most. "There are few in whom the silence of existence causes a listening, the absorption in voices which comes from their innermost selves, who lose their rest and ask to repair, to change, to shock, to cause to repent; even these who hear the cry 'rise and go to Nineveh', who ask questions, see visions, who are called, in fact, even these hesitate, fear, wait. Jonah is one of these, who senses a mission, who is called to action . . ."[19] this time against the mindless automatism of modern man. In the fish Jonah had made the statement that there are too many onlookers but too few who act, too few fighters in the arena, too many who applaud. However, with all this, he is afraid of change despite his awareness of its ultimate good and would rather shun the responsibility for any change at all. The failure of his mission lies therefore in his lack of confidence in the efficacy of the individual in a society dominated by the mass voice.

[19] Adir Cohen. *Modern Hebrew Poets.* Mizrachi, Tel Aviv. (No date.)

Amichai denies with justice an often repeated accusation that his play is "anti-God". On the contrary, it is God's voice that makes Jonah aware of his mission which is essentially a good and moral one. Yet on the ship there is an ironic parody which conceives of prayer as a useless but customary exercise. The ship's captain says irritably:

> . . . pray to whomever you wish, but pray, and loudly. I want to hear resounding cries . . . sighs and flagellations until blood streams . . . forward! to pray. *(He goes to the table and throws the earphones onto the map.)* [He notices Jonah and asks] Why are you walking about here? Sit in your box and pray.

Jonah: I am thinking. I am considering.
Captain: That isn't prayer. *(To a sailor)* Pray, you!

Only a little later the young radio officer on the same ship makes Jonah aware of God's omnipotence from which, just as in the Biblical story, there is no escape.

Amichai's play is not unique in its being "difficult, oblique and garbled"; every article to be read about Beckett's *Waiting for Godot*, for example, offers a different solution to its obscurity and critics have contradicted each other vigorously, meaning that no one except Beckett understood it at all. The Israeli critics do not seem to have made much more sense out of *Journey to Nineveh.* Arising out of the apparent unintelligibility of modern plays has been so much contention about this problem of over-subjectivity in the drama that it forms a massive symposium in print. The case for the playwright is expressed by John Osborne when he says, "It's possible to write for yourself and to write for a few people at the same time. It's also possible to write for yourself and write for everybody. But it's not my job as a dramatist to worry about reaching a mass audience, if there is one, to make the theatre less of a minority art. So much of that, in any case, depends on other factors, like new buildings with good restaurants, service and other amenities. If you're going to do what other people think or say you ought to do, it's a waste of time. Ultimately, after all, the only satisfaction you get out of doing all this is the satisfaction you give yourself."[20] This attitude is questionable because of the very nature of drama as an art. A play cannot exist in a vacuum and no playwright who is honest composes a play without the idea of its performance before an audience. "Stories of artists who toss their manuscripts into the fire . . . or refuse their works to be published should be examined with a certain amount of skepticism. If an artist does destroy or withhold his work it is probably because it has not fulfilled his need for self-expression, or because he fears disappointment or ridicule. In either case it is evident that he attaches enormous importance to communication, for if he were concerned only with the act of creation he would not care whether anyone saw his work or not . . . With respect to drama, the essential requirement of communication is simply stated: plays are written to be performed before an audience in an auditorium."[21] An individual artist whether painter, composer, writer, poet or sculptor can perhaps allow himself the luxury of creating without any thought for contact with the audience of his day but, should this be his will, for the coming generations. But the art of the theatre must be immediate and represent direct communication between the playwright and his public. These are the eternal conditions for the existence of drama at all.

Israeli audiences are either spoilt or misguided. Their initial response to new plays has been conditioned by years of conventional entertainment, conventional in the sense that it makes few demands

[20] Brandt, *op. cit.*

[21] Elmer Rice in Bentley, *op. cit.*

on them as interpreters and their habit of forming immediate judgement is difficult to break. Much of their antipathy towards the new writing is derived from the shift in the artist's intention, in the context of Israeli writing undoubtedly a sudden and shocking change, one exemplified not so much by Yehuda Amichai since drama is not his primary form of expression as for example by Nissim Aloni.

Still one cannot with confidence attempt to explain all the intriguing complexities of Amichai's symbolism: the constant recurrence of the trinity, for example – three Jonahs, three women, three surgeons unless, like the Jonahs, the others are all different facets of one entity; however, this would not apply to the surgeons because they are so perfectly alike that one could suffice; or they may represent the identical, faceless and soulless machines of government. The effigy of a goddess that becomes a dead woman is also a disturbing enigma in the play; constant fog is perhaps symbolic of Jonah's bewilderment, the boxes, the ship, the fish are all aspects of his desired security.

Amichai's *Journey to Nineveh* contains no happiness, little love, no pleasure and no humour. One of the characteristics of Absurdism, according to Albee, is that it is "often wildly, wildly funny". *Journey to Nineveh* is not "funny" in situation or dialogue. Even Amichai's rather heavy irony does not lighten its mood. The closest approach to humour occurs when the ship's captain asks, "How is it outside?" The radio man puts his head through a porthole and looks at the audience, representing the sea and replies: "Terrible. Terrible. Soon it will swallow us." There is a certain amount of satire in the barber's descriptions, particularly that of the king who descends from his throne followed by an army of reporters and photographers, to reside in the desert in a cottage with a telephone, hot running water and, under heavy guard, to read ancient books. The reference can only be to Ben-Gurion. There is satire in the volley of questions some reporters fire at Jonah without giving him an opportunity to reply before they disappear. On the whole *Journey to Nineveh* is reminiscent of a nightmare in which the dreamer sees himself wandering from one grotesque situation to another. A scene in the play has Jonah trying desperately to telephone for help and unable to get through – the Kafkaesque nightmare of not being able to contact the unseen implacable powers in order to beg their aid. Like Alice, Jonah is constantly encountering people who want to push him around; he wanders through the distorted landscapes of Hans Andersen and E.T.A.Hoffman, struggling against the ubiquitous yet elusive force determining his actions. In this, too, the play employs some of the typical metaphysical crises of Expressionism. Yet for all this the little man fails to evoke sympathy without certain reservations because he is too much of a symbol to be a man; the humanity of a dramatic hero is vital if the play's purpose is to offer a universal message through him. This play dispenses altogether with characterisation and dramatic conflict nor does it employ any climaxes. As a whole it functions on too many levels. Act 1 deals with the problem of privacy, Act 2 with the nature of Jonah's mission, Act 3 is a social satire with the symbolic significance of Nineveh's totalitarian regime in question unless Amichai is saying that all of mankind represents a kind of totalitarianism, for Jonah is not "prophesying" against the rulers but against the nature of man himself. In the first act Jonah's wife appears and reappears, walking in and out of the room to say a word or two but she serves very little further purpose. Amichai's greatest fault, which he shares with Yehuda Haezrachi in *The Refusal*, is overstatement: where he could leave ideas to the audience for their deliberation he explains them too well, for example in the section already quoted which describes Jonah climbing out of the box and standing with one leg inside and the other out. He talks about it and his companion the prostitute talks about it so much that its point is all but lost. The same happens in Nineveh when the woman is to be taken away and set free against her will. This is a powerful point, well made, until Jonah's comment to the "operator" who has just given the order to dispatch the woman to freedom: "You say that as if you were saying take her out to be killed." There are a number of long monologues which even in context seem to be more like interpolated poems, particularly one at the end of the first act which is filled with philosophical material and directed solely at the audience.

In their discussions of Amichai's language in the play Feingold and Haim Gamzu make the comment that on many occasions the playwright used pretentious poetic acrobatics (sometimes "pseudo-poetry") for no purpose except hyperbole and this often heavily and clumsily. Many of the lines – and here the two critics agree although they have given different examples – are irrelevant pieces of verbal ornamentation, "surplus ink", exoticism without significance and often incomprehensible. And deserving their strictest criticism is the frequent use of vulgarity, crude language used apparently for its own sake or perhaps for the purpose of presenting the corrupt world of Nineveh as realistically as possible. While in the light of modern dramatic trends one can no longer be prudish about "bad" language on the stage it is true that Amichai uses sexual imagery with far less poetry than Aloni, for example, does in *The King is the Most Cruel*. He includes many modern conventions once considered shocking but which have since become commonplace commercial enticement: a variety of prostitutes, sailors discussing their sex life in voluptuous detail, scenes of explicit eroticism.

Dr Gamzu, known in his time as the most powerful theatrical critic in Israel, commended the playwright on his choice of an excellent idea but criticised his usage of it. "In drama," he said, "an idea alone is not enough and a play is not original only because the heroes may be walking on their hands or standing on their heads. A good idea deserves the correct expression and in the right place. There are no substitutes for clarity." He concluded by stating flatly that the *production* of *Journey to Nineveh* was the worst seen on the Israeli stage for fifteen years. This fact is probably responsible for the comparatively unenthusiastic reception of what has since come to be regarded as a great play and a classic of the Israeli repertoire.

Israel's Biblical drama has developed to conform with current trends in theatre. The representative examples selected here show three distinct areas of playwriting: the "straight" historical play which, like Shakespeare's, shows the conflict of individual characters within the boundaries of historical reality; secondly, satire in which the Biblical story is used as an ironic device or satire as an exposition of the Biblical story. Thirdly, the Biblical story told allegorically in contemporary socio-political terms. This has become the most popular form of Biblical drama. In fact in its later development the Hebrew Biblical play has formed a bridge leading to what could be called the Israeli theatrical avant-garde, a combination of ancient national-religious sources cast in the most modern exposition and form. It is as yet the only truly original contribution to dramatic art that Israel has made and a unique one because although the Old Testament is Hebrew in origin and spirit it is so universally well known that any play based on any part of it has the added impact of having its allegorical source-material immediately familiar to any audience. *Journey to Nineveh* was the first true link between the Biblical play and the avant-garde proper, that of Beckett and Ionesco and their disciples. A later play of this type was Benjamin Galai's *Sodom City*, the story of Lot and the destruction of Sodom and Amorah and its parallel in our nuclear time. It describes the cold war between the two sinful cities whose inhabitants tended to ignore the terrible holocaust threatening them and did nothing to avert it. The message of the play to its twentieth-century audience is obvious, and pessimistic regarding the future of mankind.

A few other Biblical-historical dramas of varied styles achieved popularity in the sixties. *The Night of the Moabite* by Moshe Shamir (Haifa Municipal Theatre, 1962) resorted to a modern version of the idealised and idyllic epic tale of Ruth and Boaz. It was a highly stylised treatment that introduced new interpretations and explained behaviour patterns in the light of modern psychology, but in the main it followed the Biblical story. *The High Season* by Aharon Meged (Habimah, 1967) presented the case of Job projected as an allegorical study of the Jews and their relationship with Germany. *The Rebel and the King* by Israel Eliraz (Haifa Municipal Theatre, 1968) told the story of Absalom's revolt against King David. The most notorious play of this genre whose Biblical original is all but imperceptible is Hanoch Levin's satirical *Queen of the Bathtub* about which more will be said in a following chapter.

2 The Plays of the Holocaust

The Chatelaine

Hebrew drama tended in the early years to fall into clearly demarcated categories. Firstly the "Palmach" plays, those immediately following and directly concerning the War of Independence, then the plays of social realism, the "regional" plays of the decade after the war. Surprisingly few dramas have been written about the Nazi persecutions, the memory of which will always hang oppressively over Israeli consciousness. Those that finally dared to tackle this subject are with few exceptions excellent, being far removed in form and theme from the customary social melodramas. Characteristic of them all is that they do not directly touch on the Second World War but discuss its influence, after it has ended, on people who are not necessarily direct victims, both in Israel and the diaspora. However, the central figure or proposition in these dramas is the Holocaust itself; it is this which determines the behaviour and ultimate fate of the plays' characters.

With these works the Hebrew drama seems to have found the creative impetus it had been seeking so long for with each of them it took a qualitative leap forward. They each successfully solved the problem of "universalising" specifically Israeli and Jewish problems because their creators had something vital and deeply felt to say and they said it in a drama of ideas which for once was discursive and filled with conflict. Their form was experimental, attempting to suit the writer's analysis of insoluble problems and conflicts of attitude and the combination of profundity of theme with the playwright's new awareness of structural possibilities gave these plays their originality. But the way to consistent progress was not yet clear, even at this point, for the playwrights still had their audiences and critics to contend with.

The earliest in this group of plays was Leah Goldberg's *The Chatelaine* (*The Lady of the Manor*), produced by Cameri in 1955. Thematically it was relevant to its era generally while at the same time relating specifically to a number of particularly Israeli problems: the rehabilitation of Jews after the war, the recovery of Jewish property confiscated by the Nazis and a statement of what the new land of Israel offered as compared with the irreversible decay of post-war Europe.

It tells of two emissaries from Israel who arrive at a castle somewhere in Europe in order to search for books stolen from Jews by the Germans. A storm is raging outside and the two Israelis, Dora

Ringel and Zand, are compelled to remain at the castle despite the obvious reluctance of its custodian, Zabrodski, to put them up. The drama progresses over three hours while the storm continues outside. Zabrodski reveals that he was once the owner of the castle and that it had belonged to his distinguished aristocratic family for generations but had subsequently been taken over by the State. Later the two visitors make the climactic discovery that for four years Zabrodski has been concealing a young Jewish refugee in the confines of his castle, keeping her there by convincing her that the war is still continuing and that the Nazis constantly lurk outside. He loves her, but even more than that he reveres her as a symbol of youth and the past which he is unable to relinquish. She, in turn, regards him as her protector and has developed a certain affection for him. She has become the chatelaine and over the years the two have acted out in secret the conventions of a vanished time, a vanished world.

The major portion of the play deals with Dora's attempts to convince the girl, Lena, that the war has been over for years, then to persuade her to accompany her and Zand to Israel where a new life awaits her. Opposing Dora is Zabrodski who nevertheless finally allows Lena to make the decision on her own, so losing his single remaining link with the past he is unable and unwilling to forget.

Leah Goldberg has created a drama which is not by definition "Israeli" despite the fact that it is concerned with problems relevant to Israel and the Jews and that its protagonists, Zand and especially Dora, are types that can exist only within the reality of Israel. She has successfully "universalised" its local problems by bringing them to bear on universal issues: the past versus the present, old values versus the new, reality versus fantasy, the nature of love and possession, fear, age and deceit. She herself declares that "the land of Israel and Jewish life were not a solitary and exotic island isolated within the problem of man's existence in the world at that time. Their particular problems could not be solved without association with the general fate of that period. Therefore the presentation of the problems in *The Chatelaine* did not have to be within the environment of Israel which is usually symbolised by the character of the kibbutz treasurer and the *hora*. And so, in the trio, the voice of a stranger is heard – Zabrodski, the European Count."[1] Yet this stranger appears to be no less a victim of the war and the Nazis – except in degree – than the millions of Jews who suffered for so long.

The overall subject matter of the play is a specific historical fact – the Holocaust and the resulting need to gather European Jewish

[1] *Orot*, March–April 1956.

children from the various refuges they had found during the war. Many of these children, who had of necessity converted to Christianity, did not want to be removed from their new lives and on this point the play turns: the conflict between the old repressive European values and the new materialistic world of pragmatism and freedom for all.

Dora: If you had to deal with children hiding in strange families, in monasteries – you'd see how this "beauty" still grips them! Can you imagine what I go through every day? A constant war. The dead, with skeleton hands, have fastened on the living children and are pulling them down to the grave.

Yet the issues are not clearly defined nor seen in terms of absolute negatives and positives. Leah Goldberg has invested her play with a certain irony by means of the characters she has chosen to represent her opposing values. The old, decadent, all-but-vanished culture is portrayed through the figure of the Count, a truly noble gentleman, having all the courtesy, elegance and gentle sensibilities of the healthy aristocracy. The new is Dora, an unlikeable, practical, forty-year-old woman with no time for dreams, intent on bustling her way through the job she has taken on and so representing the ideal world as something mechanical and devoid of subtlety or sensitivity. She trots out the tenets of Zionist ideology while the playwright appears to be mocking her.

Dora: We're here and we're going to help you leave this place. You'll come with us to Palestine. You'll join a group your own age. You'll live, work, you'll be healthy and free and happy like all the other young people.

It does not sound attractive and it is not surprising that Lena answers her with a blunt "No" although, to be fair to Dora, Lena is, at this stage, still bewildered and suspicious.

Conflict clearly rests in Leah Goldberg herself. While aware without doubt that the life offered by Palestine to the young refugees from Nazi brutality is the correct and desirable one she is saying at the same time that the down-to-earth, practical outlook need not be devoid of beauty, that beauty is in itself not necessarily decadent or evil and that the past still may have something to offer the present and should not be rejected. As a Jewish writer Leah Goldberg must stand on the side of the new and in the end Lena, dressed in street clothes, leaves the castle with the two Jewish emissaries; yet the author's depiction of the Count in his lonely splendour is sympathetic enough to convince her audience that she retains some love for the "castle" as representative of an era, a lifestyle and an environment.

The setting and story of *The Chatelaine* provide, on the surface, an unflawed example of nineteenth-century European romanticism. It has a beautiful old castle set in magnificent gardens, a stormy night, a heroic nobleman living on memories of the past, suffering his doomed love for a beautiful young girl, fairy-like in her innocence and wholly dependent on him; secret doorways and passages leading to a strange confinement, perhaps even a dungeon, in the recesses of the castle; hints of dark deeds and passions; an amulet of poison; tragedy and redemption. Dora is a kind of "villain" who comes to rob the heroine of her home, her splendid dreams and tender lover. Yet on a deeper level the play offers an inversion of this stereotypical melodramatic romanticism: the castle once housed Nazis and even before that it was a symbol of the oppression of the poor by the titled rich. It retains a patina of evil from its days as German headquarters. The sad, ageing Count has imprisoned a young girl, probably seduced her and certainly denied her the natural life due to her. He has housed her in a prison of deception because of his own need to recreate a dream. The "villain" who shatters this dream is, in fact, a representative of life and sunlight, purity, cleanliness and health. The play as a whole is a commentary on the decadence implicit in romanticism, decay as a necessary outcome of too much self-analysis, indulgence in fantasy, mysticism, a useless yearning for the past and an obsession with death not only as the ultimate and most satisfying result of human action but as a *welcome* destroyer of all that is natural and consequently unpredictable in life.

Zabrodski: Death. Both of us – you and I, Lena, knew so much about death, that this bit of poison faded to insignificance in all the real death that surrounded us. This you learnt here . . .

The issues of the play are represented by the characters and are, in fact, almost personified by them. Dora, middle aged and practical, is a devoted socialist. She is unimaginative and mouths propaganda without a breath of originality to broaden her narrow horizons. She has little perception about people and no tolerance whatsoever of ideas not her own – and those she voices are not even her own but have been instilled into her, rendering her a self-righteous propaganda machine. She is impatient of everything but her limited, constricted world. It is doubtful that she feels any true pity for Lena – the girl is merely another soul to save, another rubber stamp signifying a job completed. Dora is like a hound on a trail, without compassion, only compulsive duty. At times her practicality is comic: for example, after Lena's long quasi-mystical depiction of her dream and her dreamlike memory of walking outside, Dora says: "... you can't walk in town in these shoes ... But tomorrow, when we leave this place – you'll have to go into a shop and buy shoes." Dora's down-to-earth preparation of a cup of tea contrasts sharply with the sudden tension between Zabrodski and Zand when they discuss the sleeping arrangements upon which they cannot agree. Her preoccupation with her own social stature reveals itself in her rather childish comment, a non-sequitur, that when she was young only "fashionable society" drank tea. The masses – including herself – drank coffee.

Dora hates the Count for many reasons, above all because he represents her past as well as his own and reminds her of her own early suffering as a Jew in Europe. For the same reason she hates everything ancient ("all these old things") retaining the atmosphere of the past because it brings to mind the world wherein she grew up. "In decent society," she says with sarcasm, "it is customary to believe that the older anything is the more beautiful it is." And, to Zand: "For you this is indeed a strange country. But for me – this was my birthplace. Palaces and ruins always live side by side! Perhaps I lack an aesthetic sense. Perhaps I have seen too much sorrow and suffering and poverty these past years in my work, searching for children without a home, abandoned, consumptive, lice-ridden. But I hate all this antiquity, this useless dust." She extends her hatred to Zabrodski because he is not Jewish, because she is a socialist and he an aristocrat and partly because of the old deeply instilled fear and distrust of the European Jew for the European nobility. In short, he is the fearsome figure of her youth: the man up in the castle above the squalor of the ghettos. Part of her loathing for Zabrodski stems quite understandably from her suspicion of his association with the Nazis and his apparent corruption of a young girl, a Jewess. Dora's hatreds and resentments are valid but nevertheless her uncompromising subjectivity limits her outlook on life. Her antipathy to the past and its connotations is what makes her so unequivocal a convert to the Israeli way of life; her new nationalism is based on rejection of the past rather than a natural aspiration towards the future. Now that she has her own society, one in which she is wholly accepted, she dismisses all others, extending to them her distrust and suspicion and exhibiting the possessiveness of an insecure person who will hide within the boundaries of the world he knows best.

Zand, the watchmaker's son, is more of a realist, able to appreciate the values of others because he is blessed with empathy and because his travels and knowledge gained through reading have taken him beyond the limits of prosaic daily experience. He pities Lena but he appears very much to dissociate himself from the entire conflict except for one occasion on which he could hardly have remained aloof, when he attempted to take a phial of poison away from her. Zand also pities the old man and respects him for what he once represented. However, he is an onlooker more than a participant and although he comprehends the situation he does not contribute very much to it except as an irritant to Dora and a foil for her arguments. "In the past," he says to her, "there are many things that even watchmakers' sons must know and even love. Even in Zabrodski's past. What we are to take from this past is for us to decide. But to argue with him about it? That I don't want to do. Why? He has the right to love what he wants to and to hate what he wants to . . . this is his end. This is his condition. And we – we are very many; therefore we are permitted to be mediators and do what we must in silence." It is Zand who makes the statement upon which the play is based: "We're already of a different time and different place. That's all." Almost the entire body of contemporary Hebrew literature stresses this idea of *this* time and *this* place, but it cannot conceal a longing for the past and its spiritual landscape, a need to reveal and return to roots.

Zand is the intermediate point between Dora on the one hand and Zabrodski on the other. He declares that one can still dream on a basis of reality, that is, that reality and illusion can be mingled without material harm to oneself. He does not seem at all certain, in the light of this belief, that Lena should leave the castle.

While achieving an uncommon depth of character Zabrodski is a symbol, one repeated in many plays and novels, of failure to accept the new order, the changing world. He clings to the past, its people, its values, its way of life. He despises and fears the masses and hated the Nazis not only for their brutality but because they too were part of a blind senseless mass that dirtied his traditions. He dreams about the noble elegance and standards of past ages and the times when the castle was not only his home but a repository of the tradition of generations. He admires the Jews for being "the only ones in the world today who are still capable of understanding the meaning of tradition". He believes firmly in the individual and is therefore the natural opponent of the bright young socialism and its welfare state, the mass-life which is symbolised by Dora.

Leah Goldberg has – perhaps despite herself – drawn him with a measure of affection. He has tremendous nobility, a natural graciousness which his early reluctance to house the unwanted guests cannot hide and it is precisely this old-world courtesy that enrages Dora. Initially he seems to possess all the qualities of a romantic hero: he has exhibited great courage and daring by hiding a Jewess under the very eyes of the enemy and he has a deep reverence for the beauties of the past. His hopes for the future are founded on his mystical obsession with the Book of Revelations. Now he is a sad, lonely, handsome nobleman, living among his dreams in his Castle with his ethereal Lady . . . The romanticism alters to become pathos when, at the end, he seeks refuge, almost frantically, in illusion and reveals that to him the reality of the mind is more desirable than objective reality because fantasy is controllable and can be constructed at will. Zabrodski suffers from a touch of Pirandellian madness in wanting to create his own world in order to have control of events. "*I* gave you a true dream! The dream was true – and if there was something false in it . . . who was the one who lied, Lena?" By shutting themselves away from reality they need never cease their ritualised worship of the grandeur of the past, and death will come only when they call it. In Zabrodski's eyes they are already dead, entombed in a setting which no longer exists in the "polished . . . smooth and electrical! Above all – electrical!" world outside.

His imprisonment of Lena is morally indefensible but dramatically convincing. But for him she would certainly have perished, therefore in terms of his ancient code her life belongs to him. She represents to him the time of his youth when he was the scion of the castle and not its ageing custodian.

Zabrodski: One day she came to me – and it was as if the days of my youth had returned; and in this castle it was like in those days . . . the nights were . . . as if the light of the moon were inside . . . the prophecy was fulfilled: there would be no living and no dead, old or young . . . the only truth was in memories that became flesh and blood . . . a life that could not be replaced was still here in reality . . . and if one of us had suddenly died that would have been just a step in a different, stronger reality. Because the reality was a dream . . .

Lena could have escaped by taking the poison she kept always in a locket worn around her neck, but she did not for Zabrodski provided her with a fantasy that banished cruel reality. Had her life with him been intolerable she could have ended it either by committing suicide or – what would to her have amounted to the same thing – by daring to open a window and go out into the fresh air she loved, into the apparently waiting arms of the Germans. But the Count gave her refuge and a haven and stilled her need and desire to think for she is neither intelligent nor strong-willed. Once she says: "I like my dreams . . ." They allay the need to face the truth, for as long as Zabrodski provides her with dreams she has no need to burden her mind with responsibility of any kind. She is content to be a victim and there is no doubt that as far as she is capable of feeling anything she has developed a certain tenderness or at least concern for her jailer. At the end one cannot help but recognise a sense of betrayal when she turns her back on Zabrodski and walks out with Dora and Zand.

Initially Lena wards off knowledge of the "new" world and seeks to remain with the Count who is her security. But one breath of fresh air, ironically still part of her poetic delusion of air, sun, light and the moon, is sufficient to sway her. She has no conception of the implications of living among people in this promised "new" life but is, rather, exchanging one illusion for another. She herself declares that her abiding fantasy is one of running barefoot and free outside in the sun and the only thing that prompts her to leave with the two strangers is the promise of clean, fresh air. Ordinary human relationships have become impossible for her, enclosed as she is in fantasy. Never once does she question Zabrodski or express any horror at what he has done to her, nor does she attempt to understand him or his need. At the end of the play it seems that she has merely replaced him with Zand as her protector and mentor. "The disturbed world of Lena," says the playwright Leah Goldberg, "is a human world that bears within it all the possibilities of a sense of the past, the present and, because she is young, the future. Because of this Lena was for me – more than the three other points of view – a point of departure, and of focus in the play."[2] Professor Shaked[3] regards Zabrodski, not Lena, as the focal point and the only fully realised character in the play and, with respect, he is right for Zabrodski clearly appears to have overstepped the playwright's original purpose and taken on a life of his own. On one level he exemplifies the message that it is upon the destruction of the world he represents that the new may be built. On another he reflects the playwright's own dialectical tension in her views on the validity of the past. He cannot on any account be dismissed merely as a grotesque, pottering old eccentric given to nasty thoughts about young girls, or as a point of departure for acceptable and topical Zionist ideology or the tenets of Youth Aliyah. As to Professor Shaked's second point, Zabrodski at the end has retained his inherent

[2] *Ibid.*

[3] "In the Paths of the Hebrew Play" by Gershon Shaked. *Bamah*, July 6th 1960.

nobility and despite the decay of his world and perhaps of his mind some vestige of the old gentility remains. His rejection of reality in which pathos is mixed with his natural dignity throws into relief the extreme shallowness of Lena and her two visitors.

Together with the gothic romanticism of *The Chatelaine* are mingled certain elements of nineteenth-century realism, primarily the importance of the environment which, despite its melodramatic associations in this play, has vast symbolic importance and conditions the behaviour of each one of the characters according to his or her particular standpoint. The environment here is both the distant past, seen in the material fact of the castle and its relics, and the immediate past which has brought these four diverse characters to their meeting-point. Secondly this is a play of evaluation and analysis, of insight into people's minds through discussion not action. The importance of discussion has been repeatedly stressed as a feature of modern realism: dialogue has replaced a complicated plot as the determining force of the drama. Never had discussion and debate held a place of such eminence in Hebrew drama until the production of *The Chatelaine* with its fierce arguments about the nature of reality and the place of the past in the life of the individual.

Because of this preoccupation the play has been compared to certain of Ibsen's dramas, also because of its haunting, brooding atmosphere and the enclosure of the action within the stuffy confines of four walls. I believe this comparison to be unfounded. Although Ibsen was concerned with the question of freedom and imprisonment, sometimes self-imprisonment, he examined it through the presentation of highly individualised characters functioning in relation to the unbearable strictures of a recognisable society. The conflicts of Lena, Dora and Zabrodski are externalised: Lena's imprisonment is an actual one, as is her liberation. Ibsen's people, in the tradition of dramatic naturalism and nineteenth-century realism, are not representatives or types but beings with explicit biographies extending sometimes two generations back. Whatever their function – to expose lies and hypocrisy, to reveal the anomalies of self-delusion, to fight for spiritual freedom – they remain individuals who have survived over a century of analysis both literary and Freudian, to take their place as the immortal products of man's creativity. The audience may not grasp the finer implications of Ibsen's ideology yet the characters will live for them in their own right. Not so those of *The Chatelaine*. They are representatives of specific groups, types, and only Zabrodski is perhaps tormented enough, sufficient of an anti-hero to endure. For he is both admirable and loathsome, at once a figure of pathetic dignity and a monster of deceit and depravity. He is real and human, multifaceted and indefinable and, like Aloni's Rehoboam, one of the great characters of Hebrew drama.

While the play's major concern is at face value an Ibsenite one, to challenge apparent truth and destroy the ghosts of the past, the levels of exposition are vastly different in Ibsen's plays and in this one. Moreover Leah Goldberg has a positive solution to Lena's unique problem and a message for the audience which was particularly appropriate at the time. Ibsen offers no such solutions.

The Children of the Shadow

The "children of the shadow" are those immigrants with a history of suffering in the diaspora who try to settle in Israel and to identify on all levels with the Israelis; on the surface they succeed, but their memories still condition their behaviour and place them apart from their *sabra* companions. Such a "child" is Yoram, the hero of the poet Ben-Zion Tomer's profound play (Habimah, 1962) and his is a complex drama of guilt which has its foundation not in a deed but in the history of his people.

Yoram was despatched to Israel at the age of fourteen by way of Samarkand and Teheran while his parents were compelled to remain behind in Poland and face the horrors of the Nazi war. He grows up on a kibbutz struggling all the while to forget his past by pretending to be a *sabra*, by changing his name from Yosele to Yoram and aping the prototypical kibbutznik, a youth called Dubi. He marries an Israeli girl (Dubi's girlfriend) who only partially understands his emotional chaos, having been told very little about his origins. Then unexpectedly his parents, brother and sister-in-law, all thought to be dead, arrive in Israel as new immigrants and Yoram-Yosele has to re-examine the precarious façade he has created for himself and learn to come to terms with a spectre of memory suddenly invested with flesh and blood.

"His drama," says Ezra Zusman,[4] "is not a drama about awareness but takes place on the threshold of awareness. The clinging environment of his distant youth begins to erupt in the form of nightmares. The feeling of collective guilt lying dormant in the mass-conscience awakens in him as a personal guilt, in order to torture and condemn him. Subconscious delusions of guilt rise to the surface and he strives to conquer them by means of awareness and understanding . . . the dichotomy between Yosele, the boy in the village, and Yoram in Israel is able to be reconciled but Yoram does

[4] *Davar*, December 7th 1962.

not know this." He is an introverted, oversensitive and angry young man, suffering from a type of anger caused only by his special situation which can be summarised as the strain of being always on guard against the possibility of exposure. Tomer has cleverly utilised some of the themes from Shakespeare's *Hamlet* as a series of leitmotifs in the play: the concept of conscience, the value of existence without honour, the nature of revenge, assumed madness as an escape or at least a disguise, an elucidating play-within-a-play and not least of all the characterisation of Yoram, the man tormented by guilt he himself is unable to understand and hindered by inertia and the inability to take positive action.

The play is primarily an exploration of several aspects of guilt, a theme subsequently investigated in the major literature of Israel. Yoram is the representative of a general guilt caused, in his case, by the fact that he was powerless to assist his parents and friends, for while they were suffering the tortures of the Holocaust, he was thousands of miles away and comfortably secure in his new life.

Yoram: To see Helenka's eyes, every day, as if I have stolen something from her, as if it is my fault that I did not endure what she endured, as if it's my fault that I came here before her, that I am here . . . (*bitterly*) to live with them.

And again:

The [ghetto] uprising . . . what was I doing at the time of the uprising? (*Drinks from his glass*) Wait a moment . . . let me remember . . . yes . . . I was sitting here, in this cafe . . . I had two hours free . . . and I sat here and enjoyed the sunshine. It was a nice day . . . I went to the cinema. The cinemas were open, like today. The economic situation was good. The war effort. Yes, it was good. Like now. Only on the news they were playing different symphonies . . .

His guilt is further reinforced by his reluctance to accept his family when they arrive in Israel, creating a threat to his precarious security as a man belonging to and possessing a country and a society in which he is wholly accepted. He is ashamed of them. He has rebelled against identifying with them or with the past they represent and he cannot bear to hear the stories of their hardship in Europe for they sharpen his two-pronged guilt: he had not been there to suffer with them and at the same time did not want any part of their suffering.

Yoram: Almighty God! If only I knew why I do this, to hell . . . who am I? Their black tales make me the accused. Accused without accusation. Then I am sealed. Like a fortress. And

> as much as they try to burst inside me I am sealed even more. I am sealed – guilt rises in me. Guilt rises in me – I am sealed. What am I guilty of? What? . . . You are already rooted here, Janek said to me once. Like an accuser . . . and you too . . . you also said to me: from the time they came you started running away into your past – and then when I only just managed to escape from it . . . you also looked at me without understanding . . . I am not bound to offer to your lips my crown of thorns but they, they offer me their thorns day and night . . . my past filled with corpses, my past that no longer belongs to me . . . I have robbed them all. From my mother, her Yosele. Yosele is dead! From father – his son, from Janek his brother and from Helenka her secure bridge in the land of the immigrant camps . . .

His crime, such as it is, lies in wanting only to be a *sabra*, to forget the past, to pretend that he had no role in the dreadful story of his sister's murder by the Nazis or in his parents' anguish – as indeed he had not. He was young enough to have been saved and this is the paradox of his guilt. In Zusman's opinion his conscious desire to forget was his greater injustice to those who endured and it depicts a controversy raging in Israel to this day regarding the place of the camps and their attendant horrors in the consciousness of modern Israeli youth. In common with his entire generation after the War of Independence Yoram wants only to attain an identity apart from that represented by his family, but being the neurotic he is this desire leads to further self-accusation so that he is not sure in which world he should allow himself to belong. In his introspection – which takes on an aspect of paranoia – he fancies constant insult because he is or he is not part of his family, neither situation suits him. He scrutinises his *sabra* wife, Nurit, suspicious that she may be patronising or condescending to his family so injuring his pride and theirs. To complicate the emotional issue yet further Yoram feels some contempt for his importunate relatives while hating himself for his unjust attitude. Characteristically he is ready to blame Nurit for what he himself feels, as if she were confirming it and by implication including him in her assessment of the alien group. She, in turn, reacts with bewilderment to his extreme defensiveness, to a situation not of her making and which she does not fully comprehend. "I can't stand it any more," she cries. "After every visit [of the brother and his wife] you drive me mad . . . the way I looked at him was wrong . . . my gestures were wrong. I didn't smile enough . . . I didn't greet him nicely . . . what do you want of me?" Yoram's guilt stems from a third source also shared by the post-war generation in Israel. He wonders why more Jews had not resisted their persecutors in Europe and this unworthy thought torments him, for he had not been there to prove his courage or discover a lack of it.

Yoram [to Janek, his brother]: . . . immediately after the war, when they started coming, those of your lot, and to tell us what had happened I also began to ask: "Why didn't you rise?" And with an accusing finger! Do you understand? An accusing finger and more than a fraction of contempt.

. . . *Janek:* We also asked the same question.

Yoram: You had the right to. Not me.

His interrogation of Janek, a hero of the Warsaw ghetto uprising, points to a compulsive self-flagellating examination of his own honour, which he finds wanting, and then he reaches the despairing conclusion, as does Zigmund, another image of guilt in the play, that man is weak and must not be put to any test of courage and integrity.

The idea of honour, like that of guilt, is central to the play and both are clearly symbolised in the character of Zigmund, an almost-tragic hero with Shakespearean overtones, an amalgam of Hamlet and Lear cast in the mould of the grotesque.

Zigmund: . . . I have been involved in the most important art of the twentieth century, the art of remaining alive . . . and as you can prove I have been a successful artist. Have I indeed succeeded? Do you know Hamlet's famous monologue?

Yoram: "To be or not to be – that is the question."

Zigmund: Yes . . . no, no . . . permit me to present a variation on this monologue as Shakespeare would no doubt have written it had he been alive in the twentieth century: "To be or not to be – that is also a question!"

The case of Zigmund is more easily definable than that of Yoram. A respected intellectual in his own country and, unbeknown to Yoram, his brother-in-law, he collaborated with the Germans for reasons which are never clarified in the play, and now in Israel he punishes himself by forcing memory of his ignoble role on the *Judenrat* of the concentration camp and by continually arraigning himself, cursing himself with disparaging yet symbolic names, "dog", "rat" and "medusa". His behaviour is contradictory in that he cringes away from any possibility of being recognised while at the same time obsessively pursuing a means towards external judgment. The scenes of his solitary self-conducted trial are among the most powerful in the play, devoid of sentimentality and written with poetic power seldom encountered in Hebrew drama. Zigmund has set a toy dog on a bench and this is to serve as his judge:

"If you knew who I was you would also run away.
Believe me I am not guilty . . . you see, you are also angry with me. Listen I have just had an idea. You will be my judge. Do you agree? I myself will be the prosecution. There will be no lack of witnesses, like drops of rain. And so (*Puts the dog on the bench.*) get up, get up onto the bench! They called me dog . . . perhaps I should stand on all fours? (*He gets down on all fours. From offstage the sound of a barking dog is heard.*) Listen, a good beginning. You are an excellent judge! And so – begin. (*In the harsh voice of an interrogator.*) Your name!? (*In an obsequious voice.*) My name is Dr Zig . . . (*He kicks the dog with all his might. Then he throws it on the promenade.*) Come back, come back! Someone must judge me someone must! (*Suddenly to the audience.*) Mankind full of sin and shame/Take a coin and we'll settle the blame."

This final couplet is a variation on his usual refrain-like demand in his guise of a beggar to be *given* a coin and thus settle the account.

Zigmund is the pivotal character in the play. His positive guilt which outwardly he attempts to deny is nevertheless well-founded and stands in plain contrast to Yoram's neurotic guilt-fantasies. The encounters between the two men create most of the play's tension, which derives from the ironic fact of their familial relationship. Zigmund, in a parody of Buber's formula, consistently uses the third-person-singular when speaking to others, in an effective and sometimes tragi-comic device for self-alienation from all possibility of human contact.

Balloon seller: . . . aren't you afraid to sleep by yourself?
Zigmund: I don't sleep by myself.
Balloon seller: I don't understand.
Zigmund: I don't doubt that. Shall I tell him a secret? He is a happy man.
Balloon seller: Me?
Zigmund: Him.

Only towards the end of the play in a scene of almost unbearable pathos does Zigmund employ the second-person-singular when revealing his true identity to Yoram, his young brother-in-law. After one of many bouts of verbal sparring in which Zigmund is as elusive as the spineless medusa (jellyfish) he constantly apostrophises, Yoram breaks through:

Zigmund: He's very obstinate, sir, and I'm very soft . . . like a medusa . . . he must please believe me, it isn't worthwhile touching a medusa . . .

Yoram: It seems that in Lvov there was a medusa . . .

Zigmund: I thank him, sir, many thanks, will sir allow me to go? *(He gets up to go. Yoram pushes him down.)*

Yoram: Sit down, we haven't finished. *(Takes out the picture and shows it to Zigmund.)* Do you know this picture?

Zigmund: I know it, Yosele, I knew you from the first moment . . .

Zigmund's verbal tricks, his third-person-singular, his couplets, aphorisms, ironies, bursts of poetry, imagery, song and sheer nonsense constitute the major aspect of his madness which, like Hamlet's antic disposition, he employs as another defence against facing the truth, an equivocation protecting him from self-revelation and condemnation, for his own guilt is almost impossible to bear. "Thanks to this madness I was somehow able to retain a remnant of sanity . . ." He plays the role of an indigent old beggar who scrounges from passers-by in order to settle the account, as if money could redeem him – a reference to the reparations and the controversy associated with them. Zigmund's function in the play is multifaceted. He is in the first place an example of true culpability while that of Yoram is only fancied. The reason for Zigmund's collaboration with the enemy is never clearly stated in the play, but it seems that it came about through his misguided belief, even after his experience of the atrocities of the war and the murder of his wife, in the natural humanity of all men; or perhaps because the concentration camp commander had once been a respected academic friend of his and he could not accept the brutal change in him; possibly also because he thought that by collaboration he could aid his people. He does, on a few occasions, venture into self-justification, the most interesting attempt being by way of his parable of the tiger:

Zigmund: I'll tell you a parable: Once a tiger preyed on many sheep but he made a bitter mistake in that he challenged lions as well. The lions overcame him and wounded him severely. Then a trial was arranged for him and among other things he was accused of preying on sheep. They punished him, indeed not a very serious punishment, but the frightened tiger decided to repent. He said that he was going to atone. And then a great big sheep said to him: This is not the same tiger. It is another one."

Suddenly, during his endless process of self-imposed punishment, he accuses the Jewish people as a whole and again raises the spectre of the reparations as if by involving Israel and Germany in his own crime he may be even partially absolved. The important point, however, is not justification or condemnation of Zigmund as a war-criminal but the fact of his concrete guilt as against Yoram's neurotic self-immolation and Zigmund's expiation which at the same time allows Yoram insight into his own apparent need to atone. Yoram could not in the end find it in himself to deliver Zigmund to the Israeli authorities, partly because he felt that in a way he shared Zigmund's guilt and partly through his belief that by forgiving the tormented old man a much deadlier crime than his own he was to a certain extent forgiving himself. Indeed his protection of Zigmund offers him a sense of nobility, purification through an act of forgiveness and mercy, the capacity to understand and not to judge. Through the character of Zigmund Tomer may be attempting to secure a means of therapy for all the children of the shadow who are represented by Yoram in the play. Like Yoram he has forgiven Zigmund for a most ghastly crime; therefore, the lesser offence, whatever it may be, inspiring remorse and guilt without foundation in fact, only a kind of manufactured delusion arising from a dreadful set of circumstances, loses importance and becomes negated altogether.

Structurally the play is unusual and eminently suitable to its subject matter. Tomer has created an ingenious structure of parallel situations, each one adding insight to the other. An example of this is the scene between Yoram and a newcomer to Israel called Berele in which Yoram faces the indigent immigrant as well as his own unattractive attitude to this link with his past; this exactly echoes the scenes between Yoram and Dubi, where Dubi is the arrogant self-assured *sabra* and Yoram the ex-Yosele from Eastern Europe. Helenka's description of her experiences in a convent where she had been sent for protection amplify Yoram's memories of his childhood home and the slaughter of a chicken on the eve of the Sabbath. Both Yoram and Zigmund have placed themselves on trial: Yoram's self-justification is aimed at Nurit, Zigmund's at Yoram himself. Both dream simultaneously of Esther, Yoram's dead sister and Zigmund's wife, yet for Yoram she is the oppressor-accuser and to Zigmund his victim.

The play is an amalgam of realism and expressionism with a complex interweaving of thematic threads (many of them emanating from the character of Zigmund, for example, the hideous story of his wife's death and its consequences for the entire family): the contrast between courage and cowardice; Zigmund's misguided humanism and the varieties of guilt and responsibility. Through all this runs the motif of *Hamlet* and reference is made also to the Orpheus myth – a relevant metaphor since Yoram is in fruitless search of objective identity which turns out to be an elusive shadow vanishing at the point of contact. The characters are carefully delineated and possess the complex psychological background required by realism. They are not the symbolic everymen of expressionism; they have names, faces and histories. Dubi, Yoram's rival on the kibbutz and in the army, is the playwright's evocation of the tough, unimaginative *sabra*-figure, not a stereotype in this case but a cruel and mocking adversary whose insensitivity is paradoxically Yoram's spur to success. Nurit's parents are presented as the eternal do-gooders, the committee and agency people who endlessly travel on missions for *aliyah* but will have nothing personally to do with the immigrants for whose welfare they have laboured all their lives. Helenka, Janek's wife, is the self-pitying refugee, reminiscent of some of Bar-Tov's characters in *Each Had Six Wings* in her bitter disappointment at the indifference she encounters in the promised land. Janek is the hero of the Warsaw ghetto, emotionally eminently healthy and a contrast to Yoram's tortured introspection. Zigmund is perhaps an archetype, the classic case of sin and remorse to be found in literature and drama from Cain in the Bible through Greek tragedy to the contemporary drama of Sartre and Arthur Miller. But the playwright has humanised him in his awful self-hatred and he is the only character in the play to attain a measure of tragic stature, certainly one of the most authentic tragic heroes in Hebrew drama. The realistic episodes in the tangible plot of the play are interrupted by scenes containing pure expressionist dramatic devices: a symbolic chess game between Dubi and Yoram which is in fact a battle for personal dominance; a wedding party in which a character called only Guilt-Feeling summarises the major preoccupation of the play and a Poet describes in verse a "child of the shadow". A balloon seller appears time and again, serving as a kind of chorus and almost fulfilling the classic role of the messenger. Poems and songs abound in the play, notably Yoram's lyrical memory of his journey from Poland to Teheran as a child of the airlift. The vital episode of Yoram's childhood and Zigmund's crime is presented in a vivid dream which both Yoram and Zigmund dream simultaneously.

The Children of the Shadow was the first Hebrew play of its kind to be produced in Israel. In introspection and moral analysis woven together in the most modern dramatic terms it has not yet been equalled. It is an expression of something exceedingly personal yet it serves as a biography of a generation bearing in the very fact of its existence the possibilities of great drama.

"The Heir", and other plays

Moshe Shamir's play *The Heir* caused tremendous critical controversy after its first performance in December 1963 by the Haifa Municipal Theatre. Audiences objected to the choice of subject – the Nazi Holocaust and the subsequent German reparations – and most critics accused Shamir of being tastelessly sensationalist in his handling of these themes.

The hero – or rather anti-hero – of the play is a *sabra* who takes advantage of his former surname, Cohen, to claim reparations due to one Wolfgang Cohen who had been murdered by the Nazis and who had possessed great riches in Germany. Overnight the young man becomes formidably wealthy and is able to live a life of luxury, but in the end his initial lie plunges him into an enormous and complicated deception through which he loses sight of his own identity; he is trapped by the dead Cohen and his wealth and is involved too deeply, materially and morally, to be able to cry, as he does, "I am not Wolf Cohen."

Criticism varies regarding the character of Cohen. According to Haim Glückstein[5] he is a colourless individual, a chronic liar and an opportunist who has no definite attitude towards anything. He is intended to be an indictment of those who use the reparations in order to live a life of indolence and ease and, as Glückstein says, "He angers those whom the cap fits . . . and he also angers so many who are not members of the 'dolce vita', who would be prepared to accept Shamir's criticism but they are not prepared to hear these things from a negative character like Wolf Cohen." Such a character cannot be the instrument for the delivery of so powerful a message as Shamir's nor can he contribute to the creation of genuine dramatic conflict, because "a thief who steals because it is his nature to do so is not the subject for dramatic conflict. An honest man who steals or commits murder can be the subject for drama or tragedy." On the other hand, Michael Kasten[6] sees Ze'ev-Wolf as a symbol of uncertainty and bewilderment and the primary motif of this and other plays on the subject of the Holocaust: the search for identity by the present generation who, like Wolf, cry "Who am I, who am I?" and, like Yoram in *The Children of the Shadow*, are confused about their relationship to the Jews of Eastern Europe and their fate. Yoram is torn between his present life in Israel, which he lives in the guise of a *sabra*, educated on a kibbutz among other *sabras*, and his past as

[5] Glückstein, Kasten and Shamir: Symposium on "The Heir". *Orot*, April 1964.

[6] *Ibid.*

Yosele the child of the Polish village. This reflects the explicit problem of identity: who is Yoram in relation to Yosele and what part does Yosele have in the psyche of the *sabra* Yoram? But the difference between Yoram and Wolf Cohen is that Yoram knew the past and its connotations, refused to have any part of it and consciously rejected it; Wolf knew nothing of the past, was forced through his own deception to learn about it and then to accept it as part of his present identity as an Israeli.

It is the Eichmann trial which brings Wolf into direct contact with the Nazi persecutions; he comes to a closer understanding of its victims, an identification with them and with the man whose name and past he has taken for his own. This need for conscious identification by the youth of Israel with the Jews of Eastern Europe was Shamir's purpose in the play. "I myself," he says, "do not have the right to write a play dealing with people who endured the Holocaust or any direct contact with it. The only situation that I have the right to examine and to attempt to express regarding this subject is that of an individual or a community who were not there and do not know how they would have stood the test had they been there; on the other hand . . . they belong to and are bound to what was there and they have inherited the 'there' physically and spiritually . . ."[7] Many of the Israelis, he continues, lived off the reparations and they had the right to do so, to be the heirs of those who perished. "But from the point of view of our moral right . . . who are we? . . . how are we living? . . . here I see the dichotomy between the external reality and the inner identity. My problem is the person who has undertaken to accept the inheritance without accepting its implications regarding his identity." He considers this to be fraudulent. "The only way of expressing this problem can be: what happens to a man who has started out as a liar and who suddenly understands what he is playing with and what kind of identity he has assumed as his own? I wanted to bring my hero along a long and difficult road, from emptiness, from the sensations of a confused and ordinary young man, to purity." The play was also written, says Shamir, to compel us to notice that echoes of cries from Auschwitz and the "trumpets of pleasure" are still being heard simultaneously.

[7] *Ibid.*

The major criticism of the play derived from the sensitivity of many people living in Israel to any reminder of the past horrors. Mention on the stage of Auschwitz or Terezin created anger and unhappiness among a large section of Israeli theatregoers especially in the early sixties. The critics who regard themselves as the protectors and defenders of all audiences generally oppose any dramatic dealing with this part of Jewish history. No experience, so bitterly painful which so many endured and remember, must be paraded – to use a phrase from the play – like a carnival, for all to see. They claim that this particular catastrophe is too close and too intense to fall within the framework of artistic tragedy or to be the subject of a dramatic exercise and as such is almost an insult to those who knew the reality. A. Ben-Meir[8] says of *The Heir*: "... The activity of Ze'ev Bar-Nes – formerly Cohen – develops through the remainder of the story in a way that is a desecration of the holy memory of the victims of the Holocaust and causes revulsion in the viewer ..."

[8] *Herut*, December 6th 1963.

Haim Glückstein (he protests constantly about Shamir's flippant treatment of his theme): "A scoundrel is prepared to accept an inheritance to which he has no right from those who have been murdered while he himself has not suffered. When such a man protests against the Nazis and against profiteering of any kind, physical, moral or artistic, everything becomes unclean, rasping and irritating."

Israel Goor: "Only at the end of the play does Shamir say something very significant, something that affects all of us – regarding the reparations and the moral harm we will suffer through all contact with Germany. But this 'something' comes at the end of a long and tiring play and is also a distortion of the truth. Even so: the road to the terrible 'social perversion' (i.e. the reparations) was filled with good intentions, and because of this Shamir's deed is even worse ..."[9] He ends his criticism by wondering whether this play would have been produced had it been written by anyone but Moshe Shamir.

[9] "The Heir" by Israel Goor. *Bamah* 20, Winter 1964.

The apparent existence in Israel of a kind of subtle censorship of theme is still a tangible problem for the developing Hebrew drama. For example, this period, which has had so great an effect on the subsequent development of Israel and its people, appears now to be undergoing total erasure from their drama. The solution may lie in the method used by Tomer and Leah Goldberg of deriving events from the Holocaust, using it as a rationale for the play without graphic presentation of its horror on the stage. According to Shamir himself and his favourable critic Michael Kasten, *The Heir* is *not* about the Holocaust or the reparations but deals with a people's search for identity, brought into relief by the background of the camps and then the inheritance itself. In its problem the play is "universal" although its setting and theme is peculiar to Israel and the Israelis. "The best dramatic works," Kasten says, "are those which arouse anger. If a playwright throws stones through windows the public must weigh the situation and examine its own soul . . ."

Structurally the play is experimental, comprised of short scenes, vignettes that are, so to speak, "caught by accident and part of a story that has already begun and will still continue . . ." (Shamir).

Least innovative of the plays in this group is Aharon Meged's *Hannah Senesh* (Habimah, 1958), based on the true story of the Hungarian girl who parachuted into Hungary during the war in order to aid the Jews there. She was caught by the Hungarian authorities and tortured when she failed to reveal information regarding her companions and their activities. She was tried by a Hungarian military court and executed in 1944.

Her upbringing had not been specifically Jewish. Her father was a writer and an intellectual and Hannah herself was educated in a secular Hungarian school. She began to write poetry inspired by her father's idealism. The growing anti-semitism in Hungary and the suffering of the Jews there and in Palestine disturbed her and fostered her growing sense of nationalism, so that when she had completed her education in 1939 she emigrated to the Yishuv. She studied first in Nahalal and later joined the kibbutz Sdot Yam. When reports of the persecution of the Jews reached her during the early years of the war she volunteered to return to Hungary in order to do what she could for the Jewish community there.

Aharon Meged's play describes the period of her capture and trial by the Hungarians, interspersed with a series of flashbacks of her youth. Her mother is taken by the Hungarian police and threatened with execution if Hannah does not reveal the radio code the Jewish infiltrators have been using. Hannah refuses. She endures continuous interrogation and is threatened with further torture at the hands of the Gestapo. But worst of all is the torment of having to decide whether to sacrifice her mother or her companions and her cause.

The play is locked to its period not only through its static presentation of historical reality but through Meged's too-careful characterisation. The fact that he was acquainted with Hannah Senesh limited him severely, and consequently his representation of her is bound by his concern with absolute fidelity to his memory of her, whereas it could have transcended this to become a universal symbol of courage and idealism. The play was written about a period in Jewish history that fed on Zionist ideology and because it has, in a way, incorporated the propaganda of the time it is dated in its viewpoint. It calls for courage in the face of oppression, echoing Tchernichowski's credo that the persecuted Jew must die with a sword in his hand. It is also an indictment of those who were taken by the Nazis without any show of opposition. In the play Hannah talks of the "hundreds and thousands" of Jews who went to their death without saying a word, without raising a hand against their murderers, without attempting to save themselves. "They lost their lives and lost their honour." The ghetto fighters, she declares, rescued only two hundred people but through their active rebellion they safeguarded the honour of generations to come.

The fact that this play is a faithful representation of events as they happened weakens rather than enhances its dramatic impact. It has too much of event, too little of idea and conflict and is therefore a step backwards to the documentary. The playwright's approach is careful and restrained, almost inhibited, and he has created a tame newsreel instead of a powerful drama of ideas built around the personality of an extraordinary woman.

Aviva Geli, erstwhile theatre critic of *Orot*, makes the point that the language in *Hannah Senesh* is not sufficiently forceful but that it should be filled with great eloquence suitable to the eloquence of its theme.[10] This demand harkens back to the nationalistic exhortative drama of the first two decades of the century and is, with respect, incorrect, for the play's diction succeeds in its realistic simplicity despite other drawbacks of style and theme. People undergoing torture do not make impassioned speeches and exhortations. Meged does not demand this of his heroine in order to curry favour with the public and the critics, and as a result his play preserves greater realism and is given a certain limited tragic impact. Miss Geli says too that Meged did not spend enough time on explaining Hannah's sudden realisation of her Jewish nationalism, so surprising in the light of her assimilated upbringing; he did not give a rationale for her idealism. This is, however, unnecessary in the context of the play. Of prime importance is the fact of Hannah's courage, not the reason for it which was embodied in the atmosphere of Zionism during her youth in Hungary, the desire for action typical of that period and the pioneering spirit. Meged's play was not meant to be an epic. Hannah's motivation, her attitudes, her entire personality – all this is condensed into one dramatic moment, which Bentley calls a "unique concentration of reality".[11] "Drama", he continues, "tends to deal not only with antagonism but with culmination, not only with collisions but with *final*, *decisive* collisions; it tends towards ideas belonging to the extreme situations. A play may not fully analyse, for example, a world historical encounter in detail and elaboration but in proportion as it is a good play it renders the interaction of idea and

[10] *Orot*, October 1958.

[11] Eric Bentley. *The Life of the Drama*. Methuen, 1965.

event in its existential concreteness."

In form *Hannah Senesh* is unadventurous, employing devices popular in the Hebrew drama of its period: the flashback and the vignette. It is highly melodramatic, ending on an exalted note which might have suited its time but which has not worn well. The mystical conclusion, when Hannah's ghost returns to comfort and inspire the grieving mother, spoils any sense of tragedy evoked by Hannah's final and powerful cry for justice followed by her pleading, like a frightened child, to see her mother. The concluding scene is an anti-climax, a device which fails thoroughly in a play that is structurally simple and thematically factual and which could have attained something of the spiritual grandeur of Lorca's *Mariana Piñeda* instead of remaining on a plane of naiveté brought about by its earnest sincerity.

Two other plays dealing with the topic of the war and Jewish suffering achieved some distinction: Nathan Shaham's *A New Reckoning* (Cameri, 1954) tells the story of a refugee who attempts to start a new life in Israel but without success as he is haunted by the awful fact of having been a Kapo during the Holocaust. Aharon Meged's *The High Season*[12] (Habimah, 1967) is based on the story of Job and discusses the relationship between Israel and Germany some twenty years after the war.

[12] Literally, "The *Burning* Season" – a more apt translation considering the play's subject matter.

Israeli playwrights came to the realisation that there was no point to their competition with the cinema and (later) the television in maintaining perfect fidelity of description of the familiar world. Realistic melodrama had to be abandoned if the function of drama was to delve more deeply into human experience in order to reach beneath the surface of visible events. It had then to probe areas of interaction existing on a less graphically observable level. Television has inherited the task of providing mass entertainment, the cinema is yet in a somewhat anomalous intermediate stage, so it is the non-commercial theatre that has to supply the need for serious evaluation of reality and the concerns of the individual and his society. It must satisfy those members of the public who wish to participate in the living ritual of stimulus and response the drama offers in its quest for solutions to eternal problems. The Hebrew dramatists rose to this challenge once they had abandoned the strict reportage of the fifties.

This is not to say that the superficial documentary drama has vanished altogether from the Israeli stage, but playwrights as a whole are involved in analytical enquiry into occurrences which once would have been merely described and left at that. They have discovered that this new approach can be demonstrated in a variety of ways, many of which they have successfully attempted: for example, the use of myth as a subjective source; or a modernised permutation of tragedy which remains tragic only in its evocation of "heroes" such as Jeroboam, Zigmund and Zabrodski, who are comic and grotesque as well. There is a clear mixture of dramatic modes: realism and expressionism (*The Children of the Shadow*), expressionism and surrealism (*Journey to Nineveh*), poetic realism (*The King is the Most Cruel*), tragicomedy and farce (*Genesis*). Although the plays are diverse in plot and form they are built on similar propositions, adventurous themes expressive of the people in their distinctive circumstances while not limited to these circumstances alone. If the plays are tragic – and this is always open to doubt as is the entire premise of modern tragedy – then the dominating force is history and the past, a shared national and cultural past rather than individual heredity, the tenet of modern realism. Jewish social and political history is both the main motif and the protagonist of all these plays save *Genesis*. The Holocaust plays examine the effect on one person of the persecution of the Jews by the Nazis, which is dealt with without actually putting the camps on the stage. Each play presents a specific and at the same time universal problem, embodied in the Israeli-Jewish scene: a desperate search for identity; honour, cupidity and courage and especially guilt which, in differing guises, is common to all the plays of this type: that of Yoram, Zigmund and Wolf is obvious. Hannah Senesh vindicates all those who went to their deaths without protest, expiating the common guilt. Zabrodski is guilty, on a lower level, of committing a crime in order to create a life-saving illusion, Lena of accepting his protection as the line of least resistance, Dora of intolerance born of her childhood environment and Zand of escapism.

The characters of the Biblical-historical dramas as well as of the plays on the Holocaust stand for certain human elements rather than representing types, and these elements are, after all, what great drama is all about. Heroes still command the plays, ironically unheroic focal points of action and idea, while remaining people who transcend the confined framework of the play. Melodrama frequently constitutes the drama's concrete statement (Aloni, Meged, Tomer, Goldberg, Shamir), but the development of the dramatic themes is neither exclusively melodramatic, comic nor tragic but a rather ambiguous mixture of all three. The point is that playwrights had at last begun to adventure into form, to abandon their obsessive need for dramatic order and also tentatively to play with language. Hebrew dramatic diction of the sixties lagged behind that of Europe and the United States for there was nothing in the Hebrew drama linguistically comparable with Ionesco, Beckett or Pinter. The problems which their broken, inverted, non-communicative diction had been invented to express had not yet constituted the primary concerns of the Hebrew plays such as those discussed in this section, with the exception perhaps of Amichai's *Journey to Nineveh*. Verbal experimentation was to come later, with the mature works of Aloni, the drama of Levin, Sobol, Mundi and others.

Part IV. Modernism

The rhythm of theatre derives from an alternation of explosion and silence; more precisely, there is preparation, explosion and subsiding. The man of the theatre must not merely bring explosives in his bag; he must know exactly how to prepare the explosions and how to handle their subsidence. For the interplay between audacity and control produces the supreme artistic effects; the work of the masters of dramatic literature abounds in examples.

1 The Modern Drama: the Problem of Imitation

Those associated with Israel's restless theatre exhibit none of that self-satisfied arrogance which is said almost to be a national characteristic. On the contrary, despite its excessive output (167 original plays between 1948 and 1970), much of which is of a high standard even in this period of general re-evaluation of the terms of dramatic art, the Hebrew theatre seems to be uncommonly hypercritical, employing pedantic scrutiny of every detail of every new play and its production. Perhaps this lack of complacency is a healthy pointer towards greater improvement of its own dramatic value. The Israeli press plays a formidable role of its own, that of promoting the local drama and being the guardian of its standards. Its articles are not merely reviews, touching, on the most superficial level, on errors of presentation or bits and pieces of interpretation, but scholarly and detailed analysis of the plays, their authors and the production, in fact the entire process of theatrical creation. Whether the Israeli theatre likes it or not its professional critics know about the drama: scholars like the late Drs Gamzu and Kurzweil, academics like Professor Gershon Shaked, Drs Ben-Ami Feingold and Hillel Barzel, to name only a few on an impressive list, have created an awareness of what drama ought to be and this not in volumes available exclusively in university libraries but in the popular press. The standards set by these critics and the demands made by audiences will be discussed later, but always in the middle of these important forces – more often than not pulling in opposite directions – stands the drama itself, made increasingly insecure by its inability to decide what it wants from itself.

This insecurity has led to a measure of imitation aided also by the eagerness of the Israeli public to be a part of current trends in the theatre of other countries and by the fact that almost every play of note, old or new, English, American, French, German or Italian, has at some time been staged in modern Israel. In one season (1964–65), for example, audiences watched plays by Anouilh, Molière, Joe Orton, Büchner, Albee, Shakespeare, Euripides, Tennessee Williams, Hochhuth, Brecht, Strindberg, Bolt, Jarry, Ustinov, Arthur Miller, Wesker – among others. Out of 30 plays four were original. This has been (proportionately) the consistent trend.

In the 1971–72 season over 70 productions were given, among them six of the most noteworthy original plays, for example, *Hefetz* by Hanoch Levin, *The Gypsies of Jaffa* by Nissim Aloni, *The Days to Come*, a documentary compiled by Yehoshua Sobol dealing with the problems of the aged; *Comrades Talk About Jesus* by Amos Keinan, which suffered censorship because of its radical ideology; *A Summer Celebration* by Nathan Alterman and *The Bridal Canopy*, a dramatic adaptation of Agnon's novel. Despite the high quality of these local works the season was, as it always is, dominated by foreign products.

Why, asks Uri Kaisari[1], must the conventions of London and Paris be grafted onto everything in Israel – Modernism, Absurdism, Cruelty, all of these expressions of drama that grew where they did as a continuation of hundreds of years of normal theatrical life? "In Israel they can't be seen as a natural and logical development but a *jump before its time* that the dramatists and producers are unable to resist." Kaisari makes the point that if theatre is indeed the "public conscience" then the theatre of Israel is the conscience of the Americans or the English or any other creative nation. "What are we," he asks, "if not a small *moshava* of imperialists who are settling their culture in our country? If we want to know here, in Israel, what our theatres will be putting on in a few months it is enough for us to read London's newspapers and New York's to see what is playing there. And so we are revealed as imitators, like paupers who have nothing of their own."

[1] *Haaretz*, April 2nd 1965.

For many critics apart from Uri Kaisari the problem of the influence of foreign theatre on indigenous drama is as vast and alarming as was the encroaching Hellenism in the Israel of the Maccabees. They claim that because Israeli theatre is so young and devoid of roots it has eagerly tuned into the wavelength of modern drama without first reaching backwards in order to achieve recognition of its own origins. They blame the producers who see so much wrong with their own national product that they turn to foreign plays for the artistic satisfaction they seek and because of the security of knowing that these have succeeded elsewhere. There can be little doubt that it is, indeed, their task as much as that of the critics to educate the public, to whet its theatrical appetites and to guide it in its theatrical development and taste; playwrights accuse them of having failed to do so and of having allowed Broadway and the West End to think for them. If this is so it is a dangerous infiltration of foreign values on the young and independent native theatre because if the foreign criterion becomes the only criterion there can only be an abandonment of any personal and internal expression of Israeli cultural awareness and of any healthy organic growth.

Knowledge and understanding of foreign creative art is a necessary requisite for any culture; a national theatre must therefore stage plays from every country to serve as a bridge between the foreign culture and the local. But any national theatre which concentrates exclusively on the imported product stifles any possibility of developing its own, especially in Israel where drama is a new and virtually untried art. The foreign plays must necessarily still be technically superior to any Hebrew dramatic writing; comparison between them is unfair at this early stage in the Hebrew drama's development, but comparisons are constantly being made. The local playwrights are accordingly being forced into a defensive form of competition by their managements, to a certain extent by their critics and to a very large extent by their audiences.

Theatre is, *inter alia*, the reflection of an environment. Contemporary Hebrew drama may become a reflection of a foreign environment and of people who have no relation whatsoever to the Israeli. For example, 1963 saw a production of a play by David Levin called *Eyes Right, Eyes Left* which was a transplantation fibre by fibre of the French Absurd without alteration or individual contribution and above all with little psychological relevance. This marked the beginning of a spate of such copies with Levin's play as the vanguard. "I saw the first act of something that called itself 'Fables for Grown-ups' by David Levin and to this day I am sure that I mistook the address and chanced upon a play called 'Harold Pinter's Caretaker sitting on Ionesco's Chairs and Waiting for Godot'. I am not an enemy of the Theatre of the Absurd or the Theatre of Cruelty but sometimes when I read an original (Hebrew) playlet of this school I identify the foreign lady under the splendid garment of the Hebrew words."[2]

[2]Michael Ohed. *Maariv*, 1965 (month obliterated from photostatic copy).

This was in 1965. But even during the intervening years there have been few Israelis writing plays that are not in the same way the progeny of European parents. The extreme radicalism of the English and American theatre is already appearing in the latest Israeli drama although this reveals itself in political and sociological rather than in sexual daring. Protest is a popular modern theatrical genre valid in any healthy society where differences of opinion are permitted, but its form should suit the special characteristics of that society if it is to be effective. The young Israeli neo-Brechtians cannot convince their audiences if their lessons are cast in an alien, esoteric, borrowed form. The most important play about that most incredible event of incalculable historical and emotional significance, the war of 1967, was no more than a brooding essay on isolation and an amalgam of the American drama of the early sixties. Stage 2 of the Haifa Theatre and Habimah's Little Theatre have, in the past five years, seen a spate of strange, dreamlike plays with no specific point of view but filled with odd characters, like those of Joseph Bar Joseph's *Difficult People*. Even the brilliant plays of the late Avraham Raz are difficult to comprehend because of their uncertainty of form which includes a large measure of "borrowed" symbolism.

Mendel Kohansky expressed his dissatisfaction in a blazing article filled with contradictions but which nevertheless offered some evocation of the theatre scene: "The crisis in Haifa is especially serious, coming at a time when the country's stages are flooded with a wave of unspeakable vulgarity. A new kind of theatre audience has been discovered, an audience which up to now sought entertainment elsewhere, and clever producers are fast turning out shows to cater to their tastes. It is an easily entertained audience; they laugh at the oldest jokes and visual gags, they go into raptures when a fellow named Azulay has it out with a fellow named Weinstein. I reviewed here some weeks ago a play called 'Boutique of Lies' which I found abominable; only a few days ago I saw a play called 'The Idiot' (a thoroughly vulgarised version of a popular comedy by Marcel Achard) turned out by the same factory, and I found it so bad that I could not bring myself to review it. The audience, consisting mainly of young people, loved it. It breaks my heart to think that this fresh, unspoilt audience could learn to appreciate something good instead of being degraded by that kind of trash."[3]

[3] *Jerusalem Post*, July 7th 1972.

The fact behind all the managerial squabbles and the playwrights' vocal dissatisfaction is simply that no drama created by a superimposition of foreign elements can succeed as a national representive drama especially in the unique case of Israel. The drama being transposed to Israel was born in Europe and England of their societies and traditions and conditions of life. Every great playwright has deep roots in the philosophic and cultural thought of his nation. This tradition is the storehouse of theatrical styles which have evolved to become the established theatre of our time. In the light of all this it is clearly impossible merely to transplant the new theatre in a country like Israel because Israel lacks a background that is in any way similar. Its young society is still without solidity or homogeneity or a common tradition and it has suffered a spiritual severance from European cultural sources. Any copying or transplanting must, therefore, fail because it is unsuitable to the spirit and background of the people. Streams of art cannot pass arbitrarily from culture to culture. In order to benefit from implantation from outside the soil must be conditioned but this particular conditioning is necessarily absent in Israel. An illustration

[4]Quoted by Joseph Lapid in *Maariv*, June 28th 1963.

of this point is the wry statement of Moshe Levi, an Israeli producer,[4] to the effect that he would have no alternative but to look for a play about a prostitute for the Israeli stage in order to support the fashion of supplying theatrical prostitutes. This is, it seems, only a short step away from creating fads in accordance with those current in foreign drama. In the same article Haim Topol makes the comment that during the course of the play in which he was starring the audience laughed most at the only joke in it that was not obscene. The situation however is not yet irredeemable. As Kohansky says: "There is nothing basically wrong with the theatre in Israel . . . all you need is to give the boys with talent, integrity and dedication the tools to work with and see what they can accomplish." Fortunately there are a few "boys with talent" who are determined to accomplish, without recourse to sensationalism but through their own and individual creative impulse, having absorbed from foreign theatre only what is necessary to their education as dramatists. Nissim Aloni and Hanoch Levin are the most noteworthy of these, with the controversial Yosef Mundi and Yehoshua Sobol still to prove themselves but well on the way to doing so.

2 Nissim Aloni

Nissim Aloni's second play, *The King's Clothes* (Habimah, 1961) at last introduced what the critics had been seeking for so long, the truly "universal" play, into the Hebrew dramatic repertoire. It was an allegory without any relationship to the contemporary life of Israel or to Jewish history or the Bible and which was in fact derived from the folklore of another culture – *The Emperor's New Clothes* by Hans Christian Andersen, a story set in Denmark. Aloni's play took the Hebrew theatre beyond its territorial borders and out into the modern technological world, abandoning all "national" characteristics and preoccupations. It set the tone for all of Aloni's subsequent drama.

The importance of Aloni today is almost indefinable. It rests in every area of theatrecraft and dramaturgy in Israel. He was the first Israeli playwright to compose directly for the theatre and not an adaptor transposing his own novels and short stories for the stage. The best of the Hebrew plays have been conceived in theatrical terms, for the stage from the auditorium, following Ibsen's method. During rehearsals Aloni is still creating for he makes large alterations as the play is developed in production. In his case there is not the usual Israeli dichotomy between the play and its production for he is the director and the designer of all his own works.

The Absurd is clearly evident in them although he has, in his latest plays, shown signs of rejecting it. The exception to the style now always associated with him was his first play, *The King is the Most Cruel*, which is a realistic history play written when he was obviously toeing the line and creating *traditional* Israeli drama, a play based on a Biblical theme expounded by Biblical characters. Every great Israeli playwright without exception, from Shoham onwards, has done this before continuing to more individual structures and topics. Apart from this type of play being the sole traditional framework the playwright possesses it is the only truly original contribution Israel has so far made to world drama: the offering of a singular allegorical structure and a mythology of its own.

Not everything Aloni has written has been as dramatically progressive. *The King is the Most Cruel* was received with acclaim by most critics who felt that this was the first viable Israeli drama. There were, however, some who condemned the play because it tampered with Biblical material or because it criticised contemporary Israeli politics. This critical division has characterised the reception of every new Aloni offering since the early sixties, but he has remained true to his own unusual, generic, dramatic landscape. For the most part his first play was hailed as a triumph and proudly compared to Shakespeare and Anouilh. Nowadays Aloni is compared to no one – the ultimate acclamation – and has in fact created a new theatrical adjective which could be translated into English as "Alonic". But his writing is not, and cannot be, faultless. For one thing Aloni seems to have made a cult out of incomprehensibility. Although most of the themes that had already made their appearance in *The King is the Most Cruel* were repeated time and again in his subsequent plays he hid them in a kaleidoscope of symbolism, verbal trickery and electronic magic. The result has been neither realism nor epic theatre, nor expressionism, nor poetry but a combination of all of these, a clever distillation of every major European trend since the beginning of this century. There is much wrong with Aloni's theatre and drama, and yet it is in spite of all its faults and its flagrantly irritating aspects the most important and to date the most vital contribution ever made to Hebrew dramatic art.

"We are lucky," says Emanuel Bar-Kadma,[1] "to have Nissim Aloni. Nissim Aloni is a phenomenon . . . he is a generation. He is a 'stream'." "Aloni's plays are, without doubt, the most original, interesting and the best we have, and even beside names like Pinter, Albee and Genet – the name of Aloni can stand without humility."[2] These are only two examples of the almost hysterical adoration with which Aloni is viewed by his fellow playwrights and many critics, although theatre managements are not always as enthusiastic. For, in general, audiences find him "difficult", obscure and idiosyncratic. He appears to them to repeat himself out of an aridity of imagination. He is loved by the students and the theatrically orientated and educated but not by the public at large. Unfortunately a fair evaluation cannot be made from his playtexts alone (and very few of these have in any case been published) for the reader is deprived of the vivid theatrical effects that characterise his work: Yossel Bergner's decor, the music, the spoken language and the stylisation of production. He has to be content with the whimsicality of Aloni's ideas, recognising the almost obsessive repetition of certain themes and enjoying the glorious language. For in this latter sense alone he is unique among Israeli playwrights. His diction is peculiar to him, almost a kind of code that is his only and typical of his plays, its brilliance enhanced by the virtuoso performances of Yossi Banai who specialises in Aloni roles. The diction consists of short bursts of speech with words and phrases in ironic contrast, evocative images, snatches of song, slang, poetry, quotations and popular sayings mixed, in an apparently

[1] Emanuel Bar-Kadma. *Tediot Achronot, February 6th 1970.*

[2] Eli Moher. *Bamachaneh,* December 4th 1970.

endless flow, with naturalistic dialogue. The characters speak not in sentences but in rapid, truncated phrases each of which possesses a special value of expressiveness and suggestiveness. It is difficult to grasp the music of the language from the text alone. To a certain extent Aloni's contemporary poets have employed similar linguistic devices: Yehuda Amichai in particular is known for his juxtaposition of ancient and modern Hebrew, slang and idiomatic language, quotations from the Bible in a modern context and distortion of meaning. Merely reading Aloni, however, can become tedious, for the theatrical splendour of the words in their combination with visual and aural delights is lost to the reader.

Aloni has always been concerned with the conventions of tragedy although his plays are not tragic in form. Themes, some associated with tragedy, recur time and again in his plays: the killing of the father by the son; the figure of a grotesque king; a clown; nostalgia for a glorious past; the search, almost in the vein of a detective story, for a killer; a Pirandellian world of people acting parts, blurring planes of reality, donning masks to hide their real selves, seeking, like *Henry IV*, escape in role-play.

The King's Clothes[3] was one step further in Aloni's most obsessive tilting at the corruption of power. In fact all his plays so far have presented a progression of certain basic ideas, each play pursuing them further and deeper. The plot of *The King's Clothes* is too complex to be summarised. Basically it concerns a man who, being honest initially, perceives the rottenness of those in power and is unafraid to state his views; but in the end he compromises his idealism and becomes the ruler himself. There is in him a resemblance to Jeroboam in *The King is the Most Cruel*, except that Jeroboam was a revolutionary with a purpose for he wanted to free his people from a tyrannical king and from the ambitions of a theocrat; Bassona in *The King's Clothes* steps into his predecessor's place without any purpose of change or hope of personal fulfilment.

[3] Habimah, 1963.

The play is a perceptive satire on all that is ridiculous in society, the lies and rottenness of public life, politics and art, official institutions and in any newly established bureaucracy; it describes the total negation of all values in modern society and our own apathy, the emptiness of our slogans, the meaninglessness of the words we use, the degeneration of idealism and its objectives. It condemns conformism, the tendency to copy, to be alike at all costs, the readiness to see the king's clothes in order to avoid being different.

Like most modern plays this one is filled with symbolism open to a multitude of interpretations and therefore subjective and not always successful. It is clear that Aloni is stating an intensely felt idea and that, according to the critics' demands, he has something important to say. Despite the obscurity of numerous scenes, much of the dialogue and many unresolved dramatic movements Aloni's message is plain, and these critics who place far-fetched interpretations on every small detail, leaving themselves with no more than a code of complicated symbolism, are defeating the playwright's purpose.

This purpose is expressed through the characters, each of which is representative of some social ill. All of them – except Marie, a steadfast idealist – are negative, grotesque and inhuman, and each has a specific function in Aloni's uncovering of the petty nastiness of life. Their names, as in Restoration comedy, seem to be an indication of their characters and their function in the play. Most of the names are Italianate, the exception being Rabinowitz and one or two others, and this consistency seems to indicate a purpose. Corbo and Torno are the two opportunistic tailors transposed from the original folk-tale whose only interest is profit; they have initiated the whole affair of the king's clothes thus making a mockery of the entire court. *Corbellare* means "to make a fool of". Corbo is the more ruthless of the two – the other is hesitant, more sensitive; his name is Torno: *tornire* – "to turn". Collaro is the Cardinal. In his article on *The King's Clothes* Haim Glückstein[4] suggests that Bubu (or Bobo), the name of the commentator of the story, is derived from the name of a well-known French clown. It was also the title given to the fool or clown (called also *gracioso*) in the Spanish Renaissance *comedia*. Caspar (the King) is the traditional king of the puppet theatre. The name of the rebellious young poet is Hector Bassona: *basso* – "low". The tradition of relating names to character antedates Restoration comedy by more than a century, appearing specifically in the *commedia dell'arte* with which Glückstein compares *The King's Clothes* in detail. In fact Aloni's play resembles the *commedia dell'arte* only in the most superficial sense, for example in the comic grotesquerie of the characters (which is also a tendency of the Absurd drama) and the juxtaposition of a king, a nobleman and a multitude of servants. Glückstein bases his comparison on a number of features which he says are common to both *commedia dell'arte* and *The King's Clothes*: the Italianate names of Aloni's characters, the vignettes of entertainment that interrupt the main stream of the story, which Glückstein compares to the *lazzi* or standard comic diversions, tricks, of the *commedia dell'arte*. In the latter, however, love triumphed over evil and the wicked were punished – in *The King's Clothes* love is thwarted and the lovers

[4] *Two Original Plays* by Haim Glückstein. *Bamah* 11–12, Winter 1962.

parted. The *commedia dell'arte* did not have specific or profound moral intentions except the simple ones of demonstrating reward or retribution. *The King's Clothes* is a carefully structured play and if it has a moral it is not determined by the predictable results of stereotyped human action but is imposed by the author's acute intellect. Whether or not the play adheres rigidly to the conventions of the *commedia dell'arte* is less important than the fact that Aloni already established in this play his extraordinary facility for moulding diverse sources to his purpose, using ancient theatrical conventions as a framework for modern exposition.

The King's Clothes has been likened – as was everything in the sixties that involved symbolism and a fair quota of incomprehensible passages – to Beckett and Ionesco, but by definition it is not an Absurd comedy. The Absurd of the above-mentioned dramatists demonstrates the total senselessness of fate that batters man into despairing numbness. Aloni's play presents a destructive situation caused by man which can be righted by man should he find the courage to do battle with his own tendency to blunder. The message is therefore positive. *The King's Clothes* contains a plot and characters and a certain amount of social realism all of which is lacking in the Absurd. It is, however, possible that in his choice of a king posturing about in ridiculous clothes amid his grotesque court, the first of many such "Alonic" kings, Aloni was influenced by Alfred Jarry.

The King's Clothes was not an unqualified success. The critics were either ecstatic or vituperative. None, however, was indifferent. One accused Aloni of not having had enough material for an evening, hence the addition of so much irrelevant matter; others complained that the play was too long, the plot over-complicated. From the box-office point of view the play was a total failure. One reason put forward was that the Israeli audiences were not yet ready for it. Many theatregoers deliberately avoided seeing it because it was "so difficult to understand". Aloni's audiences were called upon to introduce a complete revolution in their approach to the theatre, and the claim of one critic that *The King's Clothes* was fit only for an experimental theatre did nothing to strengthen their interest. The truth is that the Israeli public was indeed not yet able to leap from nineteenth-century realism to the avant-garde of the sixties with no intermediate theatrical education. The second reason for failure – and the critics were unanimous on this point – was that Aloni himself produced his play. He was, they said, not equipped to do so. Time, however, has proved them mistaken.

Aloni's third play, *The American Princess* (Onot, 1963), proved beyond doubt that he wrote entirely in theatrical terms creating, in Israel, a new theatrical convention. It was a virtuoso piece of writing for two onstage characters with other parts played by voices reaching the audience through loudspeakers. It established him as the first Hebrew dramatist proper and created the Aloni cult, which is still gaining strength. Most of the themes in this play had already been considered in his earlier works. It concerns a pitiful and grotesque king called Bonifacius who lives in exile supporting himself by giving lessons in French, all the while dreaming of his glorious past. He has a son called Ferdinand, the Crown Prince, who proves to be his bitter adversary. The changing relationship between father and son provides the human and pathetic aspects of the play. The two men are eternal competitors, always belittling one another, each vying for authority. Then an "American princess", Dolly Kokomakis, a typical Aloni creature of fantasy, someone who could not possibly exist, arrives, with the intention of making a film of the old king's life, with his death at his son's hand as the denouement. Ferdinand is selected to play the king as a young man. The film forms a large portion of the play – again an Aloni device: the play-within-a-play. The son acts the role of the father in his youth, marries the queen (his mother), has a son (himself), then he plays himself avenging his father and the crown. The Oedipal pattern, hinted at in *The King is the Most Cruel*, is further developed here. The king, at this later stage, is played by a Hollywood actor who never uses make-up but instead undergoes plastic surgery for each part he takes. The princess demands that in the final murder scene the real king take his own part. The scene ends in tragedy, for someone has exchanged the blanks in the gun for live bullets and Ferdinand apparently kills the king.

Central to Aloni's drama is his abiding interest in the Oedipus myth and the relationships between father, mother and son. Already in *The King is the Most Cruel* he has his hero's fate inextricably bound with that of his mother, the mother being the deciding factor in his future and finally dying at his command. In *The American Princess* Ferdinand not only hates his father but kills him, although premeditation is not made clear. In *The King's Clothes* Bassona contrives the king's death. In *The Gypsies of Jaffa* the son kills the father onstage. In *Aunt Liza* Joseph Blank has killed his father, M'sieur Jacques, and returns to his native land after he has apparently atoned for his crime for thirty-six years. In *Eddie King* Eddie has killed his father, Don Laios, and married his mother.

The king as a ruler or monarch is, in most cases, burlesque or a grotesque or comic figure. Even Rehoboam, the most realistic of

Aloni's kings, is a figure of pathos, being fat and physically repulsive, a cruel, sadistic buffoon. The symbol of the king is an obvious one: father or authority or God. Killing the king does not, in Aloni, exclusively bear the implications of the Elizabethan concept of order and chaos, but refers further back to the elemental myth of fertility. Yet, in Aloni, once the act is achieved not rebirth only death and destruction can follow, so that his is a synthesis of the Renaissance and the primitive cosmic ideologies.

The American Princess like *The King's Clothes* exhibits the illusion and hollowness of power and the quality of ambition, as does *Napoleon – Live or Dead*, his play staged by Bimot in 1970. Also characteristic of Aloni's plays is that each of them is written within the framework of a well-known (or sometimes less well known but at least established) fable, myth or pattern, such as the corn-king myth, the story of Alice in Wonderland, *The Emperor's New Clothes* or the tale of Oedipus. Each one draws from diverse sources – folklore, the carnival, the cabaret, the *commedia dell'arte*, operetta and popular television detective melodrama. His play *The Gypsies of Jaffa* (1971), for example, contains an interesting collection of elements amazingly similar to those of the Polish Vagabond plays. These are given by a group of villagers who perform on New Year's Eve in a few small villages south of Cracow in Poland. Their performance – which is a series of improvised actions rather than a structured play – consists of a random conglomeration of scenes of ritual origin which begin with the ceremony of calling forth the ghosts of the dead. The improvised scenes are based on ritual actions and their characters are standardised. The central figures are the gypsies who tell fortunes with playing cards; the bear, who is a fearful figure because he "steals" the young girl; an old man who leads a goat by a chain; "soldiers" who restore order; death weaving in and out of the spectators. There are clowns, make-believe animals mingling with real ones, a devil and shepherds. Music, supplied by an accordion, and dancing are essential to the vagabonds' performances. Aloni's *The Gypsies of Jaffa* is sophisticated and structured, but the parallels in it to the Polish village plays are obvious, suggesting that the play's origins date further back in mythology than to the appearance of the tarot or 13-pack playing cards popularly considered to be its source. The scene of the play is a nightclub, with music and dancing the implied framework to the action. Gypsies tell fortunes with playing cards. A police-superintendent is the counterpart of the Polish "soldiers". All are awaiting death in the form of Smul Valigura[5] whose symbol is a bear. A devil appears onstage while the players are occupied with a card

[5]The name, by some stretch of imagination, could mean valiant warrior, for however obscure they may seem, Aloni's names always bear significance. However, the combination of *valiente* and *guerra* does not openly suit the character in this case.

game called "devil's curse". In the Vagabond play the "devil" engages a ploughman in a duel. References in the Aloni play to a goat and goatherd suggest the idea of a ritual scapegoat, a theme to which Aloni returns in his subsequent play *The Scapegoat* (1973). *The Gypsies of Jaffa* is a play about death; its characters are death images and its theme is vengeance. The Vagabonds symbolise the past dead and their spirits. Their merrymaking is a celebration of life at the traditional birth of the New Year. By personifying and then mocking Death, they allay fear.

One of Aloni's central characters in all his plays is the actor playing his role in an attempt to defeat life, as in *The American Princess* and *Napoleon – Live or Dead*. Aloni shows his indebtedness to Pirandello in his theme of life as a play with its symbol the mask or the mirror. No major character in an Aloni play appears as what he truly is but only as what he is pretending to be. In *Eddie King* (1975) the *actor* is no longer a central character although Teresa, the transvestite seer (an updated Teiresias) is, in a sense, a director of the play's action. It is not only in the concept of "play within a play" that Pirandello's influence on Aloni is so marked but in two other ideas: Pirandello's most essential character is a king who is either mad or sane, for the concept of madness is presented as a paradox; also Pirandello stressed in almost every play his own view of the relative value of art. To Pirandello art, which is static, and life, which is instinctual, organic and therefore changeable, are never reconciled except in the paradox of man's illusory creation of himself. In Aloni's *Aunt Liza* the sculptor is carrying one of his statues. He is asked "Is he dead?" and answers: "Dead is not a word. He is already art . . ." In Pirandello's *Diana and Tuda* two sculptors argue about the power of artistic form. The younger declares that art is not the same as life, that art transforms and enlarges. The older sculptor says that the function of art is also death. "Death will make statues of both of us when we lie stiff and cold in our beds or in the ground." The basic Pirandellian quest is to seek the statue that moves, the work of art that is life and he finds it only – and then to an extent – in the theatre. Throughout *Aunt Liza* and *The Gypsies of Jaffa* Aloni flings aphorisms, often ironic, dealing with the conflict between life and art, illusion and "truth". "You are true [or real] not alive . . ." or "true art is not alive and living art is not truth." These sometimes rather facile statements at least indicate Aloni's interest in the irreconcilability of reality and illusion, another of his consistent themes.

The influence of Brecht and Ionesco, of Jarry and de Ghelderode, need not again be stressed. This influence has been cited by Aloni's critics as a mark against him. And indeed, all great drama is based on a metaphor which is part of a specific national spirit and identity and with the Israeli critic's preoccupation with the constitution of a national drama it is understandable that "Brechtian" or "Ionesco-like" become condemnatory epithets. Ibsen's struggle for freedom arose out of the provincialism of the Norwegian milieu and extended to the individual in all nineteenth-century society; Chekhov's stemmed from the encroaching change in his country, Brecht's out of his society's corruption. Each artist grew out of a prominent feature or deficiency in his own social or artistic environment. Aloni seems to hover over a number of worlds far from Israeli reality, unidentifiable with Jewish culture or history. The one extreme in Hebrew drama had been its totally Israeli, Jewish parochialism, without any objective intellectual conclusion except criticism or comment on a purely temporal scale. The other extreme is Aloni whose problems are existential and who is not, in *general* dramatic terms, original. He has not explored Israeli consciousness. He has not shown any kind of alliance with a national identity. He has escaped into a European *mélange* and this appears to be either what enrages his critics or impresses them, while leading his supporters to the conclusion that he is the first "original" dramatist *because* of his distance from Israeli reality. There is no doubt that his drama is colourful, exciting, innovative and clever, unlike anything hitherto seen in Israel composed by an Israeli. His plays sometimes have a vaguely Israeli setting although, like Brecht's, Aloni's place names have little relationship to reality. His Jaffa is not geographically real. His characters in *The Gypsies of Jaffa* refer to the Holocaust; some of them are its victims, but the play is not really about Israelis or even Jews. The character of "Aunt Liza" figures in the Israeli past, the setting of the play is a *moshav* but the issues are not local. It is only indirectly that Aloni explores problems pertinent to Israeli consciousness such as guilt, the most prominent, already examined by Shamir, Tomer, Amichai and others. "Killing the King" may indeed be a metaphor for killing the past, killing God, killing the Jew or Abraham or history. Yet Aloni's contribution to Hebrew drama is not only its possible reference (or lack of it) to the Jewish past but in elements other than this or the obvious ones of "universality" or spectacle: first of all he has provided the Israeli drama with a figure which he firmly believes to be representative of its society. This is not a tragic hero for this would be unsuitable in Israel's specific dramatic context which eliminates the possibility of tragic heroism, leaving only comic heroism if heroism at all. The Israeli drama is seeking definition – it does not itself know what constitutes an "original" play. But it has slowly come to the realisation that any great playwright creates through personal expression, through need to state a case which, in most instances, has a subjective source. Aloni, of all the playwrights, has done this. He has provided an image which may not be original or to everyone's liking but which perfectly fits his creative impulse and his environment: the buffoon-king, the symbol of authority become grotesque, idealism reduced to the ridiculous, power to comedy. From the first of his plays Aloni has traced a course towards the exposure of power as one of man's crazier impulses. He demonstrates leadership to be pathetic and inept. He shows the leader to be a figure unable to achieve relevance to his environment, whose longing for the past echoes the defeated romanticism not only of his creator but also of his audience.

Secondly, Aloni has broken all the carefully structured rules for the creation of what the experts believe to be national drama. He has conformed only inasmuch as he has written a play based on a Biblical story. To this end he has used his own cultural sources. But he has taken one step further, to reach the very foundation of all drama rooted in the consciousness of mankind and not of any one specific group. He has reached into the very recesses of man's mind, to the ancient ritual of the death of the king from which all dramatic expression has grown. In effect he is recreating drama from its human sources, creating a tradition from its beginnings and allowing the specific consciousness of his own society to shape it. He has, in his plays, already explored much of the basic mythology of man, the legends and stories embodying the fears and taboos of the human mind. By means of the Oedipus myth and its implications he has begun to do what European writers have been doing for centuries: to examine his own deepest preoccupations and those of his society. By his juxtaposition of the eternal characters, father-son – woman-mother, the elemental forces of the social group and the psyche – he is indicating that an expression of self and then the nation will evolve. Aloni has obviously not considered Jewish mythic source material sufficient to his drama. His own consistent mythic foundation antedates structured monotheism and his interest turns on the primeval battle between man and hostile, incomprehensible forces that determine his behaviour and ultimately doom him to failure.[6] The implication is one of tragedy, but the plots are not tragic for the hero does not die. In Aloni's terms it is the unheroic man who must seek his *moira* in dreadful isolation (*The American*

[6] Meged made a tentative attempt at this in *Genesis*.

Princess, *The King's Clothes*, *Eddie King*, *Napoleon – Live or Dead*, *The Scapegoat*) and his end is not honourable self-sacrifice after defying his fate but a very unheroic retreat into madness or pretence, or the continuing frustration of the search. The story is also one of the group (or nation) whose fate, too, is a lonely journey towards spiritual self-recognition after having rejected the security offered by traditional gods.

Aloni is among the most culturally identified of all Hebrew playwrights for he applies a "universal" myth to his own cultural environment and attempts to reach a conclusion regarding its future. Because he is contrasting the definitely unheroic reality with the heroic archetypes his conclusion must be ironic; killing the king only leads to further chaos, to greater isolation and blindness. There is a social and political lesson to be learned from Aloni's drama, although overtly it is totally unrelated to any such temporal concerns.

So it is paradoxical that one of his later plays, based openly on Sophocles' *Oedipus Rex*, was a failure. Aloni seems to have arrived at an almost pre-ordained climax to his creative process in *Eddie King* (Habimah, 1975); for after hinting at it in so many plays he has finally brought into the open the Oedipus story in which Oedipus unwittingly kills his father and marries his mother. This is precisely why the play was so roundly criticised. Gidon Ophrat makes the observation that Aloni has always used a kind of code which has tantalised audiences and critics alike. "In 'Eddie King'," says Dr Ophrat, "he has in a sense given the key, which spoils the play."[7] "Here Aloni no longer speaks in riddles, those beautifully dressed-up riddles which delighted by their brilliance and irritated by their impenetrability; his language no longer dazzles . . . and there is none of the enchantment of mystery, an Aloni trademark, left here."[8] "In Aloni's play the cards are revealed from the first moment . . ."[9] This critic is referring to the fact that unlike Sophocles Aloni reveals the murderer at once. But he is also stressing, as are the others, that Aloni's own creative cards are shown face up for the first time.

Eddie King combines two myths: the ancient Oedipus story which is the moral humanisation of the corn-king rite; and the gangster myth which has been glamorised by the media and exploited by popular novelists until the Godfather has become a modern folk-hero. In a sense it seems entirely logical that in terms of his king-fixation Aloni should have taken the Godfather as his protagonist, or rather, antagonist, in *Eddie King*. For this persona is not a cynical romanticisation of crime in the style of the popular fiction of the USA but the artistic choice of a viable symbol. The godfather-figure is

[7] *Meeting Jerusalem*, May 1976.

[8] Mendel Kohansky. *Jerusalem Post* (details obliterated from photostatic copy obtained from Genazim).

[9] Joseph Netzer. *Chotem*, August 22nd 1975.

possibly the most powerful king in the world, whose dominion is universal, whose might is feared by all and who brings death and destruction far beyond the boundaries of his own territory. He is the supreme father on earth. For the first time the "king" is not a buffoon in an Aloni play, neither is Eddie King, the gangster who aspires to the throne.

From Sophocles Aloni took the motifs of family, blindness, inescapable fate – which, in line with modern tragedy, rests in the human psyche – and the search for identity. From more ancient mythology he derived the story of the father who must kill the son before he is killed by him, a seminal motif in the lives of Moses and Jesus and countless other great men. This is Aloni's attempt to rationalise Eddie-Oedipus, the parricide, for "it's always old riddles . . . who rises who stays who falls . . . and it always goes, it's funny, with a son . . . a father . . ." says Eddie, and continues: "A son, Joe said to me, what he has in this life is to finish off daddy . . . sometimes daddy finishes him off first . . . in wars . . ." Here is Aloni's clear (if a little banal) reference to paternalistic and murderous authority.

Every man is a son and his fate is therefore irrevocable. Eddie describes how the gangster-chief Don Laios taunted him until he shot him in the head.

Eddie: I told him . . . I came here to do great things and he said good, that's good, boy, begin with the tongue I certainly didn't understand. Because he shoved his whole foot together with the shoe in my face. Funny, I saw a shoe and even so I didn't understand very well. Because someone said, one of them: go ahead, Eddie King. I went ahead. I shot Don Laios right in the head. And afterwards all of them.

Later, Creon says: "You probably got into the bed that was still warm from the king you killed."

Yet Laios returns again, a living corpse representing Eddie's sudden knowledge that he was his father. "The fact of a man being a son to a father is a trap which is impossible to escape from," says Aloni. This is, as already mentioned, not an entirely new idea in Hebrew literature since 1948: the conflict between generations already apparent in the first play of the State of Israel, the new rationalism, the disintegration of the figure of the bearded Orthodox Jew whom Amichai, for example, satirised so effectively in his novel *Not of this time, Not of this Place*. This father-figure (אב) recurs almost obsessively in contemporary Hebrew poetry and is by turns rejected, mourned or appealed to.[10] Guilt and longing mingle in the writers'

[10] See particularly *New Poetry* (*Hashirah Hatzeira*). Eked Books, Tel Aviv, 1969.

memories of their fathers, a conflict that Aloni has crystallised in his constant image of the slain father whose (Oedipal) son may or may not be the slayer.

Aloni's irony is subtle and clever. The ancient myth grew from a rite celebrating the resurrection of the god and the promise of fertility and life to come. The Oedipus story placed the myth on a moral foundation where the effect of mortal sins – incest and murder – were examined. The outcome of the investigation is the lifting of the plague ravaging Thebes, the cleansing and purification of a group suffering the effects of another's sin.

Aloni's "new world", however, is one of improved vice: Creon says near the end of the play: "There's a lot of work. We must organise everything. From the start. Prostitutes. Corruption. Gambling . . . And there's competition, boys. Lots of blacks. Lots of dirty children from Puerto Rico." The new kingdom is one of darkness. The new king is that of the Underworld.

The playwright's comment extends to yet another "new world", New York itself, representative of the America that gathers in the poor and stateless. Eddie speaks about the city that presents "riddles" and he calls it the Sphinx. For the poor remain poor and the dispossessed turn to crime. The plague in the city is poverty. And out of the plague grows the awful kingship of the gangster.

Despite its cleverness, its use of myth, its language, *Eddie King* is not without puzzling inconsistencies. It is clear that Aloni wrote with some specific, obviously ironic idea in mind but he does not always clarify his intention. This is true of most of his work, but even greater clarity is required for understanding *Eddie King* because of its mythic and Sophoclean basis. Aloni tends generally to be self-indulgent and this presupposes a certain contempt not only for his audiences but for his readers as well. He is inclined towards intellectually sophisticated game-playing which leaves his audience uncomfortably behind. This is no less true of *Eddie King*.

Joseph Netzer's comment that "to write a new mythological play on an old mythological play – this seems to me to be redundant . . ."[11] is, however, not a reasonable criticism, for the reinterpretation of myth or the creation of myth-based drama is always valid, as has been demonstrated by the French Symbolists and Absurdists, by O'Neill, Miller, Lorca and many others. The definitive question regarding *Eddie King* must not be the choice of myth but of theme: Why has Aloni selected a gangster to portray Oedipus? The choice of the Godfather as representative of a king has already been discussed. But only irony can account for the story's

[11] Joseph Netzer (details obliterated on photostatic copy).

new setting in New York's criminal underworld. When the god dies, according to Jung, he goes down to the secret depths of the underworld, there to be transformed. Eddie, the tragic hero and semi-divine Oedipal figure, has been born into the underworld and remains there to play out his tragic story. Through a series of paradoxes *Eddie King* then becomes a kind of mirror image or perhaps dark reflection of classical tragic drama. Firstly, Eddie's fate is determined for him because he was born into a certain world. It is not directed by morally defined beings but by those most inimical to social morality. Secondly, the play begins with the solution to the mystery, whereas *Oedipus Rex* ends with it. Thirdly, in classical tragedy the act which sets the tragic process going must be primarily a violation of the moral law. By making his protagonist a criminal prior to the murder Aloni is twisting the validity of moral law. But then the paradox becomes less explicit: Eddie's universe is an immoral one, the negative of the upper, moral universe in that everything which is conventionally immoral is moral to "them", the gangsters. Therefore, Eddie's guilt is a problem. Is the sin, then, not murder but solely parricide, regicide or deicide – a sin common to both worlds?

One of the purposes of tragedy is catharsis brought about by the arousal of pity and terror in the viewer. Through placing his protagonists in the fearful American gangsterland Aloni alienates his audience, restricts the emotions of pity and terror and the ultimate catharsis, for Eddie – the gangster not the parricide – receives his just deserts. Aloni is playing games with tragic form, diminishing the elements of tragedy by inverting them, by stressing opposing values: an evil world as a setting for tragic action instead of a moral one, bad gods instead of good ones, a criminal hero with whom no audience can identify or suffer. "The tragic hero has normally had an extraordinary, often nearly divine destiny almost within his grasp."[12] Eddie's destiny is no more nor less what is expected for a man of his type: there is no surprise and there is nothing extraordinary in the outcome of his story.

[12] Northrop Frye: "The Mythos of Autumn". *Tragedy – Modern Essays in Criticism*, ed. Michel and Sewell. Prentice-Hall, 1962.

Aloni is without doubt the most controversial figure in the Israeli theatre. Biblical heroes long ago ceased to be sufficient for him and he began to seek a new hero. He seems, for the meantime at least, to have found him: his pathetic little man aspiring to kingship. Also, by returning to mythology, to the celebrated collective unconscious, Aloni seems to be on the right path in terms of dramatic creativity. Audiences, however, do not understand him. They are fascinated by his entertainment, the colour, spectacle and music, but that is all.

The question to be asked is whether the Israeli theatre can permit itself the luxury of this kind of esotericism, pandering to the chosen few. Its audience is still, after only three decades, in the process of education. They have not moved with the theatre in a natural line of evolution to its natural conclusion in the modern theatre of protest and paradox, Brustein's term. This is, however, a moot point, preoccupying many of the writers and critics in Israel. Not so the comment made by Boaz Evron[13] in his criticism of *Eddie King*:

> "All these pleasures do not eliminate the rude question, whether the theatre subsidised by public funds is entitled to give any playwright a blank cheque for exercises like [*Eddie King*]. Rumours about the size of the amount spent on this project, whose artistic value is very debatable, specify sums of a half a million to one and a half million *lirot*. In my opinion, sums like this from the public pocket, not from the pocket of an eccentric millionnaire, in a country in such a situation as ours – are scandalous . . . If he had been offered an absolutely limited budget and production time – that should he exceed it the contract would be nullified – it is possible that this would force him to be organised and clearer."

He goes on to say that the management of Habimah must consider whether the rope (free rein) they have given Aloni is not so long that he will hang himself with it.

When the critics judge plays by such criteria, their *monetary* value, the Israeli theatre is indeed in trouble. Admittedly there must be a limit and it seems certain that the very capable managements are aware of this. Aloni does not appear to be the type of popular entertainer who will waste money on spectacle for its own sake. The criteria of "organised" and "clearer" (מאורגן וברור יותר) are too subjective to be considered. By whose standards are these qualities to be judged? The critics' function is to analyse a theatrical presentation in terms of their own superior knowledge of the art form – in comparison with that of the average audience – and this knowledge is always, and more often than not mistakenly, attributed to them by their readers. The critics' function is not to decide how much a production should cost. The public will in any case eventually let the playwright know when they are no longer prepared to continue paying for "exercises" like *Eddie King*, simply by staying away from the theatre. So far they are not doing so while an Aloni play is on the boards.

[13] *Yediot Achronot*, June 5th 1975.

3 *The Inn of Ghosts*

Not all experiments have been by way of the popular Absurd and one modern play in particular was unusual in its style and evocation of a legendary environment in the tradition of the great masters of imaginative fiction: the poet Nathan Alterman's *The Inn of Ghosts* (Cameri, 1962), which was ahead of its time in the Israeli context because of its lyricism – befitting a famous and well-loved poet – and its mixture of genres.

If the fine distinction may be drawn, *The Inn of Ghosts* is even more "universal" than Aloni's *The King's Clothes* for it is an allegory founded on original material not well-known folklore, with an exposition that moves into realms of philosophical abstraction also new to Israeli drama. It deals with a variety of themes: the alienation of the artist from customary life, his essential homelessness, his search for fulfilment, various types and qualities of love. It is also in part a Brecht-like satire on modern society which has turned art into a consumer commodity and artists into objects of snobbish adulation while the artists themselves are presented as ghosts occupying an inn at the crossroads.

The three acts of *The Inn of Ghosts* express the past, present and future in the fate of one man and emphasise the tyranny of time in the lives of all mankind. Hananel is a young violinist who decides to abandon his mistress, Naomi, in order to seek his fortune as a concert artist. He has come to realise that art, not love, is his pre-ordained destiny, that he has no other choice for his talent has committed him, leaving him no alternative but to accede to its demands no matter where they lead him.

Hananel: I cannot but go from here tonight, to the purpose of my life. For this I was created.

Act One, therefore, represents the future. Hananel has made his decision inasmuch as it is his to make; he sets his face against what is to come and prepares to venture out onto the road, filled with expectation and ambition, yet there is an inevitability about his action foreshadowing the inevitability of his fate. In order to assist him Naomi sells herself into bondage to a money-changer for a period of twelve years. The money-changer's son is an intense young man who is almost mad with love for her. Hananel promises her that he will return to redeem her in twelve years' time, come what may. He takes up his violin and leaves her.

On the first day of his travels he reaches an inn at the crossroads and meets, among others, a fortune-teller and a beggar whom he believes to be Death and who becomes his impresario. There is also the innkeeper, a beautiful woman who exists only when a man looks at her with desire. The inn itself is at the point of juncture between Hananel's immediately past decision and what still awaits him, midway between his aspiration and its realisation. The beautiful innkeeper is a symbol of the present, the ephemeral "now", for her rule is solely the moment: when one looks away from her she vanishes.

Innkeeper: Among all the vision's people
I am one the future owes nothing
keeps nothing for her and gives her nothing
I am one in whom the end of the story
dwells in her today, at this moment.

Together the beggar, Hananel and the innkeeper set out on the road towards Hananel's success. At the inn the spirits "live" on, discussing art in the most intellectually jargonised terms reminiscent of modern academia, but on examination the entire discussion is abstract nonsense that sounds impressive but has no meaning. They have two visitors, a lady and a gentleman dressed for a concert, who seek out the artists in order to offer them their gratitude for giving their lives significance: "Our complete and true life/is the life of art!"

Lady: Thanks to him, to them, thanks to all the many different
performers there is meaning in our worldly lives . . .

– meaning channelled through others' ability to explore life's mysteries in terms of artistic beauty.

The beggar proves himself a successful impresario and Hananel begins to satisfy the demands of his artistic soul, the matter, as the beggar explains,

that is its own source
and its own purpose
and needs no reckoning
with the laws of man or God
the creating spirit and the virtues of art, pay attention, listen,
these dinars will be spread, will melt, will not leave
footsteps of blood, nor fingerprints and with them
the memory and purpose within them will disintegrate and from all this
will remain one unending thing
that the entire world will thank you for
the power of a righteous God that is in you, the blessing of the highest
that touched your fingers . . .

Hananel becomes a famous violinist, an idol of music lovers, darling of the concert halls yet he is aware that even having attained the success he has always yearned for he is still unhappy, imprisoned by his art, tied with its handcuffs for, as the beggar declares, "the loneliness of the artist's destiny is a prison cell in which he is chained . . ." There is no reward for it and no end to it. This, then, is the future realised, an inversion of the perspective of the first act, the obligation of the past discharged. Hananel has achieved his ruthless purpose, pushed on by his fate and yet something is missing from his life.

There is a certain parallel between his situation and that of Naomi for both are bound by chains of compulsion. She is the slave of the money-changer's son, who desires her and hopes to wrest her love by torture, while Hananel is as much a slave to his relentless public. But here the parallel ends: Naomi is sustained in her trial by her unshakeable devotion to Hananel and her faith in their meeting in some years' time. He, through the total egoism of the artist, has forgotten her in the pursuit of his art although he does acknowledge that something vital is lacking in his life – not the transitory sexual fulfilment the inkeeper offers him, passion carrying with it the shadow of decay, but true and abiding romantic love. But his inexorable fate demands that his existence be art alone and love may make no demands on him.

In his insane jealousy the money-changer's son seeks Hananel in order to kill him and then claim Naomi as his own. However, when he realises that Hananel scarcely thinks of her he abandons his search, for it has become clear to him that Naomi will love Hananel whether or not he is faithful to her or whether he lives or dies. Meanwhile Naomi grows weak and ill, but her hope and faith burgeon as the appointed day draws near.

The time comes for the two to meet. The innkeeper attempts to dissuade Naomi and the money-changer's son brings policemen to arrest her on a false charge so that she might be prevented from meeting her lover but all to no avail. At this very moment Hananel has reached the very pinnacle of his artistry, having given a performance which is almost mystic in its perfection.

It happened this night!
I have waited only for this all these years.
How can I say it . . . perhaps like this . . . as if Art
ceased suddenly . . . broke suddenly beneath me
and in her place her ancestor burst forth . . . no! herself
but yet another . . . as if she is nothing

but the world, darkness and joy singing her aloud . . .
singing her . . . not her, them, but they, her . . .
and this filled me
with knowledge of uselessness
and with strength I hadn't known
a power that spread, carried me to it, threw,
swept, flung, shoved, laughed . . . like a living woman . . .

He has not forgotten their appointment although its significance is lost to him for he believes that their worlds are now far apart; but music can be an expression of love and his magnificent triumph has occurred on their appointed evening. His performance has succeeded almost in blurring the limits of art. For one moment its perfection has allowed him to guess at eternity. He transcends himself and humanity – but this moment of his highest endeavour is also his breaking-point, for when he reaches the peak he learns, like Ibsen's Solness, of all he can never accomplish and that it is impossible for him to remain for long at the summit of his experience. His art has been no more than an imitation of love, serving merely as a substitute for it. Art is, according to Dr Eli Shavid, the "imitation of eternity in time".[1] Because art merely imitates life it is false (Pirandello's "form" as opposed to "life") and Hananel must therefore fail as a man for he has sought to reach by means of the counterfeit what he has not been able to attain through the truth of love. This is the meaning of his fate as an artist and Alterman's expression of insight into the artist's lonely destiny as the intermediary between creativity (the innate perception of hidden truth) and the material world. Naomi has found her fulfilment in her abiding love for Hananel and therefore, despite her suffering, she is the more fortunate of the two. Hananel discovers another bleak anomaly of the artist's fate: the moment in performance which touches that almost sacred exaltation is instantly past and he must struggle to rise to it again, seldom reaching absolute satisfaction through this need to press ever onwards to the re-creation of that splendour.

[1] *The Inn of Ghosts* by Eli Shavid. *Bamah* 20, Winter 1964.

Hananel returns to Naomi. She perceives immediately that he cannot say the words that would finally declare his love for her; without regret or hesitation she grants him a further twelve years. Once again he leaves her and Naomi, weak and totally spent, is at last taken by the beggar. But Hananel's thirst for the future has ceased. His life has lost its meaning and begins to wane as his artistic spirit – represented by a strange symbol, the monkey – also sickens and dies. Everything has already been and the love that served as his inspiration is dead. He wants only to find Naomi again. He wanders aimlessly for years until the appointed time, where at their house Naomi is waiting for him as young and beautiful as she used to be; but she is dead and only her love exists as something tangible and real. Her life, unlike his, has been meaningful, finding its fulfilment in her years of unbreakable devotion to him.

Alterman's play is based on the most romantic of ideas: art and love, both of them themes recurring in his poetry, now woven together as a mixture of prose and poetry and complex symbolism in a carefully controlled structure based on a simple fable. He has created a visionary land with no name or geographical location, peopled by the very denizens of legend: a beautiful girl who dies for love of a dedicated young musician; the animals of fable who assume human qualities; slaves and hand-maidens, an organ-grinder (always a sinister image in Romantic poetry), a beggar-impresario reminiscent of Dr Miracle or Coppelius or Mephisto. Ghosts living at an inn on the crossroads come alive at midnight, a beautiful temptress disappears unless a man beholds her, and ends her days as an ugly hag when her lover leaves her. The periods enclosing the action are magical as well: seven years and twelve years. Naomi falls into an enchanted sleep induced by some mysterious balm and Hananel carries his violin, an object frequently invested with demonic power in Romantic fiction. On this Alterman superimposes modern elements which do not suit the world of legend but which make their point, for they deal with ephemerality of a different sort: the world of the concert hall, newspapers, critics, audiences, sensation-seekers and social "lions" and above all the academic theorists whose creativity is contrived and useless sham.

Sin and retribution are secondary themes of *The Inn of Ghosts* for it stresses the belief that guilt accompanies all of human existence, especially the attempt to escape the reckoning of the past. Alterman stated, in a discussion of the play,[2] that sin and retribution dominate all areas of life except the spiritual world of creativity where the power of sin is diminished. "In this [creative] world only the results are taken into account and these justify themselves without the ways and means to them being of importance." Hananel's guilt lies primarily in his spiritual incapacity for any love other than self-love. Even his music cannot satisfy for he has taken from it and not invested himself in it. True artistic exaltation cannot be attained if the artist is not faithful to the artistic impulse itself. If this is rejected (Naomi) and peripheral advantages are sought (fame and public adoration) the artist must fail in his quest for the ideal. Naomi,

[2] *Davar*, December 24th 1962.

Hananel's creative impetus, is also the element of love, implying that love and sensitivity must kindle the creative flame. Without deeply felt human emotion there can be no artistic expression. Hananel ends his days in search of the principle he rejected, realising too late that any achievement without it must be a hollow fraud.

In contrast to his self-deluded but honestly inspired quest for artistic truth appear those characters whose approach to all artistic manifestations is acquisitive and artificial. Music, for example, has become an Event. Far from constituting an integral and indefinable element of people's lives music and art are no more than spectacle, an excuse for impressive intellectualisation, a means of meeting the famous and achieving vicarious excitement through them. Alterman's long dialogue between the ghosts on the subject of art is a masterful parody of contemporary theorising, abounding in anglicisms, jargon and non-sequiturs:

. . . the fear of the ecstasy[3] of entering
into – why don't they give us coffee –
cessation. This morning it took me like . . .
everything I say will be an understatement[3] . . . like something
apocalyptic[3] revealed to me in elliptical[3] form,
paraboloid,[3] empty . . . or like what I feel
when I grasp, for example, in the poem
"This It and That It", the couplet in which
suddenly the pseudo-iamb[3] is shattered . . .

[3]anglicism.

and so on, a mockery of our academic pretensions. One of the spirits is a playwright and, having decided that words are redundant, merely the outer skin of a work whereas the punctuation is its body, has composed a tragedy in punctuation alone.

Spirit 3: Would you like to hear some of it?
Spirits 1 & 2: Let's hear, let's hear.
Spirit 3 takes out a crumpled piece of paper. Spreads it out and declaims suddenly: Comma!
Puts the paper back in his pocket.
Spirits 1 & 2: What? What?
Spirit 3: Comma. That's the prologue.
Spirit 1: Yes, it has a certain mood. How many acts like this have you already completed?
Spirit 2: Perhaps we could hear the entire tragedy?
Spirit 3: No. This prologue has left me without strength.

It is not surprising that many of Alterman's colleagues found his play offensive.

Hananel is the archetypal Romantic hero, single-minded in his quest for perfection like Ibsen's heroes labouring under "the claim of the ideal" or, like Hedda Gabler, aspiring to the pure Dionysiac ecstasy of wearing vine-leaves in his hair. Art holds him in glorious bondage, demanding total sacrifice and offering little satisfaction in return. He discovers that the artist is alienated from normal life and from his society, bereft of a real or spiritual home. Worse even than that, his worldly success is achieved at the price of the death of his soul. Hananel searches constantly for fulfilment yet finds nothing other than an even greater duress. He has to make a clear choice between art and love: grasping at one he loses the other. Both demand absolute subservience and he believes that no man can pledge himself to both together.

Many different kinds of love are represented in the play: that of Naomi, the abiding love, the very existence of which is its own fulfilment, the love borne by every dying romantic heroine; the innkeeper is the symbol of transitory love, growing old and faded when men cease looking at her with desire. The money-changer's son represents selfish love. Each type of love has a parallel in the play: the innkeeper and Naomi, two opposite sides of the same coin; the innkeeper and the money-changer's son representing passion without spirit; the money-changer's son and Hananel, both of them selfish and demanding. The love of the innkeeper is a substitute for that of Naomi; the inn is the substitute for the home; seeking fame and honour is a substitute for an artist's lonely destiny and art itself, the lie, is a substitute for life.

Almost everything in the play is a symbol of something else. The beggar-impresario is, like Faust's Mephistopheles, a sinister companion granting success (but not love) in exchange for the soul. He is also, like Lorca's beggar-woman in *Blood Wedding*, death itself. The inn represents the spiritual homelessness of the artist and the ephemeral present, the uncertain link between the positive facts of past and future, the symbol of chance and fleeting love. The road, a frequent image in Alterman's poetry, is fate, the hope of arrival, the continued anticipation that pulls a man without any kind of recompense, for he never reaches its end. The ghosts at the inn symbolise abstract and ridiculous intellectualism. Naomi is the artistic impetus, the internal truth that Hananel imitates. The monkey is the symbol of the irrational, uncontrollable impulse in the life of man and his creative spirit. Even the violin and the organ-grinder's barrel-organ have their place in the jigsaw of symbolism. Dr Shavid calls them "imitations". This, he says, is the secret of the organ-grinder, the parrot and the monkey who hand out fortunes:

the existence of imitation is common to all of them. The organ imitates music, the paper fortunes are monkey-like imitations of tragic destiny and the monkey and the parrot are imitations of man, just as art is the ultimate imitation of life. Above all the story itself is a symbol: none of the events are directed by psychological need but they are part of the inevitability of legend. Certain things must come to pass in this world of fairy tale predetermination and the characters are at the mercy of magical forces which have placed them on the road and set their footsteps towards its destination. Similarly characterisation in *The Inn of Ghosts* is not dramatically self-determined, arising from necessity of character and situation, but subject only to the terms of the fable. The play is therefore abstract, often obscure and leaves the reader frequently bewildered. One cannot become involved in the tragedy of lovers or in Hananel's aspirations, for the characters are moving like marionettes restricted by the fingers above them and the audience is alienated and impartial. It is a drama for the intellect not for the emotions or senses. Initially it was coolly received for this reason and also because its actors were not able to manage the poetry. Due to their inexperience with poetic drama they declaimed Alterman's verse in true romantic style so that the dialogue became stilted and unnatural, and this too served to transform the characters into no more than static mouthpieces for abstract ideas, pushing the play back in time into the dramatic conventions of the nineteenth century despite its modern and relevant subject matter.

Many comparisons can be made between *The Inn of Ghosts* and other works, Ibsen's *Peer Gynt* and *Brand* in particular, the Faust legend, the plays of Maeterlinck and Brecht and those stories of Thomas Mann that deal with the alienation of the artist from life. The play is a composite of many styles of writing – Romantic on the one hand, expressionistic on the other, as in the scenes of the ghosts' conversation, with hints of epic realism in the songs, poems, the stylisation of performance, lectures about art and tales and parables within the play.

The play opened in December, 1962 at the Cameri Theatre. Apparently the audience was restive and unenthusiastic. The actors themselves complained that they had never heard so many coughs and fidgets from a first-night audience, and the applause at the end was no more than a dutiful mark of respect for the well-known poet Nathan Alterman. Dr Haim Gamzu, long feared as powerful and outspoken and compared to Kenneth Tynan and Jean-Jacques Gautier, praised the play but tore into the production and the acting

[4] *Haaretz*, January 1st 1963.

in the most acerbic terms.[4] The Cameri Theatre considered Gamzu's review an unwarranted attack exceeding the bounds of legitimate criticism, leading the theatre's manager, the producer and the author to write bitter articles denouncing the critic from both a professional and personal point of view. Then articles were written attacking these criticisms; everything and everyone connected with the production of *The Inn of Ghosts* were included in the quarrel: the actress Hannah Meron, the Cameri's previous productions, Alterman's previous play, but *The Inn of Ghosts* itself was hardly mentioned because all the combatants agreed that as a play it was, with certain qualifications , excellent. This controversy is of minor importance as far as the history of Israeli theatre is concerned, but it does raise a most vital point, encountered time and again in any study of Israeli theatrical criticism, concerning critical method. This point will be discussed later, in the chapter devoted to criticism generally.

4 Hanoch Levin

In a country that thrives on theatrical controversy no one has yet exceeded Hanoch Levin's achievement as the most controversial figure on the Israeli stage. This *enfant terrible* began his career in 1968 at the age of 24 with a revue entitled *You and I and the Next War* which was presented in a students' club. The revue cut through the national euphoria following the Six Day War by accusing and attacking the so-called makers of war in Israel. The 1969/70 season saw his third satirical revue *Queen of the Bathtub* at the Cameri Theatre and it was, as Mendel Kohansky has noted, a ferociously biting satire of a kind the theatre in Israel had never seen before. It was a castigation not only of Israeli society in general but also of Israeli youth, the Government, the Military and the Establishment. It attacked bureaucratic self-righteousness, political inefficiency and family relationships. It was, in fact, the other side of the coin of national self-congratulation and complacency. "The curious part of it," Kohansky says, "was that the show was not presented in some students' basement but on the stage of the ultra-respectable Cameri Theatre which was about to become the theatre of the city of Tel Aviv. Though individual members of the government publicly expressed their negative opinion the authorities scrupulously kept their hands off. The Cameri eventually took the 'Queen' off the boards under the pressure of public opinion as expressed primarily in the press."[1] This was after its announcement to the press that although it did not necessarily agree with the playwright's sentiments it reserved for itself the right to present the play. This statement added more fuel to the fire of controversy already raging around the production. Press comment was not unanimously negative and much of the academic criticism was based not on the performed revue but on the unpublished text. A great deal of what critics and teachers were complaining about had already been expurgated before production, either by the Censorship Board or by the playwright himself, but public opinion was roused by the performed play. Criticism of the revue was on the whole not balanced, verging on the hysterical both pro- and anti-Levin; the mildest of Levin's detractors accused him merely of the low standard of his literature or of banality; the most violent, of presenting excrement and putrefaction on the stage. One critic, Moshe ben Shaul of *Maariv*, complained that when he praised *Queen of the Bathtub* he suffered insults and vilification even from those thought to be liberal.[2]

[1] *Israel Theatre 1969/70*, published by the Israel Centre of the ITI, 1971.

[2] *Maariv*, March 13th 1975.

[3]The first was *Solomon Grip*, 1969.

Levin's second full-length play *Hefetz*[3] (Haifa Municipal Theatre, 1972) swung much of the critical evaluation into his corner. Comment on the play was rational, based on sound dramatic and theatrical criteria. As venerated a writer as Uri Rapp gave the play serious consideration, calling it a relevant work of art.

In terms of the Israeli theatre it is a relevant work of art. It examines and dissects a middle-class family and their lodger Hefetz. The play deals with the interrelationship of mother, father, daughter, son-in-law-to-be and lodger. Its themes are said to be triumphant self-esteem within a family, the alienation of every man from the other and, a topic dear to Levin's heart, mockery of the "ideal" or idealised Israeli youth. These themes and characters are repeated in his subsequent plays *Jacoby and Leidenthal* (given in England in 1974 under the title *Dominoes*), *Vardaleh's Youth* and *Shitz*.

The situation in *Hefetz* is expounded through its characters, with a sense of loathing not often encountered on the Israeli stage. Levin hates his characters too much to permit objective assessment of them or, in fact, of his plays. He hates them too much for true creative objectivity. His people are grotesque, in keeping with his chosen genre, but without the lurking sense of compassion that distinguishes the masterpieces of the Absurd. The characters seem to be too rooted in the playwright's own psyche to become symbolic, as for example do Albee's families, of a society as a whole. "Mommy" in *The American Dream* is no more lovable than Levin's Clamansea or Ruth Shachash or Vardaleh's mother and we can cheerfully hate her in her role of tormentor of "Granny". But she is the representative of one part of American society, recognisable in many satirical novels and plays as a problematical element within the family. In *Hefetz* each character is as he is, wallowing in a kind of mindless viciousness with no one like "Granny" or "Daddy" to redeem or explain it and no past to bear on it.

Levin's play follows in every detail the precepts of the Absurd – so much so that it is almost a definition of the genre. It was written in the wake of political unrest and military upheaval, similar in some ways to the environment of the French Absurdists who had witnessed at first hand the military defeat and then the occupation of France. He presents a world in which man is lost, without identity, purpose or understanding. There is no communication or affection. The characters are base, loveless and ugly. Their actions are underlined by a comic commentary which is funny to watch or read but not at all funny in implication.

The question must be asked: is Levin saying anything that has not been said before by the masters of the Absurd? The answer is that he is not, but he is making his statement in a different environment and directing his dramatic fable at an audience which has never before been a target for this particular kind of castigation. Absurd drama presupposes that the viewer is immediately aware of the universality suggested by the action, despite any specific locale or nationally recognisable characters in the play. Levin has not localised *Hefetz* to the extent of referring to anything recognisably Israeli or even Jewish. From his subsequent plays as from *Queen of the Bathtub* the audience can *assume* that *Hefetz* is about Israel and the Israelis; the *dramatis personae* have strange names with frankly Yiddish overtones, yet nothing in the play is strictly identifiable with Israel and place names are never mentioned. Levin is, then, not obviously indicating modern Israel or the modern Israeli family: he is showing a family in a place in our time and it serves merely to restate the Absurd ideology that man is lost, without identity, communication or affection. He neither asks nor answers questions. Because of its anti-realism Absurd action becomes ritualised action, but the ritual is often without clear purpose and dependent for its communication of "message" on verbal and visual symbolism. Pinter's plays, for example, have an abundance of logical symbolism and their poetry lies not only in the diction but in their structure. Themes and symbols interweave with the patterned regularity of ritual in their distorted treatment of reality. *Hefetz* lacks the rich imagery of Ionesco, Beckett, Genet or Pinter although there are certain symbols which are important in the play, for example, Levin has clearly intended the variety of hats and clothes his characters wear to serve a symbolic purpose. He dwells a great deal on legs and feet and the major anatomical attribute of the earth-mother type who is the star of *Jacoby and Leidenthal* is already alluded to in *Hefetz*. His visual and linguistic symbolism is not rich nor poetic yet the play's principal metaphor is its most powerful element, dominating the structure, the characterisation and the language: the entire drama is a ritual of sacrifice and its climax is the appeasement of the goddess or priestess through the sacrifice of every other character in the play. Within the larger ritual is the appeasement of the lesser characters by the sacrifice of Hefetz. Confession and release are mockingly stressed in a childish formula: confess and give in. Hefetz is the scapegoat whose death will allow the others the freedom they crave. His demise binds them all and becomes the deciding factor in their lives. Their silly, miserable aspirations may be realised once he has gone as if he, in fact, stands in the way of their realisation. Hannah, the waitress, states that his tragedy will sweeten her fate because he is so much worse off than she is; Adash the perpetual hypochondriac derives strength from Hefetz' misery: "How he is going to suffer in a little while! One can burst! What is my suffering in my bed as against what's going to happen to him soon!" Hefetz will be in his dark grave while Teiglach, the father, runs from nightclub to nightclub; Clamansea, the mother, will be free to stroll with her grandchildren (is this a reference to the famous photograph of Golda Meir pushing her grandchild's perambulator?) over Hefetz' buried body. Hannah will eventually find love. Adash will regain his health for the implication is that Hefetz' death and the manner of it will give him something to recover from. Varshviak, the fiancé, will eat his fill. Shukra, the friend, can abuse Hefetz without fear of contradiction.

It is not only that these people are measuring their lives against Hefetz' death, but they are seeing themselves mirrored in him and their self-imposed obstacles to their enjoyment of life will die with his death. His weakness, impotence, dullness is a frank reflection of their own. Once he is out of the way they can return to their illusions and the panaceas that make their lives bearable. Only once does Levin abandon his cynical condemnation of each one of his characters when he makes Fogra, the daughter, say, after each of the others has declaimed on the benefit Hefetz' death will bring: "I feel that there is a need for pity in this room like air for breathing . . ." – Levin's comment on the lowliness of our aspirations, and the only moment of human warmth in the whole play.

The intended efficacy of sacrificial ritual is hinted at constantly throughout the play but is always perverted. In Hefetz' death there is release for the characters from their personal barriers to life but further bondage for all of them to Fogra; there is the possibility of rebirth or regeneration – but Adash and Hannah call off their engagement and Fogra does not marry Varshviak before the play's end. Ritual and sacrifice ironically lead only to further sterility, like in Aloni's plays.

Levin's people are stupid, vicious, ugly, selfish and helpless. They are also childlike in the most obvious and offensive manner. In fact the whole play stresses the elements of childishness in the behaviour of its characters. Fogra emerges as the bully, terrorising the other children into submission by virtue of physical superiority and braggadocio. Her wretched victim is the weakest in the group. The "children" constantly play games. First of all there is the make-believe through which Clamansea and Teiglach confront Hefetz with insalubrious episodes from his past. Then there is the dressing-up, the assumption of costume exemplifying the present role. Levin is careful to stress in detail his characters' dress with special emphasis on their hats, which appear to assume a revelatory significance. Fogra's trampling of her father's hat is indicative of her contempt for him. She also refuses to don the bridal veil which is carried for her on a broomstick, always within sight.

The "children" fight for recognition among themselves, their diction faithfully echoing childish squabbling

Hefetz: So who will come with me on the roof I'd like to know.
Adash: And who will mend my heart after your news?
Hefetz: No, no! Who'll come with *me! me! me!*
Adash: Who'll fix me up! *Me! me! me!*
Hefetz: No, me, me, me, me!
Adash: Me, Me!

And so they continue. Later on:

Teiglach: Quiet!
Hefetz: I don't want to, I don't want to, I don't want to. I don't want to!

There is generally a great deal of weeping and Adash plays ill in order to avoid participation in life although he becomes well enough to do what he wants to do. Ceremonies and oaths are also reminiscent of childhood "gangs" or "clubs". Fogra's swearing in of her mother is a shocking, strongly written climax in the play for not only is it the culmination of Fogra's hideous domination but it has the frightening intensity of children's fetishes – the oaths that may not be broken for fear of dreadful but unknown consequences. At one stage Adash actually rides a four-wheeled cart reminiscent of a children's go-kart or even a perambulator. The characters seem to descend into infantile mindlessness as the play progresses. Each one of them ceases to exist except as an instrument of Fogra's victory.

Fogra herself is the most strongly drawn character in the play. She is a satire, a kind of Nazi-youth type, proud of her physical and sexual superiority, convinced of her right to dominate, contemptuous of everyone else. Her relentless persecution never lets up. She forms the central symbol of the play, the earth-mother-priestess who consumes everyone in sight. She is extended in the central female characters of Levin's next two plays *Jacoby and Leidenthal* and *Vardaleh's Youth*. It is difficult to assess her meaning to Levin. It has been suggested that she stands for the post-1948 idealisation of Israel's perfect youth; or that she represents authoritarianism, even fascism, the master as opposed to the slave; that she is an embodiment of Levin's anti-feminism, or the typical Jewish child pampered and adored by fatuous parents; or the mother, unyielding, cruel, lacking in all compassion and understanding. None of this rings entirely true for she is too malevolent, too overdone, almost hysterically written, to be a stereotype or an archetype. She may be the symbol of universal female domination or she may be an idiosyncratic invention relevant only to Levin's personal creative need. Like all the other characters she remains static, simply repeating her own definition so that the viewer or reader feels a sense of overkill and the impact is lost.

Hefetz is, however, the archetypal Absurd victim. He appears as the obstacle to everyone's ideal and his sacrificial death releases them to live out their miserable lives without hindrance. His death is highly melodramatic, a satirical reference to the preordained end of the tragic hero. Had he not died the play's sense of futility would have been heightened and its intrinsic Absurdity preserved. For his hesitation at the end is the logical culmination of his life: cowardly, weak and typical, whereas his death to a certain extent ennobles him. His wavering at the end has comic qualities: "I'm really sorry, after all the talking and preparation . . . it's not that I want to live, but . . . it's simply hard . . . you're not angry, okay? I'll make it up to you, you'll see, really, I mean to live from now on like a rag, you'll all enjoy it. Maybe I'll even go mad in a little while. That's also something, isn't it? . . . Yes, yes, I'm sure I'll go mad! You'll see . . ." This pleading, the promises, the formula of "you'll see" is the final reversion to childhood but the female adult tormentor, the eternal mother, is adamant. Hefetz is slung off the roof and he dies.

The entire play is nihilistic. The often repeated accusation of nihilism levelled against other Israeli playwrights and poets is justified in this case. *Hefetz* is the story of destruction: of self, of others, of love, of companionship, of family, of marriage, of relationship, of communication. It is not that man is nothing, but Levin shows the process by which his people dehumanise themselves and make themselves nothing. In many instances he rouses his viewers' sympathy and then immediately destroys it with some new cruelty, such as the revelation of Hefetz' perversion, his "peeping", or Adash's rejection of Hannah after one has come to expect at least one possibility of salvation.

Levin has a masterly feel for wry and penetrating humour. In keeping with the Absurd the characters' behaviour is basically funny as is their dress and speech. Levin's satirical comments are plentiful, and his irony is magnificent.

Teiglach: This is the main advantage of married life: the wife breaks all the laws of justice for her husband's benefit. How good it is to be married!

Adash: I know that if a doctor laughs it's a sign that I'm going to die. Otherwise what makes him laugh?

In his complaint about allergies he speaks of water, birds, flowers, fruit – the beauties of nature. "All of these things," he declares, "come from nature, that poems are written about and look what they do to me." The diction is, in all cases, Absurd. Levin always demonstrates his effective manipulation of language, as in the argument between Hannah and Hefetz in Scene 6 which ends nowhere. Hefetz has ordered milk for his coffee and Hannah, who is exhausted and overworked, has pleaded with him to fetch it himself. The ensuing argument has at this point already continued for about five minutes:

Hefetz: Yes, but I'm not the waiter here, Okay? Understand that I am sitting in the café in order to be served, so that I don't have to help myself. Because if I have to be my own waiter in the café I'd rather not drink at all.

Hannah: So then perhaps.

Hefetz: What.

Hannah: Don't drink.

Hefetz: So why did I sit down in the café?

Hannah: How should I know?

Hefetz: Pardon me but my coffee is getting cold. May I have some milk?

However, as in most contemporary Israeli plays there is too much talking. Levin in *Hefetz* had not yet achieved the refinement and condensation of language that he demonstrated brilliantly in his later plays *Vardaleh's Youth* and, especially, *Shitz*.

More often than not Levin takes his characters too seriously and without humour they become meaningless, simply melodramatic portraits of strange people. Clamansea (whose name is also indicative of meaninglessness – merely letters of the alphabet in serial order), Teiglach and Shukra are written totally without humour, unless humour is honest burlesque without any kind of satirical meaning, which reduces the comedy to the level of slapstick. If Levin's intention is to portray specific people then his play is not more than a lampoon. A playwright can of course present a certain personality type and then attempt to reach a conclusion about him; Levin merely offers people who for the most part do not embody universal characteristics and whose eccentricities become funny in themselves but without didactic purpose. Ophrat[4] claims that Levin has managed to turn his caricatures into symbols (p. 233). The question

[4]Gidon Ophrat. *The Israeli Drama*. Hebrew University Press, 1975.

remains: symbols of what, if not a restatement of the eternal symbols of the Absurd?

Little thematic progress is made in *Jacoby and Leidenthal* which achieved tremendous success in a combined Tzavta-Cameri production which ran for over a year (1973–74) although its characters and setting are similar to those in *Hefetz*. The play is an attack on women, specifically the large, soft motherly woman whose only task is to castrate her men in order to subjugate them. In *Vardaleh's Youth* Levin dehumanises the characters even further by using the expressionist technique of designating titles to them rather than names: the mother, the cook, the gardener, the lover, and so on. Only Vardaleh herself is given a name and in character she is an extension of Fogra but carried to extreme: remote and unattainable, giving meaning to the lives of those whose only aspiration is to reach her. The major criticism of this and his next play was that his characters are all uniformly negative, that he allows no light at all on the blackness of human existence nor any possibility at all of redemption.

In *Shitz* Levin's anger seems to reach a peak. He returns to the overt satire of *Queen of the Bathtub* and castigates his society for its preoccupation with materialism and consumerism at the expense of all other values. This, too, is not an original idea in terms of satire on European and "Anglo-Saxon" social behaviour, but it is the first time that Israel has been accused so directly from the stage of gorging itself on possessions. Levin's symbolism in this play is likewise unoriginal, however shocking it may seem. He concentrates almost exclusively on all digestive processes – eating, digesting, flatulence, vomiting and defaecation with blatant sexual activity thrown in as well. His characters' names sound like explosions of disgust and are indicative of his own loathing for them as representatives of the objects of his satire: the people around him. Fefechtz Shitz is the father, Tzeshah the mother, Sprachtzi, the daughter, and Charches, her flatulent husband. The play is about cupidity and sterility, impotence and death. The setting is still the family, the same loveless, ugly group first encountered in *Hefetz*. One has the feeling very often that Levin is climbing onto the fashionable bandwagon of the New Left with the designation of all gain as filth and all men as no more than shit. Here and there are faint echoes of Brecht, in the play's structure and the titles of the songs, but no moral message is derived from it except by inference and the alienation is brought about purely by the eccentric character-drawing with which there can be no identification of any kind even for purely didactic purposes. Here, too, Levin shows the childish elements in his approach. His anger is directed at the "grownups" in charge of his society and he sees them as grotesque, disfigured, disgusting people who engage in nothing but the basic physical activities. Children of a certain age are preoccupied with anatomy, with genitalia and their own names for them. Big Tuches (*Jacoby and Leidenthal*) is something a child would snigger at, reference to faecal matter, something else. All of Levin's characters are enormous in their grotesquerie, as a child would see them, noting the most prominent of their anatomical and behavioural idiosyncrasies. Levin's message may be one of nihilistic despair, or New Left conviction or Absurd warning, but his approach is that of an angry child in a hostile adult world.

Levin's plays are a necessary part of Israel's developing drama. Even though they are not totally original he is at least presenting the authentic Absurd in Hebrew and showing sometimes recognisable characters to his audiences. Up to this point Israeli audiences have had to do with bad imitations or translations of Pinter, Beckett and others. Pinter's inarticulate, downtrodden working men or tramps or criminals cannot be re-rooted in the Israeli environment. Absurd diction is difficult to translate with maximum effectiveness. Levin has filled this need with original slangy, colloquial Hebrew diction and a kind of black humour which can be said to be black Jewish humour. For the most part Israeli critics still demand a "safe" drama, the well-made play with uncontroversial characters. Levin's shock value is enormous and whether or not it is nationally valid it at least opens the way to honest contemporary satire and a drama which may truly reflect Israeli reality, good and bad. But the essential requirement for this kind of drama is that it must be honest.

Levin is one of three new Israeli dramatists whose influence is growing despite the endless controversy that seems to follow every new play of theirs that invades the theatre. They are part of a generation which is coming to reject much of what was a staple foundation for the Israeli literature of the past. They have come to realise that the idealism that served the post-1948 writers is no longer of any value; it is anachronistic and has consequently been relegated to the status of myth which requires reduction because in the context of their time it has, in their opinion, become an absurdity.

Their subject matter has not changed very much, but the treatment of it is what distinguishes their work from that of their predecessors who were, first and foremost, romantics. The drama is still regional and sociological but the method of presenting contemporary reality has attained a serious level of abstraction. The major change is that the young dramatists are openly critical of issues which were never previously mentioned in the drama. They are politically orientated, writing from specific political standpoints and in fact dramatic criticism has followed suit by judging them not so much by their academic or intellectual ability but by their political outlook. This new generation of writers is concerned with shattering the old gods – the values and ideals which seem to them to be outdated and irrelevant, just as the ideals and values of the *Golah* were outdated to the generation of the Palmach. They are in open rebellion against the ideology which, they claim, has given rise to chauvinism and a dangerously misleading view of reality. They want to exhibit reality as they see it. Their drama, then, still does not transcend the *hevrah* or community to become a drama of the individual, but remains a national or social search for identity. Reality has altered, but the description of it is still what preoccupies the Israeli dramatists of the seventies. They have not shifted from the daily scene, although their means of expression have changed. Their drama has yet to mature to the extent of becoming a truly personal statement, although perhaps the social criticism – due to its frequent repetition in a multitude of forms – is beginning to exist in a "universal" sense, becoming a metaphor for social stress and the need for change. The danger of imitation is ever present. However shallow the earlier Hebrew plays might have been they were a positive attempt to find an expression worthy and representative of the people, and therefore they were Israeli plays. Now Israel is in danger of deserting these very definite foundations on which its theatre could build and adopting as its own drama the pretentious hymns to perversion that the European and British public swallow whole because they are supposed to be reflections of the reality of their time and themselves. They may very well be. But they are not a true reflection of Israel, and the Israeli playwrights have no right to graft onto their growing theatrical culture a diseased member which may eventually poison the whole.

5 *A Night in May*

Midway between the documentary drama of the fifties and the extremes of the sixties and seventies stands Abraham B. Yehoshua's strange play, *A Night in May* (Bimot, 1968), the night being one shortly preceding the outbreak of the Six-Day War. Matti Meged, in his introduction to the English translation of the play, summarises it thus: "... what stands out is [Yehoshua's] tendency to 'catch' his characters in extreme situations of nervous sensitivity to what goes on inside them or around them, to bring them together on the brink of some disaster or some pathological outburst of psychic forces which had been slumbering until the moment of this meeting, to sharpen the conflict between the over-stimulated memory and the unconscious tendency to forget and to insulate oneself against memories and their stimulations."

The emphasis, then, is no longer on the sociological or on any kind of broad social reality but on the psyche. The "extreme situation" in the case of this play is the imminent war of 1967. The narrow situation is the inner world of one house and its inhabitants, both permanent and temporary.

A radio – as was the case in Amichai's *Journey to Nineveh* – is the link between this inner world and the outer. Throughout the play it supplies bulletins about the military situation and the weather, interspersed with pieces of serious music (or the quasi-serious Swingle Singers, mentioned a number of times); the weather is hot and humid everywhere except in Jerusalem where the action of the play takes place. A number of people are gathered in a house in the Rehavia quarter and during the course of one night they examine themselves and their past lives in relation to each other. Nothing happens in the sense of dramatic action in the play; the movement is wholly interior, an endless movement of the mind going back on itself in ever-decreasing circles. There is no crisis in the play. The knowledge of war to come looms over the characters, pulling them further apart from each other instead of uniting them in a common cause.

Yehoshua's *A Night in May* has once and for all destroyed the old clichés so beloved of the Palmach writers, those of battle and its accompanying bravado, courage, enthusiasm, in fact everything which characterised the early war plays of the State was finally laid to rest in a series of ironic statements made by equally ironic characters.

Tirzah, her second husband, Assaf, her baby and her mother, Mrs Sarid, live in the Jerusalem house; her brother Avinoam arrives suddenly in Jerusalem from Tel Aviv, then her ex-husband, Amikam, his girl-friend, Noa, and finally Avinoam's mistress, Naomi. They congregate in this house and throughout the night they are shown, each in his personal isolation, withdrawing further away from reality so that finally only the voice on the radio remains to remind the audience that there is a world outside the convoluted interior of the room. This follows an accepted formula in modern drama, that of a few people being gathered together during a crisis and each revealing his own inner environment. In Robert Patrick's *Kennedy's Children* none of the characters was even aware of the others; each was shut into his own enclosure of memory. Here, although the characters acknowledge the presence of others and converse and touch and possibly even make love, there is no more contact between them than between the people in Patrick's New York bar.

The theme of the play, then, is isolation both of the self and of the enclosing world which in this case is the one room in the house. Once having entered it the characters seem unable to leave as if fixed to it, like Amichai's Jonah was in his great fish. They are bound to it by their own inertia and by the fear of what they might find outside. The coming war threatens them, but this is not the main source of their fear: their past is a far more threatening force, a vision more insupportable to most of them than the imminent cataclysm. It intrudes cruelly on the apparent tranquillity – or at least the quiet – of the present, laying bare the sham, fear and weakness in each individual.

Each of them is, in addition, suffering from madness to a greater or lesser degree. Tirzah's present husband, Assaf, is a psychiatrist who has never been confronted with this wide spectrum of neuroses and who escapes from them to the safety of his psychiatric hospital whenever possible. The character of Tirzah defines them all. She is middle-aged, tired, dry and empty. She forgets things; her absent-mindedness grows in the play to become withdrawal into fantasy, her brand of madness. Perhaps once she loved Amikam, her ex-husband, but now she cannot love at all. Even their renewed lovemaking is, according to her description, empty. Then Amikam reveals that they had not made love and so even her fantasy is sterile. Their marriage had in any case been barren – sterility had accompanied it, futility had ended it, Amikam's casual and meaningless affair with a stranger, leading to a separation and divorce which neither he nor his wife had wanted. "That whole time before the divorce is sunk in a kind of fog as if everything is covered by a gloomy cloud . . ." Their marriage and its end had brought nothing, neither sadness nor joy to either of them, only a sense of incompleteness, something unfinished . . . "I was cheated out of an ending . . . that's all." Tirzah's relationship with her present husband, Assaf, is not much warmer although they have managed to have a child who, significantly, is very quiet. He never cries nor demands attention, as if he were the living symbol of their own disinterest and lethargy. Tirzah is gradually moving toward the total insanity that has already claimed her mother. Her brother, Avinoam, is as neurotic as she, restless, childlike in his barely-suppressed hysteria, involved always in feverish and useless activity. His particular imprisonment is his need for protection and his love for Amikam which is obliquely referred to many times in the play. His hatred of Assaf, Amikam's replacement in his sister's bed, his treatment of Noa, his obvious attempt to restore Amikam to Tirzah point to his deep attachment to his ex-brother-in-law and his infatuation with him.

Amikam is the failed poet and the failed Israeli who collects folklore in an African country. His first speech is a significant statement about a people's need for roots, origin and identity, all of which he has lost. It is obviously applicable to Israel. ". . . There's quite an interesting process at work there, you see," he says about the African tribe he has worked with. "They're losing their folklore at a terrific pace, just forgetting it and starting to counterfeit so to speak. They're trying to 'culturize' it, stylize it. And UNESCO is sending over people, people like me, for example, to save whatever can be saved of those dying cultures . . ." His interviewer interrupts him before he can extend his analysis to Israel but the playwright has established it in the minds of his audience: Israel is, in the same sense, detribalised and nothing has been supplied as a substitute for its displaced culture.

Amikam spends most of the play in the storeroom offstage, going through his old and outdated poetry about which Yehoshua himself has some cutting comments:

Tirzah (to Assaf): And in his poems, mind you, he's got "Jerusalem" in every other line.

Amikam: That's a literary affectation. That's why I'm going to burn the lot.

Amikam himself realises that his particular brand of poetry is silly and passé, echoing as it does the style and language of the Palmach poetry, but he nevertheless clings to it as a healthy harvest of his past when he was young and productive, before he became forgetful and an idealistic drifter whose life's work amounts to nothing in the end. The speech in which he delineates his strange, forgetful state of mind is a valid description of the other characters; his use of the adjective "shapeless" to describe the Hebrew language – which he has all but forgotten – expresses all their lives.

The old woman is a conventional dramatic symbol in more than one way: she is the traditional madman who perceives and speaks sense and she represents the past, encroached on and destroyed by the forces of the present. First her house becomes filled with the human flotsam and jetsam of her children's lives, then the war threatens her beloved Jerusalem. She finds her refuge among the small creatures of her imagination until she is taken from her once secure home into the dreadful anonymity of an institution.

The other two women, Naomi and Noa, represent varied aspects of the society and the time, as alienated as the other people and as formless and incapable of passion. Noa is Tirzah as a young woman "in a short skirt" but even she, still in her youth, is aimless and dull, rootless, drifting from man to man and vaguely hoping to be a singer. The song she performs is an ironic accompaniment to the military code-names broadcast on the radio and an indictment of them as a mockery of nature.

Harsh fields
And night without moon
And you bury your head in the rocks
Forgotten you lie
And dead,
And those who'd remember
Are weary and spent
At daybreak – dew,
Not tears,
Will drench your body.

Assaf is the scientific foil to the poetic dreamer, Amikam, and the least defined character in the play, merely observing, stepping in and out of the action to move it further on.

Involvement on any level is impossible for these people. Their utter selfishness isolates them from any possibility of fruitful life. They have all, like Amikam, been cheated out of a "real ending" for life does not tie up loose ends and they are not capable of making the effort to join theirs together. They are victims of themselves, of the past which has suddenly imposed itself on their lives in the form of Amikam's blue suitcase containing his poems, his return to the house of Tirzah and her family, the revelation of Israel's history to Mrs Sarid at the moment when its monuments stand to be destroyed. But above all it is the war that dominates this play, woven into its texture and movement like a musical theme stated and restated in a complex work.

Yehoshua's approach to war itself is necessarily different from that of the earlier drama on the subject. There is no longer a hero, individual or group, there are no battles, sieges or personal triumphs. The battleground has shifted to become the internal landscape of fear and madness. The war itself is that of another generation ideologically removed from Uri's (*He Walked in the Fields*) or Jonah's (*They Will Arrive Tomorrow*). Attitudes have altered. Glory in war no longer exists, for the soldiers are no more than cannon fodder (p. 293) to be annihilated by the enemy (p. 296).[1] If it is meaningful in any way to the individual it is as a solution to his personal problems:

Avinoam: All the neurotics and psychotics and other lunatics are going to solve their problems in the war – and the doctors close at heel doing research on conflicts and phobias and getting promotions . . .

Later Mrs Sarid predicts that he will "end up in a madhouse" and suggests that calling him up would aid his condition. The subject of war is treated with cynicism when Amikam plans his filming of "authentic sequences" of the battles: "What do we have left of the War of Independence? A few blurred photographs, a few metres of amateur snapshots. An entire period lost in oblivion . . ." Indeed the whole play is something of a requiem for that lost era and the dream that has driven the dreamers mad. Yehoshua's cynicism becomes cruel when he and Assaf attempt to persuade the old woman to return with him to the hospital: "It's so sad for you here, lying on this couch all by yourself. And our hospital's ever so cheerful now and soon there'll be lots of people coming and going . . . lots of young men . . ." This attitude foreshadows the open rebellion of Levin and his fellow writers. Each character in this play creates the war in his own image. Avi's war is already lost, his outlook is one of fatalistic pessimism: "We're going to be wiped out" compared to Amikam's "Brothers, we'll wipe out all of them. We're strong enough . . ." Avinoam moves from pessimism to a childish denial of the fact of war and he has gone so far as to have become involved in a fist-fight in defence of his attitude. He is a sad mockery of the noble Palmachnik of 1948: in the War of Liberation he had taken a grenade (thrown at him in jest) to be a pine cone, with terrible injuries as consequence. Amikam, on the other hand, hopes through the war to restore his identity lost in the jungles of Africa. Avinoam asks: "Why is everyone so keen on having a war?" And the answer is simply that small conflicts must be subordinated to the larger issue: Avi himself

[1] *Until Winter 1974* by A.B.Yehoshua. Hakibbutz Hameuchad, 1975.

will escape from the throttling possessiveness of Naomi, from his feeling for Amikam, his fear of Assaf in his guise of the controller of all madness. Assaf himself can exercise his professional skill and avoid the necessity to contemplate his wife's possible adultery. Amikam can finally escape from Tirzah and their wasted lives. It is Mrs Sarid who presents, on two occasions, the reality of war against the silly and ephemeral dream-games of the younger people.

Mrs Sarid (goes over to the radio and listens closely): How sad. What is she saying? Dear God, if only I could understand what it is they keep saying all the time. It sounds like a prayer . . . They're praying over us as if we were dead already. *(She switches it off, stumbles against Avi and starts with fright.)* Oh God, who's this? Who's here? All over the house already . . . refugees . . . little refugees . . . *(nearly trips over Noa who sighs in her sleep)* Och, what's that? . . . must escape . . . *(stumbles against Naomi on the steps. Naomi too gives a little sigh in her sleep)*. Here too, here on the steps they leap under my feet with their soft skulls . . . Oh father, our father . . . look what is happening to us . . . I am already trampling on them . . .

Her little fantasy men have suddenly and horribly metamorphosed into the battle dead. In her dream, later in the play, she sees a castle that resembles a temple covered in blood, a symbol of Jerusalem at war.

Meanwhile the people are held in their common prison of listlessness. Each of them, when faced with an insoluble part of his own crisis, goes to sleep. Sleep is a refuge from the emotional impasses in their lives, and every character at some time or another sleeps in order to hide from his anxiety. But they cannot escape, for it appears in dreams which they recount on awakening and which summarise the preoccupations and themes of the play: alienation, guilt, impotence, madness and fear.

Stylistically the play, like so many others, is a mixture of genres. Noa's song and the intrusion of dreams and fantasies give it an overtone of expressionism. It is at the same time an attempt at naturalism, but the strange behaviour of the people, the dreams and vast amount of symbolism bring it squarely back to the Absurd. Thematically that is where it belongs, for once again the dilemmas of alienation and despair are examined and no solution is suggested. The characters are no better off at the end than they were at the start. The entire drama is a microcosmic picture of Israel as Yehoshua undoubtedly saw it before the 1967 war: romantic sentimentality about the past recalling the Yishuv generation (Mrs Sarid), neurosis (Avinoam), impractical political idealism (Amikam), bewildered youth (Noa), unrealised nostalgia together with a sharp comment on the Palmach generation (Amikam's poetry and Noa's song), inability to love (Tirzah), scientific detachment (Assaf), art and culture (Naomi). The names in themselves are ironic. "Avinoam" refers to a beautiful past, "Amikam" to the revival of the nation and "Assaf" means "gathered". "Sarid" is a remnant. The similarity of the names is in itself intriguing, seen particularly in terms of their pairing: Avinoam-Naomi, Avinoam-Noa, Avinoam-Amikam. The child is called "Aminadav", meaning a gift by the nation. "Tirzah" relates to "desire". Each name refers to beauty of some kind, either personal or national, to pleasure or power, so that each of them stands as an ironic comment on the character itself.

Yehoshua's play rests uncomfortably between the topical social drama of the fifties and the experimentation of the late sixties and seventies. Like so many other writers he has failed to commit himself: once again a greatly gifted author has refused to make a statement of firm conviction. One is not sure what he is saying other than repeating the themes of despair and disillusionment, so predominant in all contemporary drama, and of rejection of the past that has characterised Hebrew writing since the establishment of the State. His attitude to war is equivocal: while obviously not one of glorification it is also not entirely negative for war is good for some, bad for others. He sees hope for Jerusalem since the wall dividing Tirzah's *living* room (this is a direct translation into Hebrew of the English "living room" (p. 289)[2] for which there is not normally a Hebrew word) has been broken down. But the new Jerusalem will be born in blood and its fighters are "dreadful! Loud, rowdy, smelling, they filled the train with all sorts of filth. Scared to death of the situation. I nearly went mad . . ." (Amikam). Is this rather intellectual distaste for war, extreme in its elimination of any nobility of purpose, appropriate in the Israeli context where war, until 1973, was a fact of life? Or is it a fashionable anti-war cry conditioned by the Vietnam protests? No realist writing in Israel at that time, prior to October 1973, could rely on the customary and undoubtedly valid moral and humanitarian condemnation of war, for to do so would be glib and politically naive. Yehoshua has partially attempted this judgement, but he has avoided any strong comment in his play by taking refuge in cynicism which is in itself too mild to be convincing. His "family" would have had to face their private battles at any time; their states of mind were not engendered by the imminent war for it served only to bring them all together. The war has collected them in Jerusalem, that is all.

[2] חדר החיים

Robert Bolt recently made the statement that the idea for a play comes from "some very deep preoccupation" which causes the playwright to expose himself at a deep level.[3] *A Night in May* tells us little about its writer's preoccupation and it reveals almost nothing of his need to write of it. In this it conforms emotionally to the plays of the fifties and sixties. The metaphor is still lacking, the trend has not been set.

[3] Robert Bolt interviewed by Sally Emerson. *Plays and Players*, June 1977.

Part V. The Problems of the Israeli Drama

The notion has spread among writers, play-doctors, critics, producers, actors, public, that plays are "not written but re-written"; that is, not written, but pieced together, not composed with one man's passion and intellect, but assembled by the ingenuity of all who stop by at the hotel bedroom, preferably during the rehearsal period. In this way dramaturgy is demoted from the fine to the useful arts; and is unique among the latter by not really being useful.

The second mistake is to write with the audience consciously in mind, instead of in the faith that there will *be an audience for good work.*

1 Criticism

To attempt to define or summarise the requirements of the Israeli critics in respect of indigenous Hebrew drama is an almost impossible task, for these are so contradictory that the reader must merely allow the critics to speak for themselves without attempting to reconcile their divergent viewpoints. The critics seem to fall into two distinct camps: those who advocate patronisation of the Hebrew drama on the grounds that it is new and inexperienced and must be encouraged; and those who believe that it must be criticised or evaluated by international dramatic standards, in the belief perhaps that the strong will survive the stringent demands made on it because of its quality as good drama and the weak will fall away for it cannot in any case be improved by concessional criticism. There is also a school of thought urging that distinction be made between the play and its production, meaning that each should be evaluated separately and by different principles.

The arguments cannot be resolved until there is a convincing critical standard in Israel. Involved in the dilemma are two vital questions – not within the scope of this work to answer – which have not been satisfactorily settled by the greatest analysts of dramatic art: what is the function of criticism and what precisely is the nature of drama?

Hebrew drama has had no orderly chronological development to parallel that of Europe and Britain. There was, for reasons already discussed, no national Hebrew drama before 1948. Since that time conditions in Israel have been different from those of any other nation at any other period because of the particular history of the Jewish people, incorporating their multitude of traumatic experiences and the phenomenon of Israel's renaissance as a nation. The Israeli public is exceptional in its diversity of background, language and culture. Even *sabras* are rarely found to have a uniformly Israeli ancestry for their deepest roots are still in the diaspora. This society cannot be compared to any other in the world even though it has so far aligned itself with Western rather than Oriental culture. Can a comparison be made, therefore, between the social and cultural conditions of other Western countries, conditions that stimulate their art, literature and theatre, and those of Israel? Theatre is said to hold a mirror up to nature. If so, may what is seen in the theatrical mirror of European and "Anglo-Saxon" society be applicable also in Israel? Upon these questions hinges the problem of the nature and quality of the contemporary indigenous Hebrew play.

Managements in Israel are accused by critics and academics of many things: lack of concern about the original play, the lack of a serious repertoire, concentration on box-office plays, a dearth of accomplished producers, the immediate and indiscriminate presentation on Israel's stages of the current Broadway and West End offerings. The Israeli theatre of today is condemned for not contributing anything to the national revolution, for having become either bourgeois or radical, either way a mockery of dramatic art and of its audiences. On the other hand the audiences are scorned by playwrights for having too little theatrical education and no taste, and they are said to be getting the theatre that they want and deserve. In the forefront of this battle stand the critics themselves. Theatrical criticism may not (and should not) be powerful enough to make or break a national drama, but its tasks and functions are of importance as a commentary on its development. Mendel Kohansky calls the critic the natural enemy of "those criticised" even when he "wields little or no power over their reputations and careers".[1] The fact is that in Israel critics wield a great deal of power, probably because of their unusual erudition in matters of the theatre. Israel Eliraz writes: "Only recently has criticism become a serious whip and we are becoming afraid of it . . ."[2] This is, of course, not peculiar to Israel. Bernard Shaw once complained that nobody likes a critic: ". . . instead of looking up to me as their guide, philosopher and friend [managers] regard me merely as the author of a series of weekly outrages on their profession and their privacy." But Shaw had perhaps a greater right to "outrage" the profession, being himself a playwright.

[1]Mendel Kohansky. *Jerusalem Post*, December 22nd 1972.

[2]From correspondence. Quoted with permission.

During the early years of the State of Israel when Hebrew drama was emerging as a new art form, local criticism of it was uniformly concessional, meaning that it was sufficient that the playwright was young and his play written about a local topic for the critic to evaluate it by means of criteria far less strict than those applied to foreign plays. During the sixties Israeli society itself became more self-critical regarding every field and aspect of its life and this attitude was transmitted to theatrical criticism as well. People were travelling a good deal more, visiting other countries and broadening their artistic horizons with the result that they began to compare the homegrown products with the foreign, and local drama and theatre was inevitably found wanting. Today criticism is lively and controversial. Every newspaper has a regular theatrical column in addition to the existence of numerous periodicals devoted entirely to the theatre, the best of these being *Bamah*. Articles on theatre appear regularly in other cultural organs and in the weekend supplements to daily newspapers, which are in themselves cultural journals of a very high standard. The attitude of the critics towards the Hebrew original play is at all times ambiguous. Some of them are pessimistic about its value as an art form, others are prepared to praise and encourage it; others evaluate it solely by the foreign yardstick and spend their time on fruitless comparison. There are still some critics who overlook every fault a play may possess but praise it lavishly because it is a Hebrew play.

"Israeli theatres," writes Joseph Lapid, "often complain that the critics judge them by the best Western standards, not making allowance for the shortcomings which are not entirely the theatres' fault. This is true to some extent since critics, by travelling abroad, do acquire new tastes and standards which are not easy to follow. But I believe that demanding critics are an incentive towards excellence: the fact is that the standard is improving and I believe that part of this is due to fear of the reviews."[3] The question here is whether critics ought to possess this power of ordering drama according to whichever personal criteria they employ. Drama critics "from the time of Aristotle have bound and fettered [the drama] and have then urged it impassionedly to soar. Yet despite its shackles it has triumphed and each triumph has been a derision of one of its most famous and distinguished critics."[4] Great drama did not ever come about through critics' teaching and explaining dramatic methodology – that is, how to write or how not to write a play – for the critic's influence is not directly on the creative act but on public opinion. Admittedly public opinion is what in the final analysis makes or breaks a playwright, but hopefully the creative writer will take the courageous decision to remain true to himself rather than to set out to please his audience, while remaining aware of the fact that his audience should be pleased. The Israeli critics appear to be working from a multitude of propositions, many of them subjectively aligned to the circumstances of Israel's existence, the high emotionalism which is part and parcel of every detail of life in Israel. Their critical criteria are not yet sufficiently independent; they do not derive from critical principles alone. For example, Israel Goor, editor of *Bamah*, feels that Israeli critics must not make undue allowances simply because the play is written in Hebrew but on the other hand they must not use what he designates as Shakespearean criteria; the play must be judged on its merit but at the same time the critic should be aware that it is original.[5] This practice, were it observed, would allow the playwright the best of all possible worlds

[3] From correspondence. Quoted with permission.

[4] George Jean Nathan. "The Drama as an Art". *European Theories of the Drama*, ed. Barrett H. Clark. Crown Publishers, reprinted 1975.

[5] "On Theatrical Criticism" by Israel Goor. *Bamah*, November 3rd 1959.

and criticism of this nature would be too indulgent to be of any value to his development.

Professor Gershon Shaked: "One must describe the literary reality as it is and only after the objective description of what is there is it possible to evaluate according to European principles. Surely one must evaluate 'the accused' by all the judicial means possible, but one can of course consider the extenuating reasons: the lack of a theatrical tradition, a sectional public, the eternal opposition of the Jewish people to theatre . . ."[6] This opinion is perhaps more realistic than that of Ben-Ami Feingold: "In my view one must distinguish between the evaluation of a production (or performance) and a play. A production, in my opinion, must be judged by a definite and strict rule, as they do in London and New York. In this aspect criticism must strive for perfection and professionalism in order to develop the theatre and in order to urge it to greater achievements. Because in this instance criticism evaluates a craft, and this must be judged in keeping with its character and traits without taking into account limitations of time and place. Opposed to this, one must appraise a *play* in accordance with its limitations and with objective encouragement. The task of the critic in Israel is, in my opinion, to stimulate the development of national original drama so he can't in this instance evaluate it according to those same criteria he uses to evaluate a play by Arthur Miller and Duerenmatt."[7] Surely this attitude is also to a large extent "concessional". Should a talent such as Duerenmatt's emerge in Israel it will not be due to the aid of criticism. The point is that a playwright cannot be created by the critics and an original drama cannot and should not be made to order. Playwrights must not expect always to be nursed and pampered: Dr Feingold is imputing a rather fond, paternalistic attitude to criticism which is as impractical as the opposite view: condemning a play out of hand because it is not as good as Arthur Miller or Duerenmatt. There is undeniably a serious problem confronting the critic in this regard: when evaluating a new work is he to apply strictly dramatic criteria to his analysis, regardless of the fact of the play's nationality? Or must he evaluate it in terms of what he knows about its audience, in terms of what it may mean to the audience according to their experience?

There is little doubt that the general standard by which Israeli theatrical critics judge the merit and value of its drama is exclusively foreign. It is only according to the yardstick of theatre and drama outside of Israel that original Hebrew drama is considered poor, and this opinion comes not as a result of sound critical practice but rather

[6] Correspondence. Quoted with permission.

[7] Correspondence. Quoted with permission.

comparison, which is a vastly different matter. "What our critics do is that they compare our productions with those in New York, Paris and (particularly) London. This, of course, is unfair. Neither have we the human nor the material resources to compare with the best in the world and we lack theatrical tradition, schooling particularly. Moreover, our theatres are importing from abroad only the most successful new plays – or the classic repertoire – while the public and the critics are presented with the whole range of indigenous plays, for the simple reason that for those there is no other place for advance selection. Unwittingly the critics are judging the world's best with our average and the result is quite often disastrous."[8] To render the situation even more anomalous most of the derogatory criticism is levelled primarily not at the plays but at their production. The critics are not prepared to distinguish, for the purpose of just criticism, between a play (מחזה) and its production (הצגה).

[8] Correspondence. Quoted with permission.

Generally Ben-Ami Feingold is not optimistic about criticism. The failure of Israeli criticism, he writes, finds its expression *especially* regarding the original play, in that the critic judges the play by means of the production without attempting to understand the play that is inside the show. "The Israeli critic is not able to distinguish between the play and its production. An average production of a good original play changes the play in his eyes also to average and he is not able to differentiate between the development of the drama and between the limitations of the theatre, until at times this reaches a paradox when he praises the play through a good production even though the play is weak and condemns a better one because of its terrible presentation." It is possible, therefore, that the critics are in fact impeding the growth of an indigenous Hebrew dramatic literature by judging the plays mainly on the technicalities of production. In their reviews most critics devote a good deal of space to the production of the play, and in many cases this is censured in the strongest terms. Ben-Ami Feingold, in his long and comprehensive discussion of *Journey to Nineveh* written *before* the staging of the play, praises it and gives his reasons for doing so: at the end of his article he expresses the hope that the production will do justice to the play.[9] Apparently it did not for the reviews unanimously condemned it. All critics, including Dr Gamzu, came out unanimously in favour of Alterman's *The Inn of Ghosts as a play*, but the entire controversy between the playwright, Dr Gamzu and his defenders began because Dr Gamzu called the production of the play appalling. He also said clearly[10] that the play on the stage was not the same play that he had read. Michael Ohed makes the comment[11]

[9] "The Journey to Nineveh" by Ben-Ami Feingold. *Bamah* 20, Winter 1964.

[10] *Haaretz*, January 1st 1963.

[11] *Maariv*, December 29th 1965.

that when he read Shabtai Tevet's *Don't Touch Naumann* he immediately realised that there was far more in it than what had been given form on the stage. Nissim Aloni was scolded for having produced his own play *The King's Clothes* because his theatrical experience was not up to it, but there was little dissidence about the fact that his play was one of the finest Hebrew plays written. These are only a few of numerous examples of similar anomalous criticism. It seems therefore that as a rule lack of experience in production is detracting from what are major pieces of theatre, excellent and original works. Looking only at the production without taking the text into account does the playwright a disservice, for while the critic must not be "concessional" he must also not be biased.

Israeli critics on the whole are pessimistic about indigenous Hebrew theatre and find little in it that is truly original or favourably comparable with foreign examples. But they seem to be judging only by production, being blinded by a lack of technical experience that is obscuring the essential qualities of the play. They are not giving the playwright a chance; he is damned from the beginning because of the directors' inexperience. Paradoxically the main reason now for Aloni's prodigious success is not the quality of his plays, because few in the audience understand them, but in the brilliance of his productions. Although in his case the dramatic material is at least equal to the theatrical, the terms of his popularity touch dangerously on the *other* extreme, that found in Europe and America where technical finesse and long experience of theatricality often hide the sterility of the dramatic material.

Many of the younger playwrights are of the opinion that the Israeli critics do not know enough about the theatre. Joseph Lapid, being both a critic and a playwright, makes a number of contradictory statements: whereas previously he declared that the improvement in the dramatic standard was attributable to fear of reviews, now he says: "The distance between Harold Pinter and an Israeli playwright is certainly not greater than the distance between Kenneth Tynan and an Israeli critic. Most of the critics have a set of values: all the classics are great therefore a fault in the performance must lie with the theatre; that a drama is inherently a better thing than a comedy; that anything that succeeded abroad should have been a success here as well but for the incompetence of our theatre.

"By and large they are out of touch with public taste . . . they discount the public as if the theatre could exist without it. The public senses it and this diminishes the critics' influence: there is very little relation between the success of a play and the reviews."[12]

[12] Correspondence (Joseph Lapid). Quoted with permission.

These views – expressed a year apart – illustrate in their contradiction not only the conflict in the ranks of the critics themselves but also a possible decline in critical standards with the corresponding loss of credibility.

Israel Goor, in his article on criticism, makes a brief but important point about its constant and general use of the troublesome and undefined term "universalism". Hebrew plays, he says, fall into two distinct categories, "The Universal" and "The Regional" as if these were, in fact, two styles of playwriting. That all the Israeli plays have an element of universalism, despite their specific setting, is indisputable. "Lately," says Goor, "every bad play whose environment is London or Paris or New York is called 'universal' but specific Jewish works are called 'provincial'. Is this snobbery? The universal value of a play does not depend on the size of the country but of the work! We know that great art is universal but before universalism it must be regional, it must be signed with the signature of a nation and its way of life."[13] On the subject of "universalism", Arnold Wesker has this to say: "There are secondary truths contained in great art in any one age that will survive till the end of time; and very often when critics dismiss an artist it is because they are confusing the two truths, and expecting primary truths in areas where only secondary truths can exist."[14] This applies both to time and place. It is interesting, in this regard, to compare the self-conscious attempts to achieve "universalism" on the part of the nineteenth- and early twentieth-century Spanish dramatists Perez Galdós and Jacinto Benavente, who travelled through Europe in order to become what they called "cosmopolitan", with the achievement of their successor Garcia Lorca whose great tragedies did not ever leave the environment of the isolated Spanish villages.

Israel as yet has no Ibsen, but it does boast at least one greatly talented playwright, Nissim Aloni, who has every right to be evaluated by means of criteria relating to the drama as an art, divorcing critical principles from the emotional issues of nationalism and Jewish culture. His plays are able to survive such criticism; those of many other Israeli playwrights are not. Are critics obliged, therefore, to compromise their critical norms in an attempt to generate confidence among these writers?

[13] Israel Goor, *op. cit.*

[14] Arnold Wesker. *Fears of Fragmentation.* Jonathan Cape, 1970.

2 The Director

If Israeli drama is regarded by its critics as being weak because of bad writing or production or its failure to attain "universality", the critics in turn are blamed for contributing to this weakness by their negative approach to the homegrown work. There is another entity to be added to the list of the accused: the director. The majority of writers in Israel do not yet see drama as their most comfortable means of expression, and the play was for many years (according to Giora Manor[1]) a kind of stepchild of literature that had to be fed from time to time. Many of the writers therefore depended entirely on the director as a kind of play-doctor, in much the same way as a sick man will put himself into the hands of his physician, with the result that today insufficient attention is paid by the director to the playwright when he does attempt to have a hand in the staging of his own plays. And so the director becomes included in the catalogue of those guilty of impeding the healthy development of the Hebrew drama. Throughout the world the function of the director, as that of the critic, is the subject of ongoing controversy, no less so in Israel. "We live at a time when the formal surface is esteemed above what used to be called 'content' . . . The relationship of shapes and surface, the naked interplay of light and line is held to be what 'art' is about, more or less exclusively . . ."[2] The director is not only able to enhance a good play but also to improve a weak one by means of the devices at his disposal. However, according to Walter Kerr the playwright's major concern must be with the organic unity of the play as a subjective work of art. "Any absorption on the part of the writer with the mechanics of performance, any reliance upon these mechanics to supply a substantial portion of his effort, is a sign of creative faltering." It depends, of course, on what Kerr means by "mechanics" for he does concede that "manipulation of the tools of sheer 'theatre' is a valid way of revealing drama". Brecht and Ibsen and the Absurdists have proved that the playwright's concern about the mechanics of performance and production is vital to the organic unity of the work. Brecht particularly made little distinction between the drama and the theatre and Kerr suggests that it was precisely this "creative faltering" which caused him to use theory and stage direction as an escape from his insecurity relating to text. Generally what Kerr means is that the playwright should not concentrate to the detriment of his dramatic message on theatrical devices in order to conceal any faults in his drama. This is precisely the conflict hampering the development of the Israeli theatre: how far

[1] *Bamah*, November 3rd 1959.

[2] *Thirty Plays Hath November*. Simon and Schuster, N.Y., 1963.

into the theatre must the playwright extend his dramatic vision? How much must the director supply to intensify this vision? So far only Nissim Aloni has solved the problem by creating his drama in totally theatrical terms, by utilising theatrical terminology in its realisation. Many younger Israeli playwrights such as Levin and Amos Keinan, for example, are following suit.

Most of the Israeli writers are of the opinion that the onus is on the director, for he is the one best equipped to nurse a new national drama into secure existence, but they claim that too many of the Israeli directors lack a sense of daring regarding the original play, being professionals who are not prepared to endanger their reputation in theatrical adventures, and are deficient in enterprise. Uri Kaisari goes so far as to accuse them of stifling original drama by turning the public against its own local talent.[3] It seems that critics are joined by directors in equal responsibility for this injustice. Israeli directors are further accused of lacking the ability to assist the playwright by guiding him and becoming part of a necessary playwright-director-actor collaboration that brings a good theatrical work into being, the collaboration emphasised by the activities of the Group Theatre, for example, which prodded so many brilliant unknown American playwrights into creative existence. In Israel playwrights and directors suffer equally from a lack of experience in the living theatre, a lack of basic knowledge of the rules of the theatre which demands from the author particularly an adjustment to a totally unfamiliar framework. The Israeli director's want of sound knowledge of the medium leads him to concentrate on foreign plays, those which have succeeded in other countries and which give him a precedent for production. The lack of cooperation and knowledge of the director has raised a most serious point in the evaluation of modern Hebrew drama, one already alluded to: the distinction made between the quality of the play itself and the quality of its production.

Mendel Kohansky made the blunt and rather high-handed statement in an article about the original play written as late as 1973 that in his opinion the standard of the Hebrew stage is not particularly high.[4] Giora Manor admits that before the curtain rises on each new production he says a little prayer: that he should not have to denounce the play or lay bare its weaknesses and omissions. "But," he adds, "in the nature of prayers – they are only answered occasionally and rarely."[5] Admittedly he is referring to productions in general on the Israeli stage, but by implication his prayers are seldom answered in respect of the original play as well. These and

[3] *Haaretz*, April 2nd 1965.

[4] *Jerusalem Post*, April 13th 1973.

[5] "A Theatre Critic Confesses" by Giora Manor. *Bamah* 50, Summer 1971.

other critics appear still to be judging by production; they are not giving the playwright a chance for he is damned from the start because of his director's inexperience. A playwright needs more than money and a backer; above all he needs a guiding, directing hand and a stage that will accept his works. Directors the world over and no less in Israel have to keep an eye on the box-office, particularly when they are dependent on it for their existence. In Israel directors are wary of experimentation; the prognosis for acceptance of every new original play is questionable for very few of them have been unqualified successes. Now young unknown playwrights are forced to struggle to find a producer or a director willing to take a risk, and too many new plays are remaining hidden in top drawers as a result of their authors' discouragement. Writers find that the directors are unwilling even to read their new works but this is a malady of directors the world over, particularly those who have had notable success with well-known "safe" works.

3 Audiences

The audience constitutes yet another obstacle to be overcome by the writer of Hebrew plays, a problem which to an extent affects the standard of his works. Theatre is by its nature dependent on the public for its success; it is a social art relying for its effect on the collaboration of playwright, performer and spectator. The dramatic experience takes place during a confined time period presupposing immediate response. Drama is a living art; if it is not seen and responded to it does not live. It is a ritual and if there is no participation there can be no ritual. The greater its communication with its audience the greater is its validity. It is a collective art because the spectator is an active participant in what is happening on the stage. "No great artist," says George Jean Nathan "has ever in his heart deliberately fashioned his work for a remote and forgotten cellar, dark and stairless. He fashions it, for all his doubts, in the hope of hospitable eyes and ears . . ."[1] If this is true of all creative endeavour, how much more so of the performing arts. The nature of the "eyes and ears" of the theatre-going public determines the nature of the theatre, and the cultural level of the audience sets its standard. Theatre that is not a necessary aspect of the artistic life of its people is valueless as an art form. In short the achievement of a nation's artistic standard depends to a large extent on the ability of its drama and therefore its theatre audience bears a good deal of responsibility for this achievement.

[1] George Jean Nathan, *op. cit.*

The society in which the artist lives and works provides the background to his work and supplies him with a starting-point. He is speaking of his society to his society and in order to understand and derive value from what he is saying his public should have a common background, a common language, common associations and experiences. Drama mirrors the society out of which it grows; that reflecting only a portion of that society cannot be national, representative drama.

In Israel the public is comprised of a multitude of communities, tribes and groups originating in every country in the world and representing various cultures and stages of civilisation. There is no Israeli milieu as there is an English milieu in England or a French milieu in France. The word "Israeli" connotes a variety of contrasting situations unparalleled in a nation with old traditions. The difference between the groups is vast and their attitude – if any – to the theatre is as varied. They have come from Eastern and Western Europe, from sophisticated capital cities, from the *shtetls* of

Russia and Poland, from primitive and isolated North African and Middle Eastern communities. For some of them, those from central Europe and the "Anglo-Saxons" from Britain, the United States, South Africa and Australia, theatre has been able to constitute a vital and integral part of their cultural life with theatrical classics a compulsory feature of their education. Most of those living in the little isolated villages of Eastern Europe were familiar only with Yiddish theatre. Certain immigrants to Israel, particularly from African and Oriental countries (the immigrants once described as "a painful and dangerous concept – the Second Israel") had never had any contact whatsoever with the theatre. As a potential audience the total heterogeneous community has nothing in common, neither taste nor theatrical experience. Their demands for theatrical fare vary enormously according to what they are accustomed to and how they differ in general in their cultural needs. The multitude of languages spoken by them further complicates the issue. Meanwhile a new generation has reached maturity, one born and educated in Israel, learning to take definite social and political viewpoints which are then reflected in its literature. These young people have grown up with the growing theatre; they are critical and sophisticated and apply new and varied criteria to their evaluation of indigenous drama. They scorn the bourgeois theatre and demand from the stage a more meaningful expression of themselves and their lives. All the while immigrants are continuing to settle in Israel.

This is the public for which the playwright has to write – a polyglot community without, for the most part, a common background, language, tradition and with no unified cultural direction. This is the public that has to be forged into a cultural unity from sectionalism and self-imposed cultural apartheid, lack of intercommunal understanding or sympathy, intolerance and ignorance.

At the moment Hebrew theatre serves only a portion of this community, that comprised of older settlers from Western countries, the audience that Leonard Schach once called "pure", and the Hebrew-speaking youth. Those who know little or no Hebrew do not attend Hebrew-language performances but those given in Yiddish, Rumanian, Arabic, Polish and so on. The Yiddish theatre has undergone a revival mainly because Yiddish was for so long a common language among the immigrants. Also, now that Hebrew is established as a spoken tongue there need no longer be fear, as there was in the Yishuv days, as to the possible supremacy of Yiddish. Until the early seventies there was no theatre provided for English-speaking settlers. They had organised themselves into a number of amateur theatrical groups which were not entirely successful, but in 1973 "the english stage" was established, sponsored by the British Council, the Council for Arts and Culture (the Ministry for Education and Culture), the Histadrut and the United States Information Centre. This theatre is run and supplied by the English-speaking immigrants, most of whom have had experience in professional theatre.

By the time the more primitive immigrants have attained fluency in Hebrew and know it well enough to attend Hebrew-language performances their general intellectual standard has been raised and not only Hebrew but the entire vista of Israeli life is part of their achievement. But in the meanwhile there remains a large section of the community outside the circle of theatregoers and consequently beyond the experience and interest of the playwright. He is therefore limited, unable to write for the public as a whole, only for that part of it best conditioned to receive and appreciate his works. If he intends to draw the entire public he must give them entertainment that requires little accomplishment to enjoy. Obviously there will always be those who prefer light entertainment to any serious statement a playwright may make, and the Hebrew play is, with few exceptions, certainly not light entertainment.[2] The serious or artistic plays will never attract a large popular audience because of their comparative difficulty. However, the playwright must still be aware of his audience's needs so that he can write something which could be meaningful to all of them, not only to the few who are especially attuned to the particular communion the theatre provides. This is a problem concerning drama in our time and not confined solely to Israel. Until this century great drama appealed to the analytical as well as the general audience. The same play was able to be both art and mere entertainment. Nowadays there is no such thing: the serious play appeals only to the discerning and the entertaining play does no more than entertain. The great playwright was and should still be an original artist who places no arbitrary limits to his statement, in other words, he does not seek out any one specific audience. "In our time," Ibsen said, " every new creative work has the task of shifting the boundary stakes." Proof of the general appeal of what we now unrealistically consider to be the "specialised" drama of the past is that in Israel the immigrant communities settled in rural areas do not necessarily prefer light entertainment; plays by Shakespeare, Ibsen, Duerenmatt and Lorca, for example, have proved to be extraordinarily successful in these areas, but the Absurd and

[2] Apart from the work of Ephraim Kishon, constituting a comic genre all of its own, described by Joseph Lapid as "mild and loving social criticism".

later experimentation is rejected.

It is not the critics nor the actors nor the directors nor even the playwrights alone who will ultimately be responsible for the successful establishment or failure of the original drama and for its image but the theatregoers themselves. And if their theatrical standard is consistently low, for whatever reason, the standard of the drama will not be able to rise. Throughout the ages of theatre the audience has determined its function: for example, in Greece it was a religious institution, in Elizabethan England a place for intellectual stimulation as in Spain during the sixteenth and seventeenth centuries; in seventeenth-century England it became a pastime for the aristocracy and did not revive until much later as an element in the lives of the general populace. Now, particularly in the United States, it is becoming a sociological and political forum with the audience a more integral part of its performance than ever before. In Israel the theatre has no obvious function other than entertainment due to its public's lack of knowledge of its meaning and capacity. It is not sufficient for them merely to watch plays, for too many eager spectators enjoy everything without discrimination or reject anything requiring more than an initial emotional response. The ideal spectator, according to J.Stavi,[3] is one who does not see the theatre solely as a place of entertainment but as an experience in the Aristotelean sense. He must add to his visual knowledge of the play by reading and learning about drama even when away from the theatre; he must not be passive or accept and digest everything given to him. He must have taste. This is perhaps an over-idealisation, for not everyone wants to become a drama student and moreover such an ideal audience would lead playwrights to even greater obscurity than they offer now. The kind of spectator needed in Israel should be a product of consistent theatrical education which until recently was not regarded as vital. For example, very little drama appeared in the prescribed syllabus for the high schools and surely the youth of the country is the potential ideal audience. Now they study a work by Sophocles or Euripides and one Hebrew play, but from the literary not theatrical point of view. For many years no Shakespeare was prescribed except in English for their final examination. They could hardly concentrate on the artistic aspect of the play having a foreign language – at that level! – to contend with. There was no Shakespeare in Hebrew translation prescribed. There is still an enormous disproportion between poetry and prose on the one hand and drama as drama on the other. A person who has studied the dramatic classics at school, who has seen many of these in live

[3] *Bamah* 20, Winter 1964.

production on the stage, has developed a certain judgement, a theatrical intellect. He will set the standard for this drama. A public that accepts everything without discrimination destroys any possibility of creating sound theatrical and dramatic criteria. Israel has no dramatic classicism of its own and has therefore to study the great works of other cultures and try through them to forge some kind of a standard in its audience. The Israeli theatre has demonstrated that it is aware of this need and has shown certain ways of filling it: both the Haifa Municipal Theatre and the Jerusalem Municipal Theatre offer lectures relating to current productions and informal public "chats" with actors and directors, in order to stimulate interest and understanding in the audience. Children's theatre offers consistently good productions given by professional groups, in addition to the two permanent children's theatre companies who work to ensure an educated and theatrically-aware public for the future. All the permanent theatre companies regularly visit the rural areas of Israel, the kibbutzim and the villages populated by new immigrants. Regional councils have been established in certain areas central to groups of kibbutzim and villages for the purpose of coordinating visits of the city-based companies. In 1950 an organisation called TELEM was founded with the intention of bringing theatrical performances to immigrants from the Middle East. In 1966 TELEM was replaced by the "Art for the People" programme, founded and maintained by government bodies, which brings theatre and concerts to every outlying area. These performances are as integral a part of the settlers' lives as they are necessary to the city dwellers.

4 Tradition

Critics in Israel have frequently cited the Hebrew drama's lack of tradition as a reason for its artistic weakness but without stating explicitly what they consider the value of tradition to be. One of the problems regarding "tradition" in Israel's contemporary theatre is the clear dividing line between past and present in Jewish culture. Generally tradition teaches familiarity with a medium, in the case of drama both from the audience's point of view and the playwright's. No art arises suddenly in a vacuum. It is a development, a progression from one form to the next and constant innovation with its roots in what has gone before. In Israel the conscious desire of most of the young writers has been to break with a tradition that they associate with an ignominious past which, they feel, has no relationship to them at all. The Jews of Eastern Europe are not the Jews of Israel, the language of the diaspora is not the language of Israel nor are its conventions those of the Israeli. In no other country is the distinction between consecutive cultural periods so marked.

What little Jewish theatrical tradition exists is in any case of small help to the contemporary dramatists. The Yiddish theatre absorbed certain features of nineteenth-century European drama, including Polish and German expressionism (*The Dybbuk*) and symbolism, but in the main it adhered to the tradition of nineteenth-century realism. Its dramatic form was a combination of elements culled from Central and Eastern European plays. The Yiddish theatre was therefore not a step in the evolution of a Jewish theatre, with Hebrew drama as the next logical development, but an offshoot of European theatre adapted to the needs and spirit of the Jews.

Had the new theatre in Israel a dramatic tradition blessed with great works through which it could study the gradual development of its individual dramas the quality of today's original play might have been different. As yet it is weak because of a lack of basic knowledge of the theatre together with a lack of experience in dramatic form, for Israel's dramatic tradition is so meagre that little can be learned from it. A link with the past affords a sense of security which Israeli dramatists lack. They have consequently been compelled to learn from traditions not their own. This applies primarily to the technicalities of dramatic construction: there is, however, no justification for artists' dismissal of the *spiritual* heritage of Jewish tradition maintained in a continuous line from Biblical times, when considering the development of Hebrew drama and the prognosis for its survival. Yiddish theatre, for example, should be no less a part of the consciousness of today's Israelis than the plays dealing with tractors, guns and early bureaucracy. So however static the material written and performed before (as well as immediately following) the emergence of the State seems in the light of current Western dramatic trends, it is still a valid reflection of the people and the time. Leah Goldberg believes that tradition is a matter of progress and must be constantly cultivated.[1] No play should be forgotten but deserves to be kept alive as part of a traditional cultural heritage. Whenever an original play succeeds, she says, the critics hail it as the first truly "original play". In one fell swoop everything else that was previously created and staged is forgotten. The Israeli public itself, she continues, is causing the past to be forgotten and preventing the continued existence of plays that were once successful. This applies even to recent plays, those only ten or fifteen years old. This attitude destroys every possibility of establishing a tradition as it does little to encourage the cultivation of the few shoots the theatre already has.

[1] Leah Goldberg. *The Fashioning of Plays and the Loss of Tradition*. Lamerchav, June 28th, 1963.

It is quite possible that other writers regard the Jewish literary tradition, being foreign to the contemporary spirit, as more of a burden than an asset; but the great cultures of the world did not grow and develop through a dismissal of the past. It is unreasonable to expect that the new reject the old for one may not put the past out of the national (and cultural) consciousness. Diaspora and Statehood are still bound together and nourished from one another. With every wave of *Aliyah*, from the First Aliyah to the smaller immigrations of the present time, the diaspora has been joined with the local environment in a combination of influences. And for all its talk of rejecting the past, one of the most characteristic features of the modern Hebrew drama is precisely its preoccupation with the past, whether national or individual. The action of the plays is firmly set in the present, but the events of the past provide the motivating forces for present action. The heroes are beset by history which dominates their lives and presses them into decision. In many cases (*Tura*, *The Refusal*, *Children of the Shadow*) this awareness propels them to a destructive outcome. Yet their dramatic moment remains an episode in the all-embracing pattern of Jewish history. Even when past events are not related directly to Israel or the Jews (*Eddie King*, *The Gypsies of Jaffa*, *The Inn of Ghosts*) they force themselves onto the present and complete the story with the inevitability of tragedy. Modern Hebrew dramatists, despite themselves, cannot reject their people's past and in this way attain a certain measure of the much sought "universality" without realising that they are doing so.

Original Hebrew drama faces enormous obstacles on its path towards full fruition as an art form worthy of the noble culture in which it is growing: managerial intolerance, lack of funds for experimentation, an audience devoid of theatrical standards led by critics who often mistake production for creation; young, frustrated playwrights who see greater possibilities overseas; a largely polyglot and mainly conservative public some of whom do not even understand the language the artist is writing in, or even if they do they are unable to understand what he is attempting to say. Furthermore he has constantly to contend with the works of great foreign playwrights, plays which have been produced all over the world and which reach Israel fully fashioned, well tried, borne on a comet's tail of success and eminence.

But Israel's lack of a Hebrew theatrical tradition can in a way be regarded as an advantage, for the theatre can now work to establish new forms to suit its particular society. All the great playwrights solved the problems that were characteristic of the theatre of their time: every generation is faced with new problems and each needs a characteristic drama to express them, for a living theatre thrives on contemporary writers.

Hebrew theatre has the extraordinary quality of both reflecting and moulding life. It is a paradigm of theatre-in-the-making, a vital aspect of a new literature. It has the unique opportunity, given to no other theatrical culture since the beginning of the century, to develop culturally as an individual, learning, as it must, from its contemporaries, then having the maturity to discard all that is unsuitable and alien to its spirit; to develop an artistic culture which will reflect its originality and *set* a trend, not be a mirror-image of the idiosyncrasies and conventions of older countries and totally unsimilar societies. In the words of Mao-Tse-Tung: "We must not reject the legacy of the . . . foreigners and refuse to learn from them [but they] should never take the place of our own creative work . . ."[2] The synthesis of "strong Western influences and local elements . . . are the distinguishing mark of the Israeli aesthetic. So, too, the very attempt to link the present and the past is an essentially Israeli characteristic. It is these interlockings that create a distinctive Israeli style, if there is such a thing . . ."[3]

[2]Yenam Forum on *Literature and the Arts*, 1942.

[3]Gidon Ophrat. *Jerusalem Post*, May 6th 1973.

Part VI In Search of the Original Play

"Live dangerously!" The artist follows Nietzsche's recommendation. Ortegay Gasset says there is some vulgarity in it because life is of its nature dangerous. True; but as the fact is ignored and implicitly denied by modern culture as such, Nietzsche was fully justified in shouting it from the housetops. Even now . . . that fundamental complacency of middle-class culture – the most imperturbable of all imperturbabilities – is still with us . . . The artist's sense of danger [has not dated]: precisely from his "subversiveness" stems his utility to society.

The problem of the original Israeli play has not yet been solved and the critics' strong complaints against it endure to the present day. In fact the terms of the conflict have not altered at all, almost thirty years after the first performance of *He Walked in the Fields*. The arguments which were explored intensively from 1948 until well into the seventies have likewise not changed: problems of "tradition", "audience" and "universality" are still preoccupying the experts with the same lack of conclusiveness as in the earliest years of Israeli dramatic criticism. Writers complain that Israeli theatre is still busy with imitations of European Absurd drama and American commercial farce; meanwhile "in the streets there is explosive dramatic material. We are a marvellous microcosm of all the problems preoccupying the sick world: racial conflict, strife between generations, the conflict of East and West and wars of oppression."[1] Too many plays of the sixties and seventies still concern themselves with trivial reality; as late as 1972 Michael Ohed asks whether anyone has seen an Arab presented on the Israeli stage. Some critics demand that the Hebrew play transcend the day-to-day problems of Israeli society and move into a realm unconnected with specific time or place; others condemn the new playwrights like Mundi, Levin and Aloni for having attempted, with varying degrees of success, to do just that. Moreover, cry the critics, there is no playwright in Israel comparable to Ibsen or Brecht. Yet, as Isaiah Weinberg pointed out,[2] other countries with similar population numbers have also not produced great playwrights and he cites modern Sweden, Norway, Denmark, Holland, Finland and Austria. These are countries older than Israel, with firm and admirable dramatic traditions.

No one has yet defined exactly what is required from the Great Israeli Playwright, nor the structure and content of the ideal Israeli play, and indeed it is questionable whether such definition is at all possible. Aloni has made the point that any good original play is a valid and acceptable model of Israeli drama. The problem seems to lie not in the age of the society or the size of its population but in the nature and quality of its communal psyche. Most Israeli writers are occupied with realism but not with truthfulness. Ibsen's realism implied total honesty, fidelity to the time and environment, for good or ill, but above all fidelity to his vision of them. Neither Ibsen nor Chekhov nor Lorca nor Brecht nor any of the modern writers so frequently cited by Israeli dramatic criticism were afraid to insult their audiences with the truth, no matter how close to actual *social* treason they came. The tenor of Israeli society does not permit this kind of honesty, for it exists tenuously on myth, and it is still too

[1] From the files of the Israel Theatre Museum: photostatic copy of article dated 1972. "This Evening an Original Play" by Michael Ohed.

[2] *The Original Drama in the Israeli Theatre*, I. Weinberg, *Davar*, 6–7, 1972.

immature to have its myth exposed. When a society is mature it can face criticism. Israeli society dare not expose itself to honest criticism from the stage; no society, in fact, wishes to face itself in the mirror of the dramatic platform. Israeli writers must of necessity be afraid to shock their public, for shocking the public implies confronting real social problems. Levin is renowned for his audacity, but his shock value is childish and unspecific and it is the lack of specificity that robs Hebrew drama of any lasting effect. In South Africa, whose culture is one of the youngest in the world, one dramatist has grown out of its deeply troubled society and given voice to some of its problems: Athol Fugard, working in conditions that could never arise in Israel, of strict censorship and fear of official reprisal, yet creating, through a deep need, a picture of *specific* oppression which is nonetheless relevant not only to South Africa but to any number of societies in today's world. It is the need that has created the drama. Fugard may or may not be popular in his native country, but his plays embody a universal metaphor that will outlast his society and its problems. No Israeli writer has yet achieved this although the dramatic output in Israel far exceeds that of South Africa. Moreover, Israeli dramatists have not yet created any memorable characters who exist as symbols of a society, such as Ibsen's; or who represent aspects of humanity common to any society, such as O'Casey's or Chekhov's or, indeed, Fugard's. The characters of Israeli drama, with certain exceptions, are vague, pasteboard types without individuality.

Throughout this discussion of contemporary Hebrew drama it has been revealed that what it lacks above all is a certain inner dynamic which gives it an individual life detached from its author. The early Israeli dramatists were skilled in accurate observation, but they did not ponder their problem nor seek to discover its wider implications. Their plays remained records, not expressions. The reason for this is that they failed to achieve detachment from them, to exceed the world they described. The set of experiences enabling the writer to move himself to a distance from his subject is what provides the metaphor through which he expresses his expositions or his *ideas*. It is the ideas that Hebrew drama lacks. With Ibsen the metaphor was the so-called "woman problem"; with Hemingway it was war and human courage; for Lawrence it was sex, for Conrad, the sea. Arthur Miller utilises the family, Pinter, an intruder or intruders, Tennessee Williams, degeneration and decay. Nissim Aloni alone of the Israeli dramatists has found such a metaphor and through it moved into a realm of analysis touching on mankind as a whole. It does not matter that he is not *overtly* concerned with Israeli localities and personalities, for his pathetic, grotesque little king has grown for him out of some aspect of Israeli society, his own society, the one he knows best.

Meanwhile playwrights accuse the "Establishment" (audiences and managers) of wanting them only to tackle the uncontroversial events of the day as they have always done – by means of dramatic reportage. The "Establishment", they say, has created an ideal reality which it wants to see reflected and it rejects everything else, ". . . a counterfeit and artificial criterion that has come to create a metaphor which is idealised and non-existent."[3]

[3] *The Original Play* by Emmanuel Bar-Kadma. *Yediot Achronot*, February 6th 1970.

The "Establishment" in its own way confirms this view by saying that one of the main reasons for the deficiency of the original play is the "relatively low standard of its social relevance. The few plays that deal, in a realistic manner, with subjects taken from the life of Israeli society receive enthusiastic encouragement from the audience . . . the trouble is that most of our playwrights prefer, these days, to escape to the historic past, to psychological depths or to the sphere of the Absurd, instead of dealing with the concrete problems of Israeli society."[4] Weinberg makes the interesting point that this lack of involvement with society in the plays is in direct proportion to the playwright's identification with this society – for the totally identified writer will not be a critic or "militant", to use Weinberg's own word.

[4] Weinberg, *op. cit.*

It is incorrect to maintain, as so many writers and critics do, that the criterion for greatness is that a play "lives" outside of Israel. For if this is so then Ephraim Kishon is the greatest dramatist Israel has yet produced, which may be true but he is not the greatest serious dramatist. The Israeli critics are, however, probably too pessimistic, for the dramatic outlook is changing. Writers like Aloni, Levin, Yehoshua Sobol and Yosef Mundi are unusually outspoken. Aloni's gentle lyricism and beauty do not detract from what appears to be a demand for change; Mundi is another Israeli dramatist to have employed a true theatrical metaphor in his discursive play using images of Herzl and Kafka, two characters representing aspects of Israeli society. His writing generally is an analysis of political reality and not merely a presentation or description of reality. These writers are spoken of disparagingly by the established theatrical commentators and deprecated as spokesmen for the New Left. The point about them is that they are expressing opinions which are not necessarily the prevailing and popular opinions; they are in fact opinions regarded as dangerous to the Israeli social body. These writers are adored by the young, vilified by the older and conservative, sometimes dismissed as merely fashionable offshoots of the radical extremists of the U.S. and Europe. But even this extremity of political thinking in the drama is progress of a sort and in their plays these writers are demonstrating that, for whatever reason, they have ceased worshipping the gods of convention and intellectual safety.

Until recently Israeli theatre was not able to afford total honesty. 1973 proved that honesty is not necessarily destructive. From now on the Israeli theatre can only reflect a society maturing into awareness of itself as it is and not as it thinks it should be. The safety of Romanticism can be abandoned if the theatre is to be a viable and durable limb of Israel's immensely healthy and active cultural body.

Plates

He Walked in the Fields	courtesy Cameri Theatre
Inn of Ghosts	courtesy Cameri Theatre
A New Reckoning	courtesy Cameri Theatre
Tura	courtesy Cameri Theatre
The Children of the Shadow	courtesy Habimah Theatre
Journey to Nineveh	courtesy Habimah Theatre
The Gypsies of Jaffa	courtesy Habimah Theatre
Eddie King	courtesy Habimah Theatre
Programme Covers	courtesy Habimah Theatre

"He Walked in the Fields" by Moshe Shamir 1948 *Cameri Theatre*

Left: *"Inn of Ghosts"* by Nathan Alterman 1962 *Cameri Theatre*
Right: *"A New Reckoning"* by Nathan Shaham 1954 *Cameri Theatre*

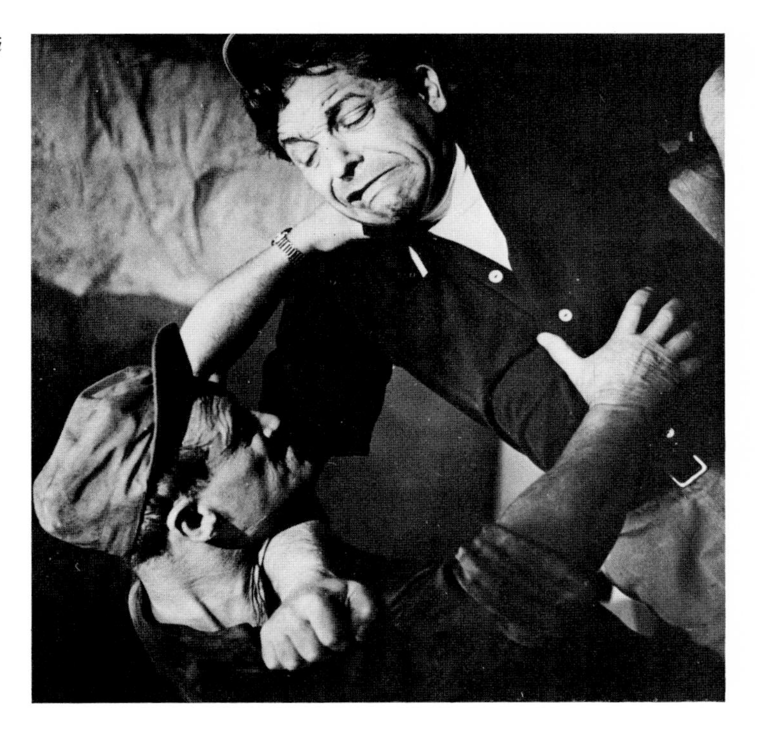

"Tura" by Josef Bar Josef 1963 *Cameri Theatre*

"The Children of the Shadow" by Ben – Zion Tomer 1962 *Habimah Theatre*

"Journey to Nineveh" by Yehuda Amichai 1964 *Habimah Theatre*

"The Gypsies of Jaffa" by Nissim Aloni 1971 *Habimah Theatre*

Programme cover for *"The Gypsies of Jaffa"*

Right and overleaf: *"Eddie King"* by Nissim Aloni
1975 *Habimah Theatre*

Programme cover for *"Eddie King"*

Selected Bibliography

History

Hengel, M.	*Judaism and Hellenism*	SCM Press Ltd, 1974
Kallen, Horace M.	*The Book of Job as a Greek Tragedy*	Hill and Wang, N.Y., 1959
Kaufmann, Y.	*The Religion of Israel*	George Allen and Unwin, 1961
Molinari, Cesare	*Theatre Through the Ages*	Cassell, London, 1972
Nicoll, Allardyce	*The Development of the Theatre*	
Ribalow, Menachem	*The Flowering of Modern Hebrew Literature*	Twayne Publishers, N.Y., 1959
Sachar, H.	*The Course of Modern Jewish History*	Weidenfeld and Nicolson, 1958

שרירא, שמואל   מבא לכתבי הקודש   מבואות תשי׳ח

Hanoch, G.   "The Hebrew Drama"   *Zion* no. 3, Nov. 1949

אלדד, ישראל   התנ״ך כדרמה   ״במה״ 8

אלירז, ישראל   להיעדרה של הדרמה העברית   ״במה״ 48–49, חרף אביב 1971

אלמגור, דן   האגדה שהפכה למחזה העברי הראשון   ״במה״ 4, ינואר 1960

דוברובסקי, יונתן   עיון מחודש במחזה העברי הראשון

Reviews

״אדי קינג״ – ניסים אלוני

רחל שקלובסקי   דבר   17/10/75

יוסף נצר   חותם   22/8/75

בועז עברון   ידיעות אחרונות   5/6/75

״אכזר מכל־ המלך״ – ניסים אלוני

חיים שוהם   קשת   סתו 1974

״בעלת הארמון״ – לאה גולדברג

ישראל גור   בין עולמות   ״במה״ 45   אביב 1970

אביבה גלי   בשדה התאטרון   ״אורות״   מרץ־אפריל 1956

״בראשית״ – אהרון מגד

בועז עברון   הרהורי בראשית   הארץ 15/3/63

מכאל קשיב   מבראשית   חרות 15/3/63

Ida B. Davidowitz. *Jerusalem Post*, 20/7/62

״גם זו לטובה״ – משה שמיר
אביבה גלי ״אורות״ פברואר 1958

״זה מסתובב״ – יוסף מונדי
יורם פורת מעריב 15/1/70

״חפץ״ – חנוך לוין
אורי רפ הארץ 6/9/74
אהוד בן עזר הארץ 30/6/72

״טורא״ יוסף בר־יוסף
חיים גמזו הארץ 26/4/63

״יעקבי ולײדנתל״ חנוך לוין
דב בר־ניר על המשמר 5/1/73
Mendel Kohansky. *Jerusalem Post*, 13/7/73

״מלכת האמבטיה״ – חנוך לוין
ב·ת· הארץ 15/5/70
יגאל בורשטיין הארץ 15/5/70
יורם ברתינסקי הארץ 15/5/70

״הנסיכה האמריקאית״ – ניסים אלוני
מרדכי בר־און למרחב 3/5/63
יורם קניוק למרחב
עזרא זוסמן דבר 1/3/63

״מסע לנינוה״ – יהודה עמיחי
חיים גמזו הארץ 31/7/64
בן עמי פיינגולד ״במה״ 20 חרף 1964

״נעורי ורדל׳ה״ – חנוך לוין
חיים גמזו הארץ 20/2/74

״סע הביתה יונתן״ – חנוך ברטוב
יורם קניוק למרחב

״עין ימין, עין שמאל״ דוד לוין
מיכאל אוהד הארץ 14/6/63

״פונדק הרוחות״ – נתן אלתרמן
חיים גמזו הארץ 1/1/63
דבורה גילולה ״במה״ 69/70 אביב־קיץ 1976
״במה״ 71 סתו 1976
Mendel Kohansky. *Jerusalem Post*, 4/1/63

״הצוענים של יפו״ – ניסים אלוני
גדעון עפרת דבר 29/10/71
״כאב כאב אחיזת עינים״ אסתר נתן·

״שיץ״ – חנוך לוין
שרגא הר־גיל מעריב 7/1/75
פ· אלף זו הדרך 29/1/75

״שש כנפים לאחד״ – חנוך ברטוב
אביבה גלי אורות אוקטובר 1958
The Quarry, Ehud Ben-Ezer
Mendel Kohansky. *Jerusalem Post*, 30/4/64

Theatre

Hatlen, T. W. — *Orientation to the Theatre* — Meredith Corp., 1972
Kernodle, G. R. — *Invitation to the Theatre* — Harcourt, Brace and World, 1967
Styan, J. L. — *The Dramatic Experience* — Cambridge University Press, 1965
Styan, J. L. — *Drama, Stage and Audience* — Cambridge University Press, 1975
Theatre in Israel — *Israel Youth Horizon* — Nov.–Dec. 1952
Rachel Engel — "Cameri"
Jehuda Hanegbi — "Dramatic Art in the Kibbutz"
Rachel Engel — "Ohel"
Ida B.Davidowitz — "Habimah"
Habimah, National Theatre Handbook — 1970
Jerusalem Sherover Theatre Newsletter — October 1971
Kohansky, Mendel — "Wanted – a Real Theatre" — *Jerusalem Post*, 11/8/72
Rosenblatt, Sally — "A World of Wonder" — *Israel Youth Horizon*, vol. vii, no. 6
Shapiro, Sraya — "The Cameri" — *Jerusalem Post*, 26/12/69
Sowden, Dora — "The New Habimah Theatre" — *South African Jewish Chronicle*, 25/9/70
Whartman, Eliezer — "Jerusalem's Impressive New Theatre" — *Jewish Affairs (South Africa)*, January 1973

גלי אביבה — בשדה התאטרון אורות נוב· 1961
גולדברג, לאה — ״עיבוד מחזות ואבוד מסורת״ למרחב 28/6/63
גור, ישראל — ״על הבקרת התאטרונית״ ״במה״ 3 נוב· 1959
וינברג, ישעיהו — ״התאטרופיליה הישראלית״ ״במה״ 40 חרף 1969
״שנויים סטרוקטוראליים בתאטרון הישראלי״ ״במה״ 50 קיץ 1971
״הרפרטואר וטעמו של הקהל״ ״במה״ 20 חרף 1964
מילא, יוסף — ״התאטרון החיוני״ ״תאטרון״ אפריל־מאי 1965

מנור, גיורא ״מבקר תאטרון מודה באשמה״ ״במה״ 50 קיץ 1971

רביקוביץ, דליה ״הבהלה הגדולה בתאטרון הישראלי״ למרחב 18/9/63

שרף, אשר ״התאטרון – בית לכולם״ ״במה״ 3 נובמבר 1959

Playwrights

אוהד, מיכאל ״הגברת עם הישבן״ הארץ 22/12/72

מירון, דן ״ניסים אלוני – ההישג והסייג״ ידיעות אחרונות 14/3/75

נגיד, חיים ״אסור לאמן לשבת על הפיסגה ולהרגיש בנוח״ ידיעות אחרונות 25/7/75

עמיחי, יהודה ״מונולוג״ מעריב 28/8/64

"The Tragicomedy of Fulfilment in Nissim Aloni's Plays." Zephyra Porat

The Original Play

אוהד, מיכאל ״הערב מחזה מקורי״ 1972

ברזל, הלל ״בעית המחזה הישראלי״ מבואות 24/4/55

בר קדמא עמנואל ״המחזה המקורי – מקור חרב?״ ידיעות אחרונות 6/2/70

האזרחי, יהודה ״התאטרון הישראלי והמחזה המקורי״ ״במה״ 5 אפריל 1960

ויינברג, ישעיהו ״המחזאות המקורית בתאטרון ישראל״ דבר 6/7/72

מנור, גיורא ״70 מחזות מקוריים״ ״תאטרון״ אפריל־מאי 1965

סנינת מיכאל ״כן לא כן לא״ חותם 26/9/73

פיינגולד, בן עמי ״מחזות מקוריים על במותינו״ ״במה״ 41

קניוק, יורם ״על מחזות מקוריים״

שקד, גרשון ״האספקלריה המאירה״ משא 11/5/73

״להתחיל כל פעם מחדש״ משא 18/5/73

״בנתיבי המחזה המקורי״ ״במח״ 6 יולי 1960

"Aspects of the Israel Theatre." Leah Goldberg. *Jewish Affairs*, July 1952

General

Aylen, Leo	*Greek Tragedy in the Modern World*	Methuen, 1964
Bentley, Eric	*The Dramatic Event*	Methuen, 1954
Bentley, Eric	*The Life of the Drama*	Methuen, 1965
Bentley, Eric	*The Playwright as Thinker*	Harcourt, Brace and World Inc., N.Y., 1946, 1967
Clark, Barrett H.	*European Theories of the Drama*	Crown Publishers, 1975
Cohn, Ruby	*Currents in Contemporary Drama*	Indiana University Press, 1969
Ferguson, Francis	*The Idea of a Theatre*	Princeton University Press, 1949

Gassner, John — *Directions in Modern Theatre and Drama* — Holt, Rinehart and Winston Inc., N.Y., 1956, 1965
Gaster, T. H. — *Myth, Legend and Custom in the Old Testament* — Harper and Row, 1969
Heiberg, Hans — *Ibsen, a Portrait of the Artist* — Allen and Unwin, 1969
Kaufmann, Walter — *Tragedy and Philosophy* — Doubleday Anchor Books, 1969
Kerr, Walter — *Thirty Plays Hath November* — Simon and Schuster, 1963
Kitchin, Lawrence — *Drama in the Sixties* — Faber, 1966
Kohansky, Mendel — *The Hebrew Theatre—its First Fifty Years* — Ktav Publishing House, N.Y., 1969
Lewis, L. — *American Plays and Playwrights of the Contemporary Theatre* — Crown Publishers Inc., N.Y., 1965
Roose-Evans, J. — *Experimental Theatre* — Avon Books, 1970
Wesker, A. — *Fears of Fragmentation* — Jonathan Cape, 1970
Clurman, Harold — "Theatre" — *The Nation*, Sept. 27th 1953
Emerson, Sally — "Playing the Game" — *Plays & Players*, June 1977
Esslin, Martin — "View from the Gods" — *Plays & Players*, March 1967
Kohansky, Mendel — "Not a Good Year" — *Jerusalem Post*, 8/9/72
Kohansky, Mendel (ed.) — "Israel Theatre 69/70" — *ITI*, 1971
Kohansky, Mendel — "Theatre in Israel" — *Encyclopaedia Judaica*
Kops, Bernard — "The Israel Theatre" — *Ariel*, July 1962
Leech, Clifford (ed.) — *Contemporary Theatre*, no. 4
Ophrat, Gidon — "Aesthetics: Developing an Israeli Synthesis" — *Jerusalem Post*, 6/5/73
Shaked, Gershon — "Hebrew Drama" — *Encyclopaedia Judaica*
World Theatre – Israel — *ITI*, May–June 1965

כהן, אדיר — סופרים עבריים בני זמננו מזרחי־תל אביב
יערי, י — המחזה העברי המקורי והמתורגם מראשיתו ועד היום (ביבליוגרפיה) 1959
עפרת, גדעון — הדרמה הישראלית צ׳רקובר מוציאים לאור בע׳ם 1975

גלברט, ס. — ״תאטרוננו ללא איפור״ על המשמר 4/9/64
גלי, א. — ״בשדה התאטרון״ אורות יוני 1961 (ועוד)
לפיד, יוסף — ״על במותיך - חללים״ מעריב 17/5/63
קיסרי, אורי — ״המילודרמה של הדרמה הישראלית״ הארץ 2/4/65

Index